THE DYNAMICS OF COMMUNISM
IN EASTERN EUROPE

The Dynamics of Communism in Eastern Europe

BY R. V. BURKS

PRINCETON UNIVERSITY PRESS

PRINCETON, NEW JERSEY

1961

TO SHERMAN KENT

PREFACE

THIS book has been in preparation for more than a decade; consequently, the list of those whom I have to thank for their assistance is of some length. The research was in part financed by grants from the Social Science Research Council for study at the Russian Research Center, Harvard University; through a Fulbright fellowship for research in Greece; and by monetary assistance from Wayne State University in the acquisition of special research materials and for the use of the university's electronic computer.

Because of the availability of firsthand observers of the phenomenon under study, considerable reliance was placed upon the interview technique. Many of those who contributed substantially of their knowledge and experience cannot, for reasons of their own personal security, be named; but I wish publicly to express my gratitude to Stanislas Banczyk, Paul Barton, A. Benaroya, Sula Benet, Stephen de Bogdan, Michael Borwicz, Sandor Brunnauer, Jan Ciechanowski, Christopher Christides, Henry H. Collins Jr., Alexander Cretzianu, Ivo Duhachek, Andor Gellert, Nicholas Georgescu-Roegen, Ernst Halperin, Michael Kirchos, Nicolas Kitsikis, Istvan D. Kertesz, Clyde Kluckhohn, Sabin Manuila, Reuben Markham, Stanislas Miholajczyk, Philip E. Mosely, Ferenc Nagy, Garim Panarity, Guy J. Pauker, Michael B. Petrovic, Gheorghe Rosu, Samuel L. Sharp, Andre Simon, Stavro Skendi, Harvey Smith, Alexander Svolos, Joshua Starr, Aladar Szegedy-Maszak, Geza Teleki, Elias Tsirimokos, Hans E. Tuetsch, Constantine Visoianu, Rudolph A. Winnacker, Stanislas Wojcik, Jan Wszelaki, and Paul Zinner. In addition to those, named and unnamed, who have given me their help, I wish to thank especially three former Communists, Ante Ciliga, Dimitrios Kolekas, and Theophylactus Papaconstantinou, as well as two career diplomats, Charles W. Yost and Robert P. Joyce; without the assistance of these five the work probably could not have been brought to completion.

My statistical advisor was John Mattila. Much of the labor of statistical calculation was done by my seminars at Wayne. John Angelopoulos, Benjamin Murdzek, James Stasevich, and George Svajda served as research assistants and translators. The final version of the manuscript was typed by Lucille Levin and Katharine M. Burks; the latter also helped in the preparation of the index.

Many have read the manuscript and proffered useful advice. In this connection I wish particularly to thank David Blair, Katharine M. Burks, T. T. Hammond, Harry N. Howard, M. M. Knappen, Richard Lowenthal, and R. C. Miller. Gabriel Almond suggested the addition of the ninth chapter on Communist movements in areas other than Eastern Europe and offered conceptual suggestions of a systematic nature which greatly improved the general argument. R. Miriam Brokaw provided helpful editorial suggestions.

None of these good people has, however, any responsibility for the opinions presented in the following pages; for these I alone am accountable. I regret that Arpad Szelpal's *Les 133 jours de Bela Kune* (Paris, 1959) and "Interview with an ex-insider. II: The party that vanished", *Soviet Survey*, no. 33, 1960, pp. 100-106, did not become available before the book was in proof.

RVB

Washington, D.C.
December, 1960

CONTENTS

CONTENTS

TABLES AND MAPS

TABLES

MAPS

THE DYNAMICS OF COMMUNISM

IN EASTERN EUROPE

INTRODUCTION:
CONCERNING COMMUNISM
AND COMMUNISTS

I N THE *Communist Manifesto*, Marx and Engels stated
flatly that the carrier of the revolutionary movement
they were launching would be a social class, one new
to the pages of history. The faltering bourgeoisie, the two
revolutionaries announced, has not only "forged the weapons
that bring death to itself; it has also called into existence
the men who are to wield these weapons—the modern working class—the proletarians. . . . Of all the classes that stand
face to face with the bourgeoisie today, the proletariat alone
is really a revolutionary class."[1] The *Manifesto* was first
published in 1848, but the notion that Communism is something essentially proletarian in character and that all working men are potential Communists has remained to this day
one of the doctrinal pillars of the movement.

In 1956, more than a century after the publication of the
Manifesto, no less a person that N. S. Khrushchev, first secretary of the Soviet Communist party, sought to prove that
a purge of the party's central committee had been a fraud.
The purged committee members had been honest Communists; they had been slandered, and the accusations against
them fabricated. Said the first secretary to the twentieth party
congress:

" . . . of the 139 members and candidates of the party's
central committee who were elected at the 17th congress,
98 persons, i.e., 70 per cent, were arrested and shot (mostly
in 1937-38). (Indignation in the hall.) What was the composition of the delegates to the 17th congress? It is known that
80 per cent of the voting participants of the 17th congress

[1] G. Max Eastman (ed.), *Capital, the Communist Manifesto, and
Other Writings by Karl Marx* (New York, 1932), pp. 327-28, 331-32.

3

joined the party during the years of conspiracy before the Revolution and during the civil war; this means before 1921. By social origin the basic mass of the delegates to the congress were workers (60 per cent of the voting members).

"For this reason, it was inconceivable that a congress so composed would have elected a central committee a majority of whom would prove to be enemies of the party. The only reason why 70 per cent of central committee members and candidates elected at the 17th congress were branded as enemies of the party and of the people was because honest Communists were slandered, accusations against them were fabricated, and revolutionary legality was gravely undermined."[2]

Nothing could be clearer. Persons of working class origin could not have conspired against a Communist party any more than African aborigines could have prayed for bad hunting weather!

The proletarian

The proletarian, in fact, finds himself at the doctrinal center of the Communist movement. He is the particular object of capitalist exploitation, and it is this exploitation which is at the root of all the suffering and tragedy in modern history. All evil, whether war, poverty, prostitution, or unemployment, is only a by-product of the exploitation of the working class. In the end, the proletarian emerges as the savior of mankind, for it is he who overthrows the capitalist system and replaces it with a classless society, one in which no evil exists because exploitation of man by man is no longer feasible. The proletarian is thus a kind of sacrificial lamb. It is he who, by the sweat of his brow, creates all wealth, and it is from him that everything is stolen. He is the victim of all evil practiced, but is himself innocent. Without the

[2] Nikita S. Khrushchev, *The Crimes of the Stalin Era. Special Report of the Twentieth Congress of the Communist Party of the Soviet Union,* annotated especially for this edition by Boris I. Nicolaevsky (New York, 1956), p. S20.

suffering of the proletarian, history would not move toward its ultimate fulfillment.

Between Communism and Christianity there are, indeed, striking doctrinal analogies. Just as Christian history begins with a state of perfection, the Garden of Eden, so Communist history commences with a primitive tribal society in which all goods were held in common. The Fall from the Garden is paralleled in Communism by the advent of private property. Just as the disobedience of God by the first human pair brought an unhappy end to their pristine state, and ushered in an age-long struggle between the champions of good and the minions of evil, so the emergence of private property signaled the differentiation of mankind into social classes and determined that all history thereafter would be dominated by the warfare between these classes. The Christian struggle has a supernatural and an ethical quality; the battle is waged by saints on the one side and demons on the other, each with human legions to back them up. In Communist teaching the struggle has an economic and mundane character; the protagonists are social classes, exploiting and exploited. At the Christian apocalypse the wicked are condemned to eternal hell-fire; in the Communist version they are led out before the firing squads of the revolution.[3]

Just as the appearance of Christ on earth gave direction and hope to the forces of righteousness, so the emergence of the industrial proletariat betokened the approach of the final and decisive engagement. As Christ has his bishops and his priests (the living church), so the proletariat has its leading cadres and its activists (the revolutionary party). If the church is frequently rent with heresy (a device of the devil for misleading the faithful), the party is as often subject to devia-

[3] Fritz Gerlich, *Der Kommunismus als Lehre vom Tausendjaehrigen Reich* (Muenchen, 1920), *passim*; R. V. Burks, "Conception of Ideology for Historians," *Journal of the History of Ideas*, x (1949), pp. 183-98; N. Berdaiev, *The Origin of Russian Communism* (New York, 1937); J. Monnerot, *Sociologie du Communisme* (Paris, 1949); cf. A. Rossi, *Physiologie du parti communiste francais* (Paris, 1948), pp. 344-45.

tions (the secret weapon of the bourgeois fiend). If, in order to protect the faithful from the fires of hell, unrepentant heretics must be sent to the stake, so must unconfessing deviationists be liquidated, to preserve the unity of the revolutionary party. The inquisition of the medieval church is paralleled by the brainwashing techniques and the rigged trials of the Communists. Imperceptibly, doctrinal analogies take on the form of organizational similarities. Perhaps doctrine and organization are the same substance, in the one case viewed perceptually and, in the other, looked at from the pragmatic standpoint.

There are, moreover, cultural parallels. Orthodox Christianity, for example, was the state church of Byzantium. As such it became the carrier of a Christianized version of late classical culture, an amalgam which it carried to the primitive peoples of eastern Europe: to the Bulgars, the Romanians, the Russians. When Orthodoxy converted these peoples, it not only brought them within the sphere of a more complex culture, a civilization, but it also subjected them to a degree of Byzantine political control. In much the same way, we may imagine, Communism, upon its identification with the tsarist state, became a serious competitor with other world religions, both sacred and profane. Communism became a vehicle for the spread of a Soviet version of Russian culture throughout a goodly portion of the Eurasian land mass, and now bids fair to set up a world civilization of its own. Its greatest successes have been achieved among peoples with cultures less complex than the Soviet. Just as Greek was once the language of religion and learning in such widely distant centers as Moscow, Kiev, Bucharest, and Sofia, so today Russian is becoming the vehicle of ideology and culture in such places as Peking, Ulan Bator, Samarkand, Tbilisi, and Tirana.

Religion, state, culture, imperial sphere: these are closely related phenomena. About this nexus there is no good reason to be cynical. Unless a given religion (or ideology) is to remain obscure and without influence, it must find its way to power, or at least to an accommodation with power. Before 1917 Communism was not much more than a curious political sect. While the mundane requirements of power have a certain corrupting influence, these are to be placed in the balance against the concessions the state will make in the interests of the faith. For if religion has need of the state, the state would have the gravest difficulties in attempting to function without the help of religion. The masses of citizenry must be motivated to the fulfillment of their duties, many of which are unpleasant and even risky, such as those connected with warfare. In a world clouded with battle and besmirched with hunger, religion (or ideology) is the seeing eye of the masses; it is their perception of what needs to be taken as ultimate.

This confrontation of the Christian religion and the Communist ideology is not meant in mockery, either of the one or (forsooth) of the other. It is meant only to bring out clearly and at the very beginning, first, the notion that Communism is a militant faith, an heretical offshoot of the Judeo-Christian tradition, still on the march; and, second, that the central doctrine of this new faith is the primacy of the proletarian, who assumes a role analogous to that of the Christ in traditional Christianity.

On the whole, anti-Communists have tended to take Communist doctrine at its declared worth, merely inverting the values. They are inclined to believe that it is a working class movement which has its roots in unemployment and low wages. They tend to think of Communist leaders as charlatans engaged in world conspiracy, and of their followers simply as misguided. The businessman often regards trade unions as the special center of Communist activity. The clubwoman simply cannot understand how someone like Alger Hiss could become involved in a movement from which his kind had nothing to gain. The government policymaker pumps money into the Iranian or the Cambodian economy on the supposition that by relieving the distress of the poorest classes he is erecting a dam against the spread of this new heresy. In short, the sacred literature of the movement is taken as an accurate indication of its character and a clear delineation of the forces which produced it.

Varieties of Communists

Anyone who concerns himself with the study of Communism will soon be confronted with the curious fact that Communists are of different kinds. This peculiarity is recognized to some extent in popular speech, which quaintly distinguishes between the "hard core" Communist and the "fellow traveller." For the sake of clarity, we must begin by defining these different types.

If we represent the Communist movement as two concentric circles, the pinpoint which is the center common to both circles will stand for the Communist leaders, the high command. Exiguous in number, the members of the high command provide the organizing talent of the movement and make the crucial decisions. Their position is elevated, privileged, and dangerous. In concentration camps their followers will provide them with such creature comforts as can be made available, the few cigarettes, the only blankets, the extra morsel of bread. If political prisoners are to be exchanged with the Soviet Union, it is these persons for whom Moscow asks, and by name. Their role is analogous to that of the general staff of an army, or to the episcopate of a church. In Communist parlance these men are sometimes referred to as "leading cadres."

Outside the pinpoint of commanders is a circle comprehending persons who devote their main energies to party work. Before the party comes to power such persons distribute leaflets, march in demonstrations, lead strikes, perform hazardous tasks of espionage. They may be ordered to storm a barricade or to take to the hills in the "little war." Along with the leading cadres, they may spend years in prison or in exile. They live in an atmosphere of feverish excitement, often go without food or sleep, and tend to contract tuberculosis or heart disease.

After the seizure of power, these men work more furiously than ever, managing "cooked" elections, building factories, supervising executions, writing propaganda, commanding military units—in short, carrying the main administrative burden (and enjoying the plush social privileges) of a totalitarian political system. They continue to burn the candle at both ends, and their faith remains high. As a last act of devotion they may be called upon to walk out before a Communist firing squad, or to end their days as slave laborers.

In anti-Communist language the people we are describing are the card-holders, but in party parlance they are referred to as "activists," "cadres," or "*apparatchiks.*" In terms of the analogy we have been pursuing, activists are comparable to the priests of a church. As the bishops and priests together make up the hierarchy, so leading cadres and activists together constitute the party "*apparat.*" As the members of the hierarchy receive their authority and power from the holy church, so the members of the *apparat* receive theirs from the sacred party. Thus the party can afford to employ the less able in key positions and can replace them almost at will. Thus also leaders of dissident factions, once defeated, tend to lose all influence and to disappear from view.[4]

Outside the pinpoint of the leading cadres and the inner circle of activists there is an outer and much fatter circle which includes all those who, for one reason or another, cooperate with the party, or sympathize with its objectives, or join the party not out of conviction but purely for reasons of personal advancement. The membership of this outer circle is both diverse and amorphous. It includes the fellow traveller, usually a prominent person who lacks the courage of his convictions. Such a man is useful to the party, both before and after the

[4] *Ibid.*, pp. 302-33, 337-42, gives an excellent description of the cadre or activist. Cf. also Giorgio Braga, *Il comunismo fra gli Italiani. Saggio di sociologia* (Milan, 1956), p. 141.

seizure of power, because he helps camouflage the conspiratorial and military aspects of party life. The outer circle includes the member of the front organization who is embittered with the existing society and anxious to take some action but not yet ready to carry his convictions to the extreme which the esoteric Communist doctrine demands. It also includes those who after the seizure of power go along with the party for opportunistic reasons: the lawyer who wishes to continue in practice, the student hopeful of matriculation at a university, the army officer anxious for promotion. One may have been a Catholic, another a Fascist, the third a Socialist, but it was impossible for these people to practice or enter the professions without becoming party members. So they swallowed their convictions and pursued their careers. When these people are needed by the party, they are referred to as "honest technicians," but when it becomes desirable to frighten or expel them they are denounced as "careerists" and "opportunists."

Then there are in the outer circle those who enlist in the ranks of the Communist guerrilla army. Enlistment is often a euphemism, but in time of war as much can be said for any army, regular or guerrilla. A typical "enlisted" guerrilla is one who dwells in the area where the little war is underway and finds that, in the circumstances there prevailing, he must join one side or the other in order to survive. Alongside the fellow traveller, the front member, the opportunist, and the guerrilla we may place in the outer circle those who, if they read a newspaper, read the one published by the party; those who can be persuaded to attend a party rally; those who are willing, with perhaps a little pressure, to contribute to the party treasury. At election time such people vote the Communist ticket, and in party lingo they are vaguely ticketed as the proletariat or the "toiling masses." If we wish to refer to all these outer elements together (the voter, the guerrilla, the opportunist, and so on), we will employ the term "soft periphery."

The relationships between all the various kinds of Communists may be presented graphically as follows:

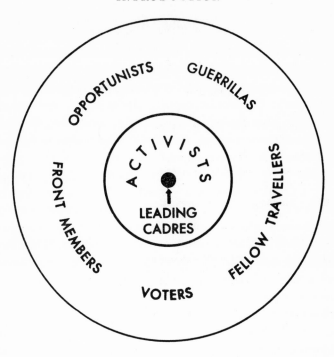

Ideally, party membership is identical with the hard core or the *apparat*, but this ideal situation occurs only now and then. Before power many activists do not have formal party membership for reasons of security or because of the difficulty of keeping records in an underground situation. After the seizure of power the party's ranks will be swollen by large numbers of opportunists and even of simple voters. The Communists themselves recognize this fact of life by speaking of the party *apparat* and the party masses, of an elite party and a mass party. To some extent each type of party has its particular tactical function and its faction of adherents within the hard core.

Fluctuations of party strength in terms of leading cadres, activists, and opportunists can be illustrated by the history of the Yugoslav party, for which relatively complete membership data are available. Perusal of the figures in Table 0.1

TABLE 0.1[5]

Yugoslav party membership

Year	Historical situation	Membership	Probable status of the bulk of the membership
1920	Newly organized, the party had the third largest electorate in the country	60,000	Activist
1923	The party was driven underground; much of its membership was in prison	6,000	Leading cadre
1932	Abandonment of parliamentary government and establishment of a royal dictatorship; police pressure increased	200	Leading cadre
1941	The party achieved semi-legal status and was increasingly popular as a foe of Nazism and a supporter of Czechoslovakia	12,000	Activist
1945	After a bloody civil war, the party emerged as the master of Yugoslavia	141,000	Activist
1952	After seven years of power	779,400	Opportunist

would lead one to guess that for each Yugoslav Communist of cadre stature there were, in 1952, approximately 20 activists and 100 opportunists.

In speaking of activists, opportunists, and so on, we are, of course, speaking of ideal types, to which only the rare individual conforms entirely. One and the same individual may at different times be a voter, an opportunist, and an activist, depending on the circumstances and his own changing views. Furthermore, the line between one type and another is often

[5] Sima Markovic, *Der Kommunismus in Jugoslawien* (Hamburg, 1922), p. 13; *The Communist* (Belgrad) for October 1946, January and September 1947, contains reports of various hierarchs in which figures concerning party strength are given; C. Kabakchiev, B. Boskovic, and C. Vatis, *Kommunisticheskie partii Balkanskikh stran* (Moscow, 1930), p. 142; Branko Lazitch, *Les partis Communistes d'Europe 1919-55* (Paris, 1956), p. 149; Branko Lazitch, *Tito et la revolution yougoslave* (Paris, 1957), p. 15.

not so sharp and so well-defined as we have traced it here. But for purposes of analysis a clear grasp of these types as ideals is essential.

Faith and responsibility

First, we must ask ourselves whether, in a study devoted to determining the extent to which Communism is a proletarian movement, it is worth while to deal with the types on the soft periphery. There are, for example, those who assert that people who vote the Communist ticket do so only by way of protest, or because the party (with tongue in cheek) has promised them a hectare of land, or because they are affected by a vague awe for distant Russia. These people, it is said, think of Communism as only another political party; they have no conception of its true nature. Six months after the party seizes power, these erstwhile voters will regret their error and become as violently anti-Communist as the remainder of the population.

It is true that the Russian peasants who at Lenin's bidding seized the landlord's land were certainly not Bolsheviks in the strict sense of that term. But could they not have waited for a legally conducted redistribution of the land, which Kerensky's liberal government was preparing? And was it really necessary to murder the landlord in the process of seizing his land?

Much has been made of the fact that the Communist-led Greek Democratic army, which kept Greece in the turmoil of civil war during the years 1946-1949, employed a system of forcible recruitment. Indeed, the commander-in-chief of this army, Markos Vafiades, once admitted publicly that from the middle of 1947, when the guerrilla army had been operating for little more than a year, recruitment was almost entirely forced.[6] This is a true statement, but it must be properly construed. Many of the forcibly recruited came from families

[6] See Vafiades' speech of 15 November 1948, in *Neos Kosmos* (Bucharest), date of publication not indicated, pp. 476-80.

who already had members with the guerrilla bands. Many of the recruits had been known in the village for their pro-Communist sympathies. These people were forcibly recruited in the sense that, like G.I. Joe, they preferred not to be involved in anybody's war, but not in the sense that they preferred the victory of the forces of the royal government. Perhaps it would be more accurate to say that the so-called Greek Democratic army was forced, after June 1947, to resort to conscription in the areas it controlled. A reliable source has insisted that 92 per cent of the personnel of the Democratic army was between 16 and 25 years of age, precisely the years of greatest military usefulness. The argument that the bulk of those forcibly recruited were unsympathetic to the Communist cause is difficult to support. The Democratic army fought on for two years after it shifted to forcible recruitment, and gave a good account of itself. Desertion in a guerrilla campaign, with its scattered bands and hit-and-run tactics, is much easier than in regular warfare.

The belief that only the leaders, or the members of the ruling party, are true Communists—are real Fascists, or what have you—is based on the assumption that the masses of mankind are generally on the side of light and reason; it is only that they have been tricked and betrayed by an unworthy leadership. This assumption underlay Wilson's view that the Germans would become peaceful and law-abiding members of the world community, if only their Junkers and industrialists and militarists could be gotten rid of. When applied to Communism, this same assumption makes it necessary to ascribe such enormous successes as the conquest of China to a truly remarkable capacity of activists for conspiracy, espionage, and battle. Is it reasonable to believe that heretical movements are consistently characterized by leadership whose moral quality is substantially poorer than that of those led? Does not the Wilsonian assumption involve the assertion that leadership produces heretical mass movements, rather than the movement producing the leadership?

It is, of course, entirely true that voters (or opportunists, guerrillas, or fellow travellers) are not activists. But the difference between activists on the one hand and all non-activists on the other is to be found in depth of conviction and in an inner necessity for acting upon conviction. The voter only sympathizes. He may harbor ideas which, if held by activists, would be regarded as deviational. By definition, the activist is a zealot. Fortunately for mankind, the number of zealots is limited and activists constitute a minority in any camp, whether religious or ideological. As a matter of social organization, only a minority can devote itself full time to the practice of a faith. Orientation to the basic uncertainties of human existence, whether these be dressed in supernatural or historical garb, is only one aspect of that existence, and the cultivation of this one aspect is a specialization, like anything else. To say that only activists are real Communists would be the same as saying that the only real Catholics are the priests and the monks, the only real Nazis those who belonged to the SS or the Gestapo, and so on.

It is a happy fact that the masses of mankind do not all sympathize with Communism. Some favor Democracy, some Islam, still others Buddhism. The point we are trying to make is that the voter who initials the Communist ballot must be placed in exactly the same category as the Protestant who gets to church only on Easter but who shudders at the thought of a Catholic in the White House, or the German who decries the excesses of the Nazis but feels, none the less, that the Jews have got to be "put in their place." It cannot be said that the Communist voter is not a real Communist any more than it can be said that the Republican or Democratic voter is no Democrat. A sympathizer is a Communist, or a Catholic, or a Democrat, or a Fascist, insofar as he is anything at all.

A Communist, then, is one adhering to an ideological faith whose doctrine constitutes an heretical version of the Judeo-Christian tradition. The central tenets of this heresy are, first, the belief that the suffering proletariat will one day save mankind from all the evils which beset it; and, second, the belief that the organization through which the proletariat acts is the Communist party. Just as there are different levels of faith, so there are different kinds of Communists—leading cadres or bishops, activists or priests, voters or communicants. It is not correct to say that people on the periphery of the movement are not real Communists. Only the few can belong to the hard core, for economic as well as psychological reasons. Each is a Communist, good or bad, effective or ineffective, in his own way and at his own station. Serious analysis could no more leave voters, or opportunists, out of account than it could ignore leading cadres or disregard activists.

PART I: THE SOCIAL AND ECONOMIC SETTING

CHAPTER I: THE HARD CORE

THIS STUDY is concerned with the nature of the Communist movement in eastern Europe. It is an attempt to discover whether in fact Communism in eastern Europe is, in any real sense, a proletarian movement, whether Marxism explains why there are Communists in that part of the world. For evidence we shall examine, not what east European Communists say about themselves and their following, but the raw data of Communist social composition.

Eastern Europe, the setting of our study, is an area roughly defined by four seas: the Baltic, the Black, the Aegean, and the Adriatic. Ethnically speaking, eastern Europe is that part of Europe which is sandwiched in between the Germans in the west, the Russians in the east, and the Turks to the south. It is, if you like, the area of the peoples "in-between," conquered and ruled first by one outside great power, then by another. Presently, as everyone is well aware, eastern Europe, or most of it, is under the domination of Soviet Russia.

More specifically, this study will concern itself with the Communist movement in eight states: in the north with Poland, Czechoslovakia, and Hungary, Catholic countries above the east European average in industry, literacy, and living standards; in the south with Yugoslavia, Romania, Bulgaria, Albania, and Greece, an area preponderantly Orthodox, largely agrarian, and in some parts as backward as anything the European continent has to show. In the time dimension, our study will reach from the Bolshevik revolution in 1917 roughly to the death of the dictator Stalin in 1953. In the present chapter we shall examine the social composition of the east European hard core, that is to say, of the leading cadres and the activists.

Leading cadres

We begin with the elite, the small group of people who make up the Communist general staff. We have a mass of

19

data which comes to us from elections held in eastern Europe between the first and the second world wars. These returns often provided information concerning the professional background of those who were candidates for or were elected to certain of the national parliaments. Table 1.1 presents this data in capsule form. N stands for the number of cases.

TABLE 1.1[1]

Interwar parliamentary candidates by class affiliation

$N = 9,943$

Party	% Workers	% Peasants	% Middle class	% Other	Total
Communist	29.4	21.4	44.8	04.4	100.0
Socialist	22.5	19.0	50.4	08.1	100.0
All other parties	07.5	40.3	44.6	07.6	100.0

The first thing that strikes us about Table 1.1 is that roughly half the leaders of all parties, regardless of ideological orientation, are people of middle class origin. In the case of most

[1] *Statistichki pregled izbora narodnikh poslanika za ustavotvorny skupshtinu kral'evine Srba, Khrvata i Slovenatsa, izyrshenikh na dan 28. novembra 1920 god* (hereafter cited as *Statistichki pregled 1920*) (Belgrad, 1921), *passim; Statistique des elections des deputes pour la XXeme assemblee nationale ordinaire* (hereafter cited as *Elections pour la XXeme assemblee*) (Sofia, 1927), pp. 94-97; *Statistique des elections des deputes pour la XXIeme assemblee nationale ordinaire* (Sofia, 1928), pp. 92-94; Vladimir Zadera, *Narodni shromazdeni ve ctvrtem volebnim obdobi po parlamentnich volbach z 19 kvetna 1935* (Prague, 1935), pp. 34-71; Vladimir Zadera, *Politicke strany v narodnim shromazdeni* (Prague, nd), pp. 34-102; *Statistique des elections a la diete et au senat effectuees le 5 et le 12 novembre 1922* (hereafter cited as *Elections a la diete 1922*) (Warsaw, 1926), pp. 8-10, 12, 14; *Statistique des elections a la diete et au senat effectuees le 4 et le 11 mars 1928* (hereafter cited as *Elections a la diete 1928*) (Warsaw, 1930), pp. xxiv, xxvi; *Statystyka wyborow do sejmu i senatu 2 dnia 16 i 23 listopada 1930 roku* (Warsaw, 1935), p. xix.

Yugoslavia and Poland published social data concerning all those nominated as candidates, while Czechoslovakia and Bulgaria published such data only concerning those actually elected. In the discussion all the persons involved are referred to as "candidates" for the sake of simplicity. In the Yugoslav election of 1920 the law provided that one-third of any list of candidates must be made up of university graduates. In Table 1.1 the category "peasant" includes, insofar as Poland and Czechoslovakia are concerned, a few representatives of the land-owning class.

parties, the other half of the leadership is mostly of peasant derivation. The Communist and Socialist parties, both of which claim descent from Marx, are distinguished by the fact that this non-bourgeois half is divided in approximately equal portions between peasants and workers. At the command level, then, the Communists in the interwar period could not claim to be proletarian.

For the period after World War II there are also leadership samples, though of considerably smaller size. Table 1.2 presents the social composition of the post-1945 central committees of four east European Communist parties. N again equals the number of cases. The middle class has acquired a clear majority. The worker element is also stronger. The peasantry has almost disappeared.

TABLE 1.2[2]

Postwar leading cadres by social derivation

Country	N	% Workers	% Peasants	% Middle class	% Other	Total
Yugoslavia	511	39.0	7.7	51.5	1.8	100.0
Poland	44	36.3	2.3	61.4	.0	100.0
Cyprus	15	33.3	.0	60.0	6.7	100.0
Albania	23	17.4	.0	82.6	.0	100.0

If we ask who these middle class people may be, the data answers that they are almost entirely professionals: doctors, lawyers, schoolteachers, and the like. Among the interwar

[2] Stavro Skendi (ed.), *Albania* (New York, 1956), pp. 323-45; *Neos dimokratis* (Lefkosia), 21 October and 11, 18, 22, and 30 November, 1951; Richard F. Staar, "The Central Committee of the United Polish Workers' Party (PZPR)," *Journal of Central European Affairs* (hereafter cited as *JCEA*), xvi (1957), pp. 371-83; *Oslobodjenje* (Sarajevo), 8 November 1948; *Slobodna Dalmacija* (Split), 7 November 1948; *Glas* (Belgrad), 22 January 1949; *Slovenski porocevalec* (Ljubljana), 6 December 1948. Of the Yugoslavs classified in Table 1.2, 456 were members of the central committees of various Yugoslav republican parties, e.g., of the Communist parties of Slovenia, Croatia, Bosnia, Serbia, and Macedonia. The other 55 were Partisan officers of field grade or higher. There may be some duplication in these figures, inasmuch as some officers of general rank were probably also central committee members.

candidates, professionals were 78 per cent of all those belonging to the middle class; among postwar Yugoslav central committeemen the percentage was 84.

In other words, the leadership of the east European Communist parties, insofar as that leadership is dominated by any class, is dominated by bourgeois elements, primarily professional. The social difference between the Communist hierarchs and their competitors from other parties seems to be that the other leaderships (except the Social Democratic) have a minority representation from the peasantry rather than from the urban working class.

Activists

It is much easier to determine the social composition of leading cadres, who constitute perhaps 5 per cent of the hard core, than to establish the social origins of the activist 95 per cent. Communist leaders are sooner or later forced into the light of day, but activists usually retain the protective cloak of anonymity to the end.

While casting about for pertinent data on activists, the author realized that the Greek prisons were overflowing with such people. As of June 1952, there were 10,569 persons held for crimes committed in pursuance of party orders. Of these prisoners, 5,053 had been sentenced to death or to life imprisonment, the rest to lesser terms.[3] What could constitute a clearer proof of activism than the commission, pursuant to party orders, of acts chargeable under the law of the land as crimes?

These 11,000 Communist prisoners must be clearly distinguished from the exiles, of whom there were at the beginning of 1952 approximately 1,500. The male exiles were held on the Aegean island of Agios Eustratios, the women on the isle of Trikkeri. In contrast to the prisoners, the exiles had

[3] This was the number of prisoners held in 1952. Within two years this figure had been reduced by pardon and retrial to approximately 4,000. There were further releases after 1955.

been convicted by no court and had been charged with no crime. They had been arrested because they were regarded by Greek authorities as especially dangerous to the security of the Greek state, and they were held at the discretion of those authorities. The law required that the case of each exile be examined annually and a new ruling made. These men were leading cadres. Their position in the party was sufficiently elevated to protect them from the workings of the law or, as the gendarmes would say, they were too high up to be caught. The men in exile had given the orders.[4] The men in the prisons had carried them out.

In 1951-1952 Communist prisoners and Communist exiles were also to be distinguished from those serving on the island of Macronissos, off the tip of Attica. Macronissos began as a rehabilitation and re-education camp for captured guerrillas. After the cessation of hostilities, draftees suspected of Communist sympathies—"involvement" is the Greek term—were stationed at Macronissos for the period of their military duty. They were free to visit nearby Athens on pass, and to return to their homes during regular leave. In addition to their military instruction, the trainees on Macronissos were given special indoctrination. In ideological terms, the trainees were for the most part neither leading cadres nor activists, but members of the soft periphery, future voters, or potential privates in a new guerrilla war. The special camp on Macronissos has since been broken up.

The Greek authorities exhibited a not unnatural reluctance to admit a foreigner within the precincts of their prisons. But in the end their curiosity got the better of their caution, and the writer, flanked on one side by an interpreter and on the other by an ex-Communist serving as contact man, gained entry. Ten different penal institutions were visited, some of them more than once. The writer talked with the wardens, interrogated many prisoners at length, and distributed ques-

---

[4] During 1953, one-half of the approximately 1,500 were released.

tionnaires among 593 so-called repentant Communists.[5] (It was useless to approach the non-repentants.)

The question at once arises as to the representative character of the 593 repentants who, only with considerable prodding, filled out the questionnaires. How representative were they of the some 10,000 activists then in prison, or of the estimated 10,000 activists not behind bars, or of the perhaps 20,000 living in true exile behind the iron curtain, in such countries as Albania, Romania, Czechoslovakia, and the Soviet Union? Might not the repentants be those with less courage, or less conviction? Might they not be precisely the non-proletarian dross which had worked its way into the party?

There are no final answers to these questions. All that can be said is that in circumstances of adversity the proportion of repentants has been high. When Metaxas became dictator in 1936, there were perhaps 10,000 party members.[6] By dint of such methods as solitary confinement, the dictator "persuaded" all but 600 or 700 of these 10,000 party members to sign repentance declarations. We would guess that these several hundred were mostly leaders, and that almost all the activists had given in. During the German occupation the bulk of these repentants applied for readmission to the party. Word was passed out that those who demonstrated their sincerity by deed would be returned to the fold. Paradoxically, many of the worst atrocities during the occupation were committed by these ex-repentants, who hoped to impress the party hierarchs with their devotion and thus gain readmittance to the ranks. At the liberation a handful were actually readmitted

[5] The results of this study were first presented in R. V. Burks, "Statistical Profile of the Greek Communist," *Journal of Modern History* (hereafter cited as *JMH*), xxvii (1955), pp. 153-58. The questionnaire used in the Greek prisons is presented in Appendix C.

[6] *1935-1945: deka chronia agones* (hereafter cited as *Deka chronia agones*) (Athens, 1945), p. 50. It seems probable that turnover in party personnel is high even after the seizure of power. Leonard Schapiro, *The Communist Party of the Soviet Union* (N.Y., 1960), pp. 436-37, shows that as of 1939 less than a fifth of 1919 party members were still members, that less than a quarter of those recruited in 1926-1928 still belonged to the party, and that less than half those who joined in 1929-1933 were still members.

to the party (and later purged) but the vast majority were turned down on the ground that the party could not besmirch itself by association with men who had committed such crimes!

Certainly the Greek authorities with whom the writer worked believed their repentants were typical or average activists, except possibly in one respect. Greek parole boards, it seems, had a tendency to favor repentants of peasant origin, on the ground that their declarations were more likely to be sincere than those of workers. If this were so, then the returns from our sample would tend to have an artificial urban bias.

Of the prisoners who made out questionnaires, only about 20 per cent admitted to membership in KKE proper, though virtually all confessed belonging to some filial or front group. Greek authorities agreed that 20 per cent was far too low, and that the prisoners feared that whatever they admitted would be used against them later. Only those prisoners whose membership was a public fact were willing to admit belonging to the party proper. On the other hand, authorities thought the true figure no higher than 50 per cent, explaining that large numbers of activists were not inscribed on the party rolls during underground and guerrilla periods for reason of security, because of the difficulty of keeping records, and so on.

The Greek prisoners

The questionnaires were so phrased as to provide information about three different standards of class status: profession, schooling, and property. The writer and his team enquired not only as to the profession of the activist himself but also as to that of his father. Each respondent was also asked to list the property owned by his father and, as well, the property held at the time he joined the Communist movement, his own property if he had already established a separate household, the property of his father if the respondent still lived at home.

By American standards, Greek youth breaks with the parental household very late. Given the over-population and

the more or less stationary standard of living which characterizes the Greek economy, it is difficult to establish a new
household. Job-getting and profession-entering are sharply
influenced by family connections, and Greek families are distinguished not only by the number of their progeny but also
by their inclusion of those who, in America, would be considered distant relatives or not related at all. Thus the profession
and property of the father might be a more accurate index to
the class affiliation of the Greek activist than the profession
or the education he put down for himself.

The returns from the questionnaires indicate that among
Greek activists, workers are two-fifths of the total, the largest
single element but by no means a majority. People of peasant
stock constitute the second largest element, roughly one-third.
After the peasants come representatives of the urban middle
class.

Comparison of parental professions with those of the activists, and of these two with the distribution of professions
among the population at large, yields some curious results, as
may be seen in Table 1.3.

It is at once apparent that the distribution of professions

TABLE 1.3[7]

Class affiliation of Greek activists (1952)
$N = 593$

Trade or profession	Distribution among fathers %	Distribution among activists %	Distribution among the population at large (1928) %
Peasants	58.7	33.8	61.1
Workers	25.8	42.3	22.5
Middle class	15.5	23.9	16.4
	100.0	100.0	100.0

[7] For N see Appendix C. The distribution of professions among the
population at large is given in *Annuaire statistique de la Grece 1930*
(hereafter cited as *Annuaire Grece 1930*) (Athens, 1931), p. 76.

among fathers is not substantially different from the distribution of professions among the population at large. If Greek activists are considered in terms of family background, there is nothing to distinguish them from any other cross-section of the Greek population. In this sense Greek activists are no more and no less proletarian than, for example, adult members of the Greek Orthodox church. What Table 1.3 reveals is that activists are often born of rural families and then shift to characteristically urban professions. This is as true of the middle class as of the urban proletariat.

To sum up: insofar as the distribution of professions among Communist activists is different from the distribution of professions among the Greek population at large, it is different because of migration from rural to urban districts. There goes into the making of the activist a certain element of deracination.

Another index of social status is the extent of formal education. Generally speaking, the lower the income group, the less extensive is the formal schooling. A larger percentage of proletarians should be illiterate than would be the case with any other class.

In respect to education, the repentants turn out to be neither more nor less literate than the population generally. On the average, male activists had had six years of schooling, female activists three. If those with one year of schooling or less are regarded as illiterate, then activist males have a literacy rate of 90.5 per cent, as compared with 89.5 per cent for their age group as given by the census of 1928. Activist females had a literacy rate of 64.5 per cent; that of their age group in 1928 had been 71.7.[8] Thus the amount of formal education received by activists points in exactly the same direction as their professional background. Greek activists do not seem to represent any one particular social class, but rather an average made up from all classes.

For a Marxist, however, the acid test of class status is

[8] *Ibid.*, p. 74.

property; the proletarian has only one possession, his muscles. Only 9 per cent of the repentants, however, indicated that they, themselves, and their fathers had been propertyless at all times. Ninety-one per cent listed their fathers and themselves as property owners.

TABLE 1.4

Mean property held by property-owning Greek activists or their families

$N = 298$

Type of property	Property owned by father	Property owned at adherence to Communism
House (by no. of rooms)	3.4	2.5
Land (in hectares)	4.3	3.3
Trees (in Greece often owned apart from the land	24.1	17.3
Livestock (head)	18.5	9.3
Shops	0.2	0.18
Employees employed (per property owner)	0.9	1.0

To begin at the bottom of Table 1.4, in nine out of ten cases either the father or the activist himself hired an employee, an apprentice, or a hired hand. This at once places the activist a full cut above the man who owns a push-cart and sells fruit, or the man who owns a kiosk and sells newspapers, magazines, and prayer beads—these, *in Greek society*, are already people with property interests.

There are, unfortunately, no statistics on housing in Greece, either with regard to the number of rooms available or with respect to home ownership. One suspects, however, that the Greek average with regard to rooms would fall below that of the Soviet Union, which, in urban areas at any rate, appears to be one room per family; in general, the Greek standard of living is substantially below that prevailing in the USSR. When, therefore, it develops that 91 per cent of the respondents' parents owned their own homes, and that the average home comprised nearly 3½ rooms (including kitchens), it is clear that Greek activists average out at the middle class or *kulak* level.

At one point, more exact reasoning is possible. The Greek bureaucracy possessed data on the size and number of landed holdings in the kingdom. This information had been collected in 1929, but no one had ever gotten around to publishing it. In due course the data were made available to the Mutual Security Administration (Greece). The average repentant comes from a family which owned 4.3 hectares (nearly 11 acres) of land. In the framework of the MSA figures, this would place the repentant's family holding in the upper 18 per cent of all Greek holdings taken by size.

Property owned at the time of adherence to Communism was substantially less, but we should not rush to the conclusion that activism was a product of the proletarianization of middle class elements. Three and one-third hectares, the mean holding at the time of adherence, is still within the upper 18 per cent of all Greek holdings, taken by size. Given the median date of Communist involvement, which is 1943, it is just as likely that the burning of houses and the slaughtering of livestock was consequence, as well as cause, of Communist adherence. The secular trend toward morselization of peasant holdings, so characteristic of eastern Europe generally, would also account for some of the difference between parental property and property held at the time of adherence.

To sum up: if the sample taken in the Greek prisons is representative, then clearly the typical or average Greek activist is no proletarian. Only one in ten is a true proletarian, in the sense of lacking property altogether. Nine out of ten are men of substance, or come from families of substance. If we strike an average, then the typical Greek activist (or his father, if the activist had no household of his own at the time of adherence) owns a three room house, a farm of four hectares, a dozen head of livestock, and an orchard of twenty trees. The activist or his father employs, either in the shop or on the land, one apprentice or hired hand. *By Greek standards*, such a man is well off. He may not be rich, but neither is he stricken with poverty.

Interview with Epaminondas Zafieris

The writer spent many hours conversing with repentants, singly or in groups. Perhaps an account of one such interview will serve to make vivid the statistical picture presented in the previous paragraphs. The reader should imagine a white structure originally built as a school for girls, now, with its windows barred, converted into a prison. (Only one prison in all of Greece was built *ad hoc*.) A courteous warden has surrendered his office for the duration of the visit, thus conferring on his guests an additional aura of authority. We have already visited each of the four *achtidas*, or divisions of the prison, three repentant, one non-repentant. We have also visited the prison workshop, a rarity among Greek lock-ups, where the inmates as a rule are condemned by custom, if not by law, to idleness. The Communists take advantage of this situation by setting up classes with compulsory attendance. It had been the hope of Athens to have at least this one particular prison occupied entirely by ex-Communists, but trouble in the central penitentiary had led to the transfer out of one *achtida* of repentants and their replacement with unredeemed hard core people from Athens. In each *achtida* the warden had assembled the prisoners and, while the Mediterranean sun burned fiercely down, made a little speech, presenting the visitors and explaining their purpose in coming. Then, as if by a prearranged signal, one of the prisoners had stepped forward and made a speech in reply, promising cooperation. The non-repentant spokesman had politely added: assuming that the investigation is truly scientific in nature, as you say.

Within the coolness and comfort of the warden's office were the prisoner, the contact man, the interpreter, and the writer. To put the prisoner more at ease, he was served coffee and given cigarettes, though this was in violation of prison rules. Interviewees were usually old-time friends of the contact man, who had himself been a party member for seventeen years, becoming, at the last, quartermaster of a major guerrilla detachment. Sometimes prisoners volunteered to give their stories; the prisoner before us now (we shall call him Epaminondas Zafieris) at one time had shared the cell of our contact man.

At the time of the interview the prisoner was still under sentence of death, though he has since been pardoned and released. He had been a member of *Steni aftoamina*, the execution squad of the party's secret police. He had personally "executed" at least six people, in line of duty. Twenty-seven years of age when interviewed, Zafieris was well above average height for a Greek, handsome, well-built, poised, clearly the leader type.

Of peasant stock, Zafieris had been born in an obscure village in the Peloponnesos. Though his parents were peasants, one grandfather had risen to the rank of general officer in the Greek army, one uncle had been an officer of lesser rank, and another uncle had become one of the most prominent artists of contemporary Greece. In 1936, when Zafieris was a boy of eleven, the family had moved to Athens. His father had quarrelled with still another of the boy's numerous uncles over the land-holding of which the two were coowners. The basic difficulty was that the plot simply could not be made to support two families. So Epaminondas, his three brothers, and his sister came to be housed over the bank at Athens, where their father had found employment both as clerk and as janitor. With his two jobs, and with the help of a loan, the elder Zafieris somehow managed to build a house which could serve as his daughter's dowry, and to send Epaminondas to secondary school.

At the age of sixteen Zafieris left school and, lying about his years, volunteered for service with the royal Greek air force. The Italians had already invaded Greece; furthermore, the lad had for some time decided upon a military career, like his grandfather and his uncle before him. With the German invasion and the collapse of formal Greek resistance, Zafieris was separated from his unit. He undertook to feed British troopers hiding out in the hills, stealing chickens for their sustenance. The next year (1942) he joined the Communist-dominated resistance movement and was assigned to the underground in Athens.

His life in the resistance was adventuresome. He was given the mission of "executing" Greeks who chose to collaborate with the Germans. He assassinated Germans, too. He joined the party. Once he was arrested by the German authorities, but they were unaware of his true identity and sold the youngster back to his father for two tons of olive oil, as of that day the ransom of a king. During the fighting against the British he served as liaison officer between ELAS[9] headquarters and the ELAS First Corps. After the treaty of Varkiza warrants began to circulate against him, and he asked the party for transfer to the special camp at Bulkes in southern Yugoslavia, where large numbers of activists had been sent for safekeeping.

In Bulkes, Zafieris was assigned to the secret police. The chief function of the camp police, some 150 strong, was the arrest and execution of malcontents and "liquidationists." Zafieris evidently did not have much respect for deviationists. Mostly they were representative of the *Lumpenproletariat*, he said. Some smoked hashish. Others wanted to escape. Still others, as he put it, wished to have sexual relations with the local girls. The prisoner insisted that he had never participated in the torture of those about to be executed.

In February 1946 Zafieris was ordered to return to Athens and report for duty to *Steni aftoamina*. This, as we explained earlier, was the assassination squad of the party's secret police. There were twenty people in the unit, the bulk of whom were students either at the secondary or at the university level. According to Zafieris, this fact was no accident. The party

[9] Initials used as the name of the Communist-dominated guerrilla army of 1941-1945.

knew from experience that "police" units composed of representatives of the *Lumpenproletariat* were ineffective. Units so composed "made mistakes" and had "few results." These illiterates would kill with an ice pick instead of a pistol, cut off the noses of their victims, and so on, thus giving right-wing newspapers an advantage in the propaganda war. Intellectuals, the prisoner asserted, knew how to kill without all these unnecessary flourishes.

Sometime in 1947 Zafieris ran across an abandoned infant. Stray dogs had chewed off one of the child's hands. Weeping, he carried the baby to his sister, and commanded her to rear it. At first he blamed the infant's mother, but further reflection convinced him that the prevailing social order was responsible. He felt strengthened in his Communist conviction.

That same year he was arrested for an "execution" committed during the occupation. The victim in question, a girl member of the Communist youth, had been liquidated in the presence of her mother and her sister. From 1947 on Zafieris was in prison.

Two years later he began to have his first ideological doubts. These were occasioned, according to the prisoner, by the party's coming out openly in favor of autonomy for the Slavic-speaking minority in northern Greece. In 1950, during his trial, a judge asked him if he would be willing to resist with force of arms a Bulgarian (Communist) invasion of Macedonia. When Zafieris replied in the affirmative, his fellow defendants turned on him and denounced him as a traitor to the cause. The attitude of these comrades filled him with deep resentment. They did not "respect his party history." He began to realize that he could no longer be a good Communist. He signed a declaration of repentance.

There was much that was typical in the story of Epaminondas Zafieris. He had been born in the village, but grew up in the city. The son of a peasant turned bank clerk, with pretensions to a military career, he could scarcely be classified as proletarian. Rather, he stemmed from the lower middle

class, and he had the driving personal ambition so often characteristic of members of that class. He joined the Communists
partly from patriotic motives—Communism had come to be
identified with resistance to the foreign invader—and he became an activist partly because he hoped for a military career
with the party. Had the Communists won out in Greece,
Zafieris, instead of being a prisoner with a sentence of death
over him, would have become a high-ranking official of the
"new" and redoubtable Communist police. His repentance was
a product of the very factors which had led to his ideological
commitment. He signed a repentance declaration *after* the
cause of the guerrillas (and his career) were hopelessly
ruined, and *after* it had become clear to him that the Communists intended to surrender Greek Macedonia to the Slavs.
As a Communist he had taken great personal risks and he had
killed without remorse, in the cause. As an anti-Communist—
if (for example) his assignment to the royal gendarmerie had
been possible—he would have taken risks as great and killed
as ruthlessly.

Comparable data

From our Greek sample we get the impression that the social
composition of activists differs somewhat from that of leading
cadres: middle class elements are no longer dominant, while
both workers and peasants have increased in importance, with
the workers having a plurality. Yet property held by all three
classes, and education achieved, together with the tale of
Epaminondas Zafieris, suggest an atmosphere which for
Greece was distinctly middle class, or at least distinctly national average. We are dealing with those workers and peasants who are better off.

How characteristic is our Greek sample of the other parties
in eastern Europe? A few scattered statistics in Table 1.5, all
from the interwar period, suggest a general answer. Our
sample from the Greek prisons seems not untypical of east
European activists generally.

The social composition of the interwar parties reveals wide variation. The proportion of worker membership varies from a tenth to a half; the shifts in peasant and middle class adherence from party to party are equally great. These differences reflect differing social environments, but they also result from the efforts of Communist statisticians to put a bad situation in a

TABLE 1.5[10]

Social composition of interwar parties

Country	Year	% Workers	% Peasants	% Middle class	Other	Total
Czechoslovakia	1927	53.4	14.6	18.5	13.5	100.0
Greece	1932	42.6	54.4	3.0	.0	100.0
Greek sample	1952	42.3	33.8	23.9	.0	100.0
Poland	1932	39.0	40.5	5.5	15.0	100.0
Bulgaria	1919	10.2	46.2	43.6	.0	100.0

favorable light. In the Polish case, the Belorussian and Ukrainian subparties have been excluded from the count, thus reducing the importance of the peasant element. Of the Greek membership of 1932, only 6.6 per cent was made up of factory workers; all the others were casually assembled under the rubric "other workers." The Bulgarians often issued statements on the proportion of "wage workers" in their membership (43 per cent in 1919!) but in this category they included landless peasants and salaried employees as well as industrial

[10] *Kommunisticheskii internatsional pered shestym vsemirnym kongressom. Obsor deiatel'nosti IKKI i sektsii kominterna mezhdu V i VI kongressami* (hereafter cited as *Shestym kongressom*) (Moscow, 1928), pp. 187-88; T. Beichek, "Vopros o profsoiuzakh no IV s'ezde kommunisticheskoi partii Chekho-Slovakei," *Krasnyi internatsional profsoiuzov. Organ ispolnitel'nogo biuro krasnogo profinterna. Ezhemesiachnoe izdanie na russkom, nemetskom, frantsuskom i angliiskom iazykakh* (hereafter cited as *Krasnyi internatsional profsoiuzov*) (Moscow), no. 5 (1927), pp. 548-56; *Pente chronia agones 1931-36* (Athens, 1946), pp. 128-30; *Kommunisticheskii internatsional pered VII vsemirnym kongressom. Materialy* (hereafter cited as *VII kongressom*) (Moscow, 1935), pp. 285, 332; Joseph Rothschild, *The Communist Party of Bulgaria. Origins and Development (1883-1936)* (New York, 1959), pp. 95, 106.

workers. If we were able to introduce the proper corrections in Table 1.5, our 1952 Greek sample might well turn out to be somewhat on the high side, insofar as industrial workers are concerned.

None the less, the message of Table 1.5 is clear. If among leading cadres it was the middle class who dominated, among ordinary activists persons of middle class origin tend to be much less important. Among activists, no single class predominates, certainly not the proletariat. Despite the ringing words of the *Manifesto*, the proletariat is not, in eastern Europe, *the* revolutionary class. Among activists, the plurality lies with either the workers (two cases as of Table 1.5) or with the peasants (three cases). From a Marxist point of view, none of the parties for which we have data can boast of a satisfactory social composition. In this connection, the very dearth of statistics on the social composition of the east European parties speaks volumes.

In another and non-Marxian sense, of course, all members of the hard core, whatever their social origin, are middle class professionals. To take a prominent example, Gottwald, the leader of the Czech Communists, may have been trained as a joiner but, from 1920 until his flight to the Soviet Union in 1938, he was in fact a journalist and editor, employed full time during much of the period by the Communist daily *Rude pravo*.[11] Vafiades, a member of the Greek politburo, began life as a tobacco worker but ended his career as the commander of a guerrilla army.[12] Imre Nagy, ill-fated prime minister of Communist Hungary, was the son of a dwarfholder but most of his adult life was spent either in administering a Soviet collective farm or in supervising Hungarian land re-

[11] US House Committee on Foreign Affairs, *The Strategy and Tactics of World Communism. Supplement IV: Five Hundred Leading Communists in the Eastern Hemisphere, Including the USSR* (hereafter cited as *Five Hundred Leading Communists*) (Washington, D.C., 1948), p. 28; Dana Adams Schmidt, *Anatomy of a Satellite* (Boston, 1952), p. 40.
[12] *Five Hundred Leading Communists*, pp. 63-64.

form.[13] To put the matter bluntly, activists, or *apparatchiki* as they are sometimes called, insofar as they have not been formally trained as lawyers, teachers, and engineers, may be regarded as self-tutored professionals who have used the party to climb into the ranks of the middle class.

[13] *Ibid.*, pp. 65-66; Francois Fejto, *La tragedie hongroise ou une revolution socialiste anti-Sovietique* (Paris, 1936), pp. 189-225.

CHAPTER II:
THE SOFT PERIPHERY

W<small>E SUPPOSE</small> that if an activist, or *apparatchik*, were to read the preceding chapter, he would fall back on the argument that the party, as *apparat*, is (as Lenin said) only the vanguard of the proletariat. The party *leads* the proletariat to the fulfillment of its historic mission. In order properly to investigate the Marxian theory of Communism, therefore, we must examine the social composition of the Communist following in eastern Europe: what we have chosen to refer to as the "soft periphery."

In a broad sort of way, the mass following of the east European *apparat* has assumed, in chronological succession, three forms. In the 1920's the most important following numerically was made up of those who voted the Communist ticket. In the 1940's, after a period of outlawry and repression, some of the parties took to the field in military operations. Consequently the effective support of the *apparat* came, in this period, from guerrillas. After the seizure of power at the close of World War II, the *apparat* opened party membership to virtually all comers, and the formal parties swelled to the bursting point with opportunists. These in turn now became the principal indigenous support upon which the *apparat* depended. We shall examine each of these groups in turn—the voter, the guerrilla, and the opportunist—in an effort to determine the class character of each.

As is argued in Appendix A, certain of the elections held in eastern Europe since 1918 have been free elections in which the Communists participated on the basis of equality. Because there is no other way to determine whether the Communist vote in these elections was cast mainly by industrial workers, we have resorted to the statistical technique of correlation analysis. That is, we have compared by means of a well-known statistical process the geographic distribution of the Communist votes with the geographic distribution of the industrial workers.[1]

The results of this comparison are presented in Table 2.1. An explanation of the statistical technique in non-technical language is to be found in Appendix A. For the reader who wishes to know only how to interpret Table 2.1 and those tables which follow, it is sufficient to know that r stands for coefficient of correlation, or the measure of comparability; that σr stands for the standard error of r; and that when any r, whether it is positive or negative, is twice or more the size of σr, the correlation is significant, that is, it probably reflects a causal relationship. A significant positive correlation (say an r of .39, where $\sigma r = .15$) means that as industrial workers increase from one district to the next, the Communist vote also increases. In this case we are entitled to suppose that workers are, in general, voting the Communist ticket. A significant negative correlation ($r = -.71$, where $\sigma r = .30$) indicates that as industrial workers increase, Communist votes tend to decrease. An r less than twice the standard error, whether positive or negative, means that there is no significant pattern; some workers vote Communist, others do not, and there is no necessary connection.

The workers and the Communist vote

With this word of explanation let us glance at Table 2.1. Of the 10 cases analyzed, only 3 show positive correlation, and these instances are all in Greece, where no significant Socialist party has ever existed. There are 6 cases in which there was no significant relation (workers voting all tickets, including the Communist) and 1 case (Czechoslovakia, 1935) when the workers simply were not voting for the Communists. In Czechoslovakia, the most industrialized country of

[1] A standard reference work is Helen M. Walker and Joseph Lev, *Statistical Inference* (New York, 1953).

TABLE 2.1[2]

Industrial workers compared with Communist and Socialist votes

(1920-1936)

Country and election year	N (no. of districts) and σr (standard error of r)	r (coefficient of correlation) for relationship between workers and Communist votes	r for relationship between workers and Socialist votes
Czechoslovakia	N = 22		
1925	σr = .22	−.19	.77
1929		.01	.78
1935		−.46	.59
Slovakia	N = 79		
1929	σr = .11	.18	.57
Bulgaria	N = 15/16		
1919	σr = .27	−.12	−.15
1920		.03	.11
1923 (April)		−.01	−.05
Greece	N = 34		
1926	σr = .17	.40	No significant
1933		.70	Socialist
1936		.59	party

eastern Europe, the worker vote went mainly to the Socialists, as Table 2.1 shows.

There is other evidence to indicate that throughout the area the allegiance of the working class was split among a variety of parties. In 1927, there were 1.4 million trade union members in Czechoslovakia. Table 2.2 shows how this membership was distributed among various political affiliations. While it is no doubt true that there is a middle class element hidden in these figures, especially among the National Socialist and Christian Socialist unions, the fact remains that, insofar as the allegiance of organized labor is concerned, Communist labor represented a small minority, while the largest single bloc of organized labor was controlled by the

[2] For the raw data used in constructing this table see the appropriate country in Appendix B. The footnotes to this appendix indicate the original sources.

TABLE 2.2[3]

Union membership in Czechoslovakia (1927)

Type of union	Percentage of total union membership
Social Democratic	40.2
National Socialist (Benes)	21.4
Without political affiliation	14.9
Communist	14.1
Christian Socialist	9.4
	100.0

Social Democrats. This substantiates the results obtained by correlation analysis.

Indeed, in eastern Europe there were working class people who much preferred the political right. Interwar, the Tatabanyi coal mining district of Hungary returned Fascist Arrow cross, as well as Social Democratic, members to the Hungarian parliament. In the Romanian election of 1937, the Fascist Iron guard picked up much of the vote cast in 1931 for the Socialist and Communist tickets. After 1945, the Romanian Communist party organized shock squads from among worker groups originally created by the Iron guard. The Greek seaman's union known by the letters OENO, so renowned for its role in the Communist movement after 1941, was opposed by a less well-known and numerically weaker but firmly monarchist seaman's union known as PNO. The Communist union was strongest among Greek sailors abroad (OENO was founded in Liverpool), while the monarchist union had its strength among the sailors who worked in Greek waters.[4] After World War II a substantial fraction of Greek workers were consciously royalist and ardently anti-Communist; they voted for such conservative leaders as Tsal-

[3] Beichek, loc.cit.
[4] Lucretiu Patrascanu, Sous trois dictatures (Paris, 1941), pp. 136-37; for the phenomenon of double unionism in Greece see Petro P-ve, "Itogi ob'edinitel'nogo s'ezda grecheskikh profsoiuzakh," Krasny internatsional profsoiuzov, no. 4 (1929), pp. 296-99.

daris and Papagos. Leaders of the Greek left when interviewed by the writer in 1951-1952 were bitterly unanimous in this assertion and explained that many of these workers had come only recently from the country, where conservative and monarchist traditions were deeply rooted.

To put the whole matter in a few words, industrial labor in eastern Europe in the interwar period by no means manifested any kind of political solidarity. While there were workers who voted for the extreme left, there were others who cast their ballots for the extreme right, and still others who, in substantial numbers, supported parties belonging to neither extreme. If east European workers were conscious of their social status, they certainly did not manifest that consciousness by their voting behavior. Could it be that those workers who voted Communist did so for reasons not connected with their class affiliation?

If the working class does not provide the bulk of the Communist vote, then we must look elsewhere.

The peasants and the Communist vote

In countries where the Communist vote was massive, the vast majority of those who initialled the Communist ticket were people who lived in rural communities. In the Bulgarian election of April 1923, 69.9 per cent of all Communist voters resided in rural areas; the comparable figure for the Czechoslovak election of 1925 was 68.5 per cent, and for the Polish election of 1928, 72.6 per cent.[5] While some of these voters were no doubt local blacksmiths, wheelwrights, and other artisans, it seems more than probable that two-thirds of all Communist voters were tillers of the soil.

This being the case, the question is, which peasants? The Communist answer here is (as usual) very flat: landless

---

[5] *Elections pour la XXeme assemblee*, pp. 15-16; *Les elections a l'assemblee nationale en novembre 1925* (hereafter cited as *Assemblee nationale 1925*) (Prague, 1926), pp. 14*-15*; *Elections a la diete 1928*, pp. xxviii-xxix. Kh. Kabakchiev, a leading Bulgarian Communist, estimated that 75 per cent of the Communist vote of April 1923 was cast by peasants. Cf. Rothschild, p. 115, n. 117.

peasants, in the first instance; then dwarfholding peasants, those whose holdings are too small to support a peasant family. (As a rule, experts on eastern Europe regard anything less than 5 hectares, which is approximately 12 acres, as a dwarfholding.) Western scholars generally have agreed with the Communist view, in the sense of believing that peasant Communism was largely motivated by land hunger. Advocates of land reform—that is, the breaking up of big estates and the redistribution of these estates among the mass of peasants —are fond of arguing that such reform is the only practicable defense against Communism in rural areas.

It was natural that the Communists should appeal to the east European peasantry with the promise of further land reform. But the Communists did not believe in land reform, except as a device for winning popular support. Rather, they believed in the restoration of the great estates, which they called collectives; and, more than that, in the introduction of tractors and harvesters, the forcible removal of surplus agricultural manpower to city factories and state-owned mines, and the reduction of the peasants remaining in the countryside to the status of landless laborers. Since it was impossible to convince the peasants of the wisdom of this solution of the agrarian problem, the Communists did not try; such things were secrets for the initiated. Meantime, they attempted to persuade landless peasants and dwarfholders that a "little" revolution would be "a good thing." The question is whether they succeeded and, if so, to what extent.

In the interwar period the only territory combining free elections and large estates with a numerically significant Communist vote was Slovakia. In the case of dwarfholders, data are more extensive. In Table 2.3 the proportion of total arable held in estates greater than 500 hectares is taken as an index to the distribution of landless peasants; while the proportion of arable held in farms less than 5 hectares in extent is considered indicative of the strength of the dwarfholding population.

TABLE 2.3[6]

Landless peasants, dwarfholders, and Communist and Socialist votes
(1923-1929)

Comparison	Country and election year	N	σr	r
Landless peasants and Communist votes	Slovakia, 1929	79	.11	−.08
Landless peasants and Socialist votes				.55
Dwarfholders and Communist votes				.16
Dwarfholders and Socialist votes				.13
Dwarfholders and Communist votes	Bulgaria, April 1923	16	.26	−.72
Dwarfholders and Socialist votes				−.38

Table 2.3 indicates that the Communists were not correct in believing that it was the dwarfholder and, above all, the landless peasant who rallied to their cause. Communist votes simply are not concentrated in the same places as the rural proletariat. On the contrary, it is the Socialist vote which is concentrated where the landless workers are found; in the one instance for which data are available, r is five times one standard error. In Bulgaria, moreover, there is a negative correlation—roughly three times the standard error—between Communist votes and those with diminutive farms.

So far as the electoral evidence we have goes, then, there was no particular or necessary connection between landless peasants or dwarfholders, on the one hand, and Communist votes, on the other. Yet the paradox remains: the bulk of the Communist vote in eastern Europe is to be found in the countryside. We must ask again the question we put in the case of the industrial worker: could it be that those peasants who voted Communist did so for reasons not connected with their status as kulaks, dwarfholders, or landless laborers?

[6] For the raw data used in the construction of Table 2.3 see Appendix B.

Communist guerrillas

In his address to the meeting of Communist leaders (September 1947) which founded the Cominform, E. Kardelj, a Yugoslav delegate and himself a schoolteacher by trade, defended the social composition of the Yugoslav Partisan army. Speaking of the Partisan struggle (1941-1945), he said:

"Even within our party there were those—hardy dogmatists—who said that a partisan war could only be a secondary means, and in no case the principal weapon, in an armed rising. They said that the cities, and not the forests and the backwoods [okrainy], must decide the fate of the armed uprising. Therefore they regarded as incorrect the sending of workers from the towns to join the partisan detachments and as even more so the departure of the [party] leadership from the city and its partial conversion into a military leadership. In actuality, these and similar theories were the reflection of an opportunism which feared cold steel. The triumph of the policy of the central committee of our party proved, in contrast to all these opportunistic 'theories,' that, in the conditions of a cruel Fascist occupation of our country, it was precisely a partisan war in combination with all kinds of activity in the cities and country districts which was the best, the quickest, and the only possible road to victory."[7]

Kardelj's position is obviously awkward. The Germans and Italians had had control of the cities. Only by going to the mountain could the party have hoped to come to power. But in going to the mountain, the party (that is, the activist element) had to base itself on backward peasants and mountaineers, and not on the forward-looking urban working classes. There had been Yugoslav comrades dogmatic enough to point out this contradiction at the time, and schoolteacher Kardelj

[7] E. Kardelj, "Kommunisticheskaia partiia Jugoslavii v bor'be za nezavisimost' narodov strany, za narodnuiu vlast', za economicheskoe vostanovlenie i sotsialisticheskuiu rekonstruktsiu khoziaistva," *Informatsionnoe soveshchanie predstavitelei nekotorykh kompartii v Pol'she v kontse sentiabria 1947 goda* (hereafter cited as *Informatsionnoe soveshchanie*) (Moscow, 1948), p. 58.

found it necessary to refute them before the highest court in the Communist world, even though the rising in Yugoslavia had been blessed with unbelievable success.

In point of fact, the city workers of Yugoslavia had remained passive throughout the war. They were treated with disdainful consideration by the conquerors, who did not wish production disrupted. Comparatively speaking, the workers were well paid (they sent financial contributions to the hard-pressed guerrillas!). Except for leading cadres and some shock units, which were heavily student and intellectual in character, the war on the mountain was fought by the peasant and the mountaineer.[8]

It was much the same in Greece, though the Yugoslavs were critical of the Greek comrades, saying that the Greek Communist party did not even try to recruit city workers for the mountain but rather prepared to paralyze communications by means of strikes. Battalions of workers, the so-called Reserve ELAS, were trained for the day when the occupying forces would withdraw from Greece. The Greek leaders, said the Yugoslavs, did not believe that a true revolutionary force could be created by a peasant-fought partisan war but only by means of mass struggle in cities. Not until 1943, according to the Yugoslav version, did the Greeks come to realize that the true revolutionary front was on the mountain and not in the town.[9] In the fight with the British for the possession of Athens (December 1944) the politburo depended primarily on ELAS divisions brought in from the country, although Reserve ELAS units were also employed.

[8] Lazitch, *Tito*, pp. 63-65. The Bulgarian Communist rebels of September 1923 were also overwhelmingly peasant. See Kabakchiev, Boshkovic, and Vatis, p. 109; Rothschild, pp. 142, 144; M. Bombal' and I. Chirkov, "Sel'skokhoziaistvennyi proletariat i krestianskii internatsional," *Krasny internatsional profsouizov*, no. 4 (1924), pp. 330-36. Everywhere the rebel columns were overwhelmingly peasant in composition. For the most part the uprising took the form of hopeless charges by scythe-armed villagers against the towns and their well-armed garrisons. The centers of the rebellion had also been strongholds of Stamboliski's peasant movement.

[9] S. Vukmanovic, *Il partito communista greco e la lotta di liberazione nazionale* (np, 1951), pp. 30-46.

As for the Greek Democratic army of 1946-1949, its chief political commissar complained to party headquarters at the height of the fighting that "our units in central and western Macedonia [where the guerrillas were by far the strongest] are made up 90 per cent of peasants and 10 per cent of city folk (not all of whom are workers)."[10] In March 1948 the Greek politburo published an open letter, urging all its urban units to organize a mass exodus of workers to the mountain. But the proletariat remained unmoved. Four months after this appeal the central committee, meeting on Mt. Grammos, formally took note of the fact that the party had been unable to break through the irresolution and the spirit of wait-and-see which had been created in the broad masses of city dwellers by the "murderous terrorism of the monarcho-fascists."[11]

But perhaps the passivity of the urban masses is best explained by geography. It is not likely that those city workers who were pro-Communist were less genuinely so than those peasants who were pro-Communist. The little war is more easily maintained in mountainous areas. During the Nazi war, guerrilla bands operated for very long only where the terrain was extremely rugged, more particularly in the series of mountain chains which reaches from Trieste in the north to Athens and Adrianople on the south. The bulk of Yugoslav Partisan operations took place in Bosnia and Montenegro, the wildest parts of all this region, and in the ungracious territories immediately adjacent thereto. With the lines of normal communication held by hostile forces, it was difficult for city dwellers, even those who so desired, to make their way to such wild and isolated places.

[10] Cited in *ibid.*, p. 124, but see also pp. 126 and 148. During the Greek civil war of 1948-1949 the United Nations Special Commission for Observation in the Balkans (UNSCOB) established six forward observation posts and interviewed several hundred captured guerrillas. Summaries of the information so obtained were dispatched to UNSCOB headquarters in Athens. The summaries usually gave the vocation of the prisoners interviewed; the overwhelming mass turned out to be peasants and shepherds.

[11] *I organotiki politiki tou KKE 1918-1950* (nd, np), *passim.*

In these regions, moreover, geography combined with a proud tradition of guerrilla warfare. *Klefts* and *haiduks* who had joined plain everyday brigandage with patriotic opposition to the Turkish overlords were still the local heroes. The Serbian rising of 1804 and the Greek insurrection of 1821 had been led by these hero-brigands, and their deeds had passed into the folklore of the mountaineer. The *haiduk* songs were still sung at weddings and on other festive occasions, and the *haiduk* dances still danced. In the culture of these mountain dwellers armed insurrection against a foreign oppressor seemed natural.[12]

What was more, many of these mountains were food deficit areas, where imports of grain from less inhospitable terrain were necessary to maintain life. Once the economy had been disorganized by military occupation, raiding the enemy encampments became a principal source of food (and weapons). As the fighting progressed, villages were destroyed, either by way of Fascist reprisal, or by one set or other of guerrillas. The survivors had little choice but to seek refuge with the guerrilla bands. More often than not, a Partisan recruit became acquainted with Communist doctrine for the first time when the commissar of his unit undertook to instruct him.

To sum up: Communist guerrillas in eastern Europe were overwhelmingly of peasant and mountaineering stock. The number of industrial workers in the ranks of a guerrilla force was downright pitiful. Yet it was these peasant guerrilla fighters who provided the motor force for the establishment of Communist regimes in Yugoslavia and in Albania, and who probably would have brought the Communists to power in Greece had it not been for Western military intervention. The writer is reminded of a conversation he once had with a leader of the Greek left, a former minister in the EAM government on the mountain. Said the ex-minister in some

[12] For a presentation of this thesis in English see D. A. Tomasic, *National Communism and Soviet Strategy* (Washington, D.C., 1957), especially chapter IV. Much better is Ernst Halperin, *Der siegreiche Ketzer. Titos Kampf gegen Stalin* (Koeln, 1957), pp. 11-15.

dudgeon: *"En Europe orientale le partie communiste n'est guere une revolution. C'est plutot une jacquerie!"*

The opportunists

During the five years following the liberation of eastern Europe from the Nazis, the Communist parties grew in size at an unbelievable rate. Incredible is the case of the Romanian party, which numbered 883 members when Soviet troops began to pour into Bucharest in 1944, and five years later was a million strong.[13] Even the largest of the parties at the time of liberation, the Yugoslav, boasted only 141,000 members, which is to be compared with a membership of one-half million when that party was read out of the Cominform in 1948.

The huge size of the postwar parties was to a considerable extent the result of deliberate policy. The Communists wished to convince a skeptical world that theirs was a grass roots movement. They were also faced with the practical problem of operating the machinery of east European government, increasingly complex as the consequence of Communist-sponsored state ownership of industry. With their characteristic hurry, the Communist leaders admitted to party membership huge numbers of persons who had only cursory knowledge of Marxist doctrine. As W. Gomulka, secretary general of the Polish party, explained to the founding meeting of the Cominform in September 1947: "We have purposely allowed mass adherence to the party, since, in our circumstances, it was easier to work with a mass organization. A cadre party does not replace a mass party, the more so since we have few party activists who possess a high political level. . . . At the time of the elections, almost all members of the party were involved in the electoral campaign. This we could

[13] Ernst H[alp]erin in *Neue Zuercher Zeitung* (hereafter cited as *NZZ*), *Fernausgabe 242*, 3 September 1953; Francois Fejto, *Histoire des democraties populaires* (Paris, 1952), p. 195.

not have done without a mass party."[14] In short, the Polish party would have had difficulty "managing" the election of 1947 had it restricted membership to activists. In Czechoslovakia the mass party achieved in 1949 the preposterous size of 2.3 million members: one of every three adults in the Czech population wore the party button in his or her lapel.[15]

Two significant groups of inimical origin were brought, by deliberate policy, into the party's ranks in this first flush of Communist power: the Socialists and the Nazis. Or perhaps we should be charitable and say ex-Nazis and ex-collaborators; at any rate, people with evil on their consciences who now thought to save themselves by crossing over to the side of the erstwhile foe. The Communists welcomed Nazi converts, so long as they had not been prominent enough to cause the party embarrassment. In Hungary, former members of the Fascist Arrow cross party were offered release from concentration camps if they would see the light and affiliate with the Communists. Anti-Communist Hungarians regaled one another with accounts of the recruiting difficulties which (they liked to believe) plagued the party. To assist a membership drive, according to one story, premiums were offered: those who succeeded in recruiting one new party member would be excused from attending party meetings; those who recruited two new members would be permitted to resign from the party; those who recruited three would receive a certificate stating they had never belonged to the party; while those recruiting four would have their Arrow cross membership cards returned to them!

There were by 1951 in eastern Europe, exclusive of Greece, some 7 million party members. The hugeness of this figure is suggested by comparison with the Soviet Union, which, boasting approximately the same number of party members, had roughly twice the population of eastern Europe. The

[14] V. Gomulka, "O deiatel'nosti tsk Pol'skoi rabochei partii," *Informatsionnoe soveshchanie*, pp. 97-124.
[15] *Rude pravo* (Prague), 27 May 1949.

TABLE 2.4[16]

Size of the Communist parties of eastern Europe

	PERCENTAGE OF TOTAL POPULATION BELONGING TO THE PARTY	
Country	circa 1938	circa 1948
Czechoslovakia	0.5	21.0
Hungary	0.3	10.9
Bulgaria	0.4	6.3
Romania	0.006	6.3
Poland	0.06	6.0
Albania	0.0	3.8
USSR	1.4	3.8
Yugoslavia	0.09	2.6

party is largest on the westernmost periphery of eastern Europe, in Czechoslovakia and in Hungary.

Since opportunists are not Communists by conviction, but rather by convenience or by circumstance, we ought not, in strict logic, to be interested in their social provenance. Table 2.5 is therefore offered as a curiosity.

At any rate there is a pattern. Those parties located in that part of eastern Europe which is most industrial had the strongest representation of workers. This was in part, however, the result of the forcible absorption of the Socialist parties. In Czechoslovakia, Poland, and Hungary it had always been the Socialists who had commanded the allegiance of the great bulk of the industrial workers.

To summarize: at the periphery of the east European Communist movement it is clearly the peasants who have dominated. The bulk of Communist voters have resided in rural districts. Communist guerrillas were almost entirely peasants.

[16] P. Korbel, "Numerical Strength and Composition of the Communist Party of Czechoslovakia," published in mimeograph by the Free Europe committee, New York, 1954, p. 24; *Neos Kosmos*, II, (1950), p. 237; *For a Lasting Peace, for a People's Democracy* (Bucharest), 2 March 1951; Fejto, *Democraties populaires*, p. 195; Lazitch, p. 149; Skendi (ed.), p. 84; Harry Schwartz in *New York Times* (hereafter cited as *NYT*), 30 April 1950 and 27 February 1949; *NYT*, 4 November 1942, p. 7, col. 3.

TABLE 2.5[17]

Social composition of east European Communist parties according
to official data (1947-1948)

Party	Date of information	% Workers	% Peasants	% Middle class	Total
Polish	1948	57.3	22.1	20.6	100.0
Czechoslovak	1948	57.0	31.0	12.0	100.0
Hungarian	1947	56.0	37.3	6.7	100.0
Romanian	1947	44.0	39.0	17.0	100.0
Yugoslav	1948	29.5	49.4	21.1	100.0
Bulgarian	1947	25.9	43.8	30.3	100.0
Albanian	1948	19.7	66.9	13.4	100.0

Even among opportunists, the median proportion of peasants
(see Table 2.5) has been on the order of two-fifths.

Nor is it possible to find a class basis for this heavy participation of the peasantry in the movement. Between those who
have no land, or too little, and Communist votes, there is little
correlation or none.

At the periphery, industrial workers have constituted a
small minority. They have been far from casting a majority
vote for the Communists; on the contrary, they have divided
their vote among all parties, including parties with the coloring of the far right. In eastern Europe the Communist following has been no more proletarian in its social composition
than was the hard core.

[17] Richard F. Staar, "New Course in Communist Poland," *Journal of
Politics*, xx (1958), pp. 64-88; Sidney Gruson in *NYT*, 10 January
1949; Rudolph Slansky's speech in *Rude pravo*, 27 May 1949; I. Revai,
"O deiatel'nosti tsk Vengerskoi kommunisticheskoi partii," *Informatsionnoe soveshchanie*, pp. 256-79; G. Georgiu-Dej, "Kommunisticheskaia
partiia Rumyni v bor'be za demokratizatsiiu strany," *ibid.*, pp. 233-55;
Tomasic, pp. 111-12; V. Chervenkov "O rabote Bolgarskoi rabochei
partii (Kommunistov)," *Informatsionnoe soveshchanie*, pp. 203-32;
Skendi (ed.), p. 84. It should be noted that the percentage of workers
has tended to decline, while the percentage of middle class persons has
tended to increase with the passage of time. Thus, in the case of Poland,
worker representation had dropped to 37.3 per cent by 1959, that of
intellectuals and "others" had risen to 46.0 per cent. Cf. Richard F.
Staar, "Third Congress of the Polish Communist Party," *The American
Slavic and East European Review* (hereafter cited as *ASEER*), xix
(1960), pp. 63-73.

Communism in eastern Europe has not been, in any significant sense of the term, a proletarian movement. It has been representative of all social classes, the peasantry and the bourgeoisie as well as the working class. Communist terminology itself inadvertently confesses to the multi-class character of the movement. In Communist literature there is not only the "working class," which is clearly differentiated from the "toiling masses," but also there is the "progressive intelligentsia."

The question is, *which* proletarian, *which* bourgeois elements, and *which* peasants are revolutionary? And why? If the classic theory of class warfare does not explain the emergence of a Communist movement in eastern Europe, then what theory does?

CHAPTER III: A LESS
ENCHANTING HYPOTHESIS

I N EASTERN EUROPE the social groups which produce above-average numbers of Communists are not difficult to discover, once the Marxian, or class, approach to the problem has been abandoned. The Communist-producing groups are rather diverse: tobacco workers (to mention a group from the proletariat), peasants producing a single cash crop for the market, schoolteachers, refugees uprooted from their traditional homeland, youth. Study of some of these disparate groups will suggest that, despite their differences, they possess certain significant traits in common.

We shall begin this examination with the tobacco worker, by whom we mean, not the peasant who toils in the field, nor the worker who stands at the cigarette fabricating machine, but rather the laborer who sorts and cures the tobacco in the warehouse. *This* tobacco worker is a special breed.

The tobacco worker as enrage

Marxism spread among the tobacco workers of the Balkans very early. In 1909, in the Greek port of Volos, a Marxist circle organized a strike of tobacco workers. In the backward and inaccessible Austrian-held province of Bosnia, a Social Democratic party led a strike of tobacco workers at about the same time. In 1917, G. Dimitrov, then the leader of the left-wing of Bulgarian Social Democracy, later secretary general of the Comintern, slipped into the Xanthe-Drama area of Greece and founded an illegal organization of tobacco workers.

Furthermore, the trade is a disturbed one. Official Bulgarian statistics for the period 1922-1926 show that, among all trades, the tobacco workers were first in the frequency of strikes, first in the percentage of workers out per strike, and first in the number of working days lost. Greek Communist data for a six-month period in 1935 show that the tobacco workers' union was the second most restive in all of Greece.[1]

The writer was able to spend some time on the trail of the Greek tobacco worker. The tobacco workers' union is among the oldest and most stoutly organized in Greece; in matters of seniority and the closed shop, the tobacco worker is among the best protected laborers in Greece. Furthermore, his work is counted as highly skilled and is among the best paid. The women, dressed in neatly pressed and brightly colored cotton prints, are reputed to be the best-dressed among lower class Greek women. On pay day, fruit peddlers and other hawkers can be seen hovering near the doors of the warehouses, doing a brisk trade in oranges and other fruits much too expensive for the purse of the average Greek worker.

On the other hand, employment among tobacco workers is highly seasonal. Much depends on the state of the world market and its ability to absorb Greek (that is, Turkish) tobacco. A tobacco manipulator may be employed only six months in the year.[2] During unemployment he must fall back on a meagre government dole. He alternates between more than average prosperity and hungry impecuniousness.

His is, moreover, a "conversational trade." A tobacco warehouse is divided into sizeable rooms. A hundred or more sorters of both sexes will sit in a circle on the floor, cheek by jowl. (Anti-Communists insist there is much sexual promiscuity among tobacco workers.) Because artificial ventilation

[1] Stella D. Blagoyeva, *Dimitrov. A Biography* (New York, 1934), pp. 28-29; *Annuaire statistique du royaume de la Bulgarie 1926* (hereafter cited as *Annuaire Bulgarie 1926*) (Sofia, 1927), pp. 172-73; Kh. Rozov, "Vseobshchaia stachka tabachnikov," *Krasnyi internatsional profsoiuzov*, no. 7 (1929), pp. 543-47; *Rizospastis* (Athens), 15 August and 28 November 1935; J. Saris, "Vseobshchaia zabastovka v Gretsii. Polozhenie rabochego klassa i levykh organizatsii," *Krasnyi internatsional profsoiuzov*, no. 8 (1928), pp. 118-23; J. Kimis, "Gretsia. Sovremennoe profdvizhenie," *ibid.*, pp. 543-48.

[2] According to the census of 1928, 62.9 per cent of tobacco workers were employed 200 days a year or less. *Annuaire Grece 1930*, p. 195. Rozov, *loc.cit.*, states that the Bulgarian tobacco worker was busy no more than 200 days a year.

is expensive, the atmosphere is humid and heavy with tobacco dust. While sorting out the leaves, the workers chatter about their personal affairs and about politics. During periods of unemployment they spend much of their time in the *kafeneion*, or coffee house, in Greece an ecumenical institution, with tables on the sunny sidewalk, free newspapers, boards for backgammon, and not infrequently an agitator or two. Thus the tobacco worker couples his cycles of prosperity and poverty with abundant opportunities for "education."

The cash cropper

In eastern Europe the single crop cultivated by the cash cropper varies from area to area. Usually it is wheat, but it may also be tobacco, or grapes,[3] or silk. Whatever the crop, it is subject to the vagaries of international trade. In boom times the cash cropper is the first to enjoy prosperity, but he is also the first to feel the cold winds of economic depression. As for his physical location, he naturally tends to congregate on plains, where the soil is fruitful and where communication with the outside world is good. All this is well exemplified in the Greek province of Drama.

The province of Drama lies in eastern Macedonia and is directly adjacent to the Bulgarian frontier. From the town of Drama northward to the frontier, the province is rough and mountainous, and its denizens practice a more or less self-sufficient agriculture. In the valley to the south of the town, however, through which the railroad linking Salonika with Turkish Edirne pursues its meandering way, the population is almost entirely dependent upon tobacco farming. On the mountain slopes the Communist vote is very low, and in the villages, perched high up, almost non-existent. The Communist vote in Drama province is almost entirely concentrated in the valley. Seemingly, the flatter the valley floor is, and the greater the ease of communication, the higher the Communist

[3] For an analysis of the relationship between vineyards and Communism see R. V. Burks, "Catholic Parties in Latin Europe," *JMH*, xxiv (1952), pp. 269-86.

vote. (It is also noticeable that the frequency of Communist voters among the villagers increases with proximity to the warehouses where the tobacco is graded.)

That Drama is not an isolated case is suggested by the correlations in Table 3.1. In the Bulgarian instance, r is not

TABLE 3.1[4]

Percentage of arable devoted to wheat compared with percentile voting strength of the Communists

Country	Election	N	σr	r
Bulgaria	April 1923	16	.27	.39
Greece	1936	34	.17	.52
Slovakia	1929	79	.11	.42

twice σr, but in Greece it is two and one-half times, and in Slovakia (where N is 79) nearly four.

Fate of the refugee

In 1920 the Greeks, seized by a typical Balkan fit of nationalist megalomania, attempted to invade Turkey and restore the Byzantine empire, the last remnant of which had disappeared in 1453, half a millennium earlier. This atavistic enterprise ended in defeat. Among other consequences, the Greek minority which had inhabited the coasts of Anatolia for thousands of years was driven out by the irate Turks and forced to "return" to metropolitan Greece. As if this were not tragedy enough, the millenary colonies of Greeks which were settled along the Black Sea coast of Bulgaria, the Ukraine, and the Caucasus were also forced to seek refuge in Greece.

There is widespread agreement in Greece that refugee elements, whether urban or rural, proletarian, peasant, or middle class, constitute the core of the Communist vote.[5]

[4] For the raw data see the appropriate countries in Appendix B.

[5] Speech of N. Zachariades in *To 7on sinedrion tou Kappa kappa epsilon* (Athens, 1945), vol. E', p. 13B.

Correlation analysis (in Table 3.2) tends to bear out the popular notion. All three rr are more than three times one σr!

TABLE 3.2[6]

Refugees from Asia Minor and
Communist votes in Greece

$N = 34 \qquad \sigma r = .17$

Election	r
1926	.62
1933	.57
1936	.67

A glance at the birthplaces of a dozen or so leading Communists in postwar Greece reveals the same relationship (Table 3.3).

TABLE 3.3[7]

Geographic origin of leading
Greek Communists

Name	Natal province
Bartzotas	Thessally
Hadjivassiliou	Asia Minor
Ioannides	Thessally
Karageorgis	Euboea
Partsalides	Asia Minor
Porphyrogenis	Thessally
Roussos	Eastern Thrace
Siantos	Thessally
Stringos	Cyprus
Theos	Thessally
Vafiades	Asia Minor
Vlandas	Crete
Zachariades	Asia Minor

Of the thirteen Communists listed, four were born in Asia Minor, one in the Turkish province of Eastern Thrace, and one in the British-held island of Cyprus, so that nearly half qualify as refugees, double the proportion of refugees in the

[6] For the raw data see "Greece" in Appendix B.
[7] *Five Hundred Leading Communists*, pp. 61-64.

Greek population generally.[8] (Those familiar with the history of modern Greece will note that most of the remaining leaders—Karageorgis from Euboea is the solitary exception—were born in those parts of the country which were liberated from Turkish rule long after the formation of the original Greek state in 1829. Except for the city of Athens, Greek Communism has not made much headway in old Greece, which is the relatively happy and satisfied part of the country.)

But to return to the refugees. All told, there were perhaps 1.2 million of these migrants: men, women, and children. The population of the Greek homeland at the time the refugees began to arrive was on the order of 5 million.[9] It was as if the United States had been forced to accept in the years 1922-1928 some 29 million uprooted and poverty-stricken English-speaking immigrants. The Greek economy, never robust, underwent severe shock. Economically, the refugees proved difficult of assimilation. Even today their villages and their suburban quarters (still shanty in part) are easily distinguishable: their architecture, their dialects, even their music continue to possess an Asiatic flavor.

In Turkey, in the Caucasus, in the Ukraine, countries as backward perhaps as Greece, the refugees had constituted a middle class of lawyers, merchants, and government officials. Their standard of living, measured against that of their Turkish or Russian neighbors, had been high. But in Greece many of these middle class people became dwarf-holders and settled on the land, while even greater numbers crowded into characteristic settlements on the periphery of Athens, Piraeus, and Salonika, there to eke out existence as unskilled laborers or as petty merchants. They resented bitterly this change in their social status.[10]

[8] *Annuaire statistique de la Grece 1931* (hereafter cited as *Annuaire Grece 1931*), p. 30.
[9] The basic work on the Greek refugee is Vasillos G. Valaoras, *To dimografikon provlima tis Ellados kai i epidrasis ton prosfigon* (Athens, 1939).
[10] William Hardy McNeill, *The Greek Dilemma: War and Aftermath* (New York, 1947), p. 31

It is said that the refugees most predisposed to Communism were not those from Asia Minor but those from the Russian Caucasus, the "Caucasians," as they are called in Greece. It is estimated that in Kilkis province, where one-third of all Caucasians are settled, 80 per cent of them voted for the Communists in the election of 1951. On the other hand, during the occupation, small numbers of Caucasians enlisted in the German-organized security battalions, or otherwise collaborated with the Nazis.

Authorities on the Caucasian problem are of the opinion that the basic reason for the greater affinity of these particular refugees for the Communist cause was the nostalgic memory of the Russian homeland. Life in Greece was so hard that the Caucasian past, even with the stormy events of the Russian revolution, became a kind of idyll. The Caucasians were ready to believe in a Soviet paradise. In the old country, Caucasian leaders had been Menshevik; in Greece they turned Bolshevik. An example of this typical transition is provided by the physician, I. Passalides, the leader of the Communist delegation in the Greek parliament in the 1950's. The greatest influence of the Caucasian idyll, however, was on the second generation, those born in Greece, who knew the far-off homeland only from the accounts of their parents.

Communism and youth

In the years after 1944, east European Communists did a good deal of juggling with existing electoral law. One of the characteristic changes was a reduction in the minimum voting age. Before the war, in 1939, the minimum voting age in most countries had been 21 years; in Poland, however, it was 24, in Hungary 26, and in Romania 30. By 1953 each state in eastern Europe, except Greece, had reduced the minimum voting age to 18 years. Even in Greece the guerrillas held a kind of election in the territories under their control during October 1947, with the minimum age reduced to 18.[11]

[11] See the articles on post World War II elections in eastern Europe,

Since the minimum voting age in the Soviet Union was 18 years, it may be assumed that the change in satellite electoral law was at least in part a matter of doctrine. Even Bela Kun, the Communist dictator of Hungary after World War I, had reduced the age to 18 for an April 1919 Hungarian election to local and national Soviets.[12] Still, it may also be possible that the Communists believed that a reduction in voting age would increase their margin at the polls in those countries where free elections were held. Others besides the Communists entertained this view. The Bulgarian opposition, announcing its intent of boycotting the election scheduled for November 1945, explained that the lowering of the minimum voting age was not only a violation of the constitution but also a device for securing more votes for the Communist-dominated Fatherland front.[13]

Balloting in the Trieste election of June 1949 provides the

---

some unsigned, by Henry H. Collins, Jr. in *Soviet Russia Today* (New York), the issues of January, February, March, June, and July 1948; A. Kristo, chief of the press section, Ministry of Foreign Affairs, Tirana, to Henry H. Collins, Jr., 29 April 1947, in the files of the National Council of Soviet-American Friendship, New York City; Sandor Brunauer, "Communist Use of the Franchise in Hungary," mimeograph publication of the Mid-European Studies Center of New York City, no. 29, 1954, pp. 4, 13; William Diamond, *Czechoslovakia between East and West* (London, 1947), p. 18; *Bulletin d'information pour les Roumains de l'etranger* (Paris), 10 February 1948, p. 6; M. B. Petrovich, "The Central Government of Yugoslavia," *Political Science Quarterly* (hereafter cited as *PSQ*), LXII (1947), pp. 504-30; *Dziennik ustaw Rzeczypospolitej Polskiej* (Warsaw), 1935, no. 319, chapter 11, article 11; AP dispatch on the Polish election in *NYT*, 27 October 1952, p. 25; UP dispatch from Bucharest in *NZZ, Fernausgabe 200*, 22 July 1952; dispatch on the Romanian election in *NYT*, 6 October 1947, special to the *NYT*, Athens, in *NYT*, 7 October 1947, p. 6. The Yugoslav party program of 1940 called for a reduction of the voting age to 18 years. Ante Ciliga (ed.), "Les decisions de la cinquieme conference du parti Communiste yougoslave (octobre 1940)" (hereafter cited as "Cinquieme conference 1940") (typescript sent by the editor to R. V. Burks in 1950), p. 27.

[12] M. Rakosi, "Sozdanie kommunisticheskoi partii Vengrii. Vengerskaia respublika (1917-1919 gg)," *Voprosy istorii* (Moscow), November 1955, pp. 41-64.

[13] "Die wahlkampagne in Bulgarien," *NZZ, Morgenausgabe 1678*, 8 November 1945. See also AP dispatch from Sofia on 16 November 1945, *NYT*, 17 November 1945, p. 9.

Bulgarian opposition with statistical support for its electoral analysis.

TABLE 3.4[14]

Age and political preference, Trieste (1949)

$N = 12;$ $\sigma r = .29$

Age group	Compared with Communists ρ	Compared with Christian Democrats ρ	Compared with Italian social movement ρ
21-24	.67	−.60	−.69
25-29	.64	−.57	−.64
30-34	.29	−.24	−.31
35-39	.59	−.64	−.62
40-44	.26	−.31	−.31
45-49	.14	−.14	−.14
50-54	−.67	.76	.79
55-59	−.79	.79	.79
60-64	−.62	.68	.74
65-69	−.38	.36	.45
70 +	−.38	.36	.41

Ideologically speaking, the Christian Democrats occupied a position to the right of center. The Italian social movement was an openly neo-Fascist party, on the extreme right. What Table 3.4 shows is that there is a necessary positive correlation between Communist votes and the age groups 21-29 years. (Presumably the correlation would be at least as high for those under 21 years.) In contrast there is, for the same age group, a negative correlation with both Christian Democratic and Italian social voters. The relationship reverses itself for the age groups 50-64: the correlation with Communist voters is clearly negative, with Christian Democratic and Italian social voters clearly positive.

[14] "Come hanno votato Trieste," *Cronache sociali* (Rome), no. 14, 1 August 1949, pp. 1-10. $\rho = $ rho, usually a less accurate measure of correlation than r. Since the source does not provide the raw data, it was not possible to recalculate and convert to r. At the end of 1919, 90 per cent of the membership of the Bolshevik party was 40 years of age or less; in 1927 over 85 per cent were under 40, while as late as 1952 about three quarters of party members were estimated to be under 45 years of age, Schapiro, pp. 233, 310, 524.

There is confirmation of this association between youth and Communism at the cadre level. We have the ages of the some 10,000 candidates who stood for election in the interwar period, and whose professional affiliations were presented in Table 1.1. The average age of the Communist candidates alone was 36.2 years, making them seven years younger than their opponents.

A Greek once offered the writer an adage: he who is young and not a Communist has no heart; he who is old and believes in Communism has no head. A police officer who for twelve years prior to 1941 was charged with the surveillance of Communists in the Athens-Piraeus area avers that among university students 40 per cent had Communist sympathies (as compared with 7 per cent among the electorate at this same time). The officer estimated that perhaps 15 per cent were actually members of the Communist youth. After graduation the percentage of members dropped to 2 or 3, and the number of sympathizers fell off proportionately. Once the student had become established, once the period of professional uncertainty, irregular meals, midnight study, and sexual experimentation had passed, susceptibility to Communism dropped off sharply. (It is an unfortunate and fallacious platitude of American culture that the period of youth is an especially happy one.)

The role of the student is clearest in Albania, the most primitive of the east European countries. Before the Albanian party was organized in 1941 the chief center of Communist ideas was the French gymnasium in Korca, in southeastern Albania near the Greek frontier. Here Socialist professors from Paris introduced the student body to the Marxist *Gedankenwelt*.[15]

One of the students at the gymnasium was Enver Hoxha, later secretary general of the Albanian party. Hoxha's father was a judge and landowner; he secured the boy a government scholarship for study abroad, despite his mediocre grades.

[15] V[ictor] M[eier] in *NZZ, Morgenausgabe* 1073, 13 April 1957.

At the University of Montpelier in southern France, Hoxha failed flatly at the study of law. From Montpelier he moved to Brussels, where he served as secretary to the honorary Albanian consul, and began to dabble in Communist affairs. In 1936 the young man came home, without academic laurels but with a deal of Communist doctrine in his baggage. He found employment as a teacher of elementary French at the Korca gymnasium.[16]

The Albanian *actif* contained a large number of Hoxhas, youths who had been sent to the West to study, who had specialized in such esoteric fields as Romance philology and corporation law, and who had returned to find unhappy employment as interpreters or schoolteachers. A sample of 27 Albanian leading cadres included 13 who had studied abroad.[17]

A further 10 of the 27 Albanian cadres had attended gymnasium or its equivalent; this fact is probably also significant. Naturally those who, like Hoxha, had actually been to the West would be more acutely aware of the differences in living standards. But the psychological effect of returning from Lodz or Jasi to the east European equivalent of Podunk would be much the same. The youngster, fresh out of lycee, approached the village and its backward ways as something to be changed, root and branch. When village tradition and village superstition and suffocating village poverty proved obdurate, conversion to apocalyptic Communism might follow.[18]

[16] Lazitch, p. 68; "History of the Albanian Communist Party I," *News from Behind the Iron Curtain* (hereafter cited as *NBIC*), IV (November 1955), pp. 3-10.

[17] Skendi (ed.), pp. 323-45.

[18] Reuben Markham, *Tito's Imperial Communism* (Chapel Hill, 1947), p. 62; Ivo Duchacek, "The Strategy of Communist Infiltration: the Case of Czechoslovakia," mimeograph publication of the Yale Institute of International Studies, 1949, p. 28. In the aftermath of the Communist uprising of 1923 the Bulgarian government dissolved a teachers' union and various student groups, closed many schools, and dismissed more than 1,500 elementary school teachers. Rothschild, p. 145, n. 146.

Backwardness and Communism

The case of youth suggests that Communism in under-developed countries may have significant characteristics which differentiate it from the Communism of industrial lands. It appears, for example, that Communism more easily captures control of trade unions where there is less in the way of an industrial proletariat. Comintern figures for adherence to Communist, as opposed to non-Communist, unions are shown in Table 3.5.

TABLE 3.5[19]

Adherence to Communist unions as a percentage
of total union membership (1921)

Country	%
Hungary	0.0
Poland	20.7
Czechoslovakia	25.0
Romania	36.0
Greece	50.0
Bulgaria	85.8
Yugoslavia	90.0

The Hungarian figure is artificially low, owing to the out-lawry of Communism in that country. The remaining figures in Table 3.5 are only rough approximations, padded in favor of the Communists by inclusion of an estimated number of workers organized in non-Communist unions but believed by the Comintern to sympathize with Communism. None the less, it is striking how regularly the proportion of Communist-minded labor rises as we proceed down the scale from rela-tively advanced to relatively underdeveloped countries.

It also seems to be true that Communism tends to swallow up Socialism in the less advanced lands. This characteristic

[19] *Ezhegodnik kominterna. Spravochnaia kniga po istorii mezhdunarod-nogo rabochego politicheskogo i professional'nogo dvizheniia—statistike i ekonomike vsekh stran mira na 1923 god* (hereafter cited as *Ezhegodnik kominterna*) (Moscow, 1923), pp. 82-83. We use the term "adherence" since the Comintern figures include estimates of the num-bers formally belonging to non-Communist unions but actually sympa-thizing with Moscow.

is worth special consideration, since Communism and Socialism both derive from the same Marxist heritage, the one being, so to speak, violence-minded, while the other adopts the gradualism of parliamentary legislation. Let us compare the Communist and Socialist votes in the three provinces of interwar Czechoslovakia (Table 3.6).

TABLE 3.6[20]

Socialist and Communist votes in Czechoslovakia (1929)

Province	Communist as % of total vote cast	Socialist as % of total vote cast
Bohemia-Moravia	9.8	22.9
Slovakia	10.7	9.8
Ruthenia	15.2	8.6

In other words, Socialists are more than twice as numerous as Communists in Bohemia and Moravia, the western, industrialized districts of Czechoslovakia; while in eastern, overwhelmingly agrarian Ruthenia, the relationship is almost reversed. Slovakia occupies an intermediate position, with Socialist and Communist strength about equal. This relationship not only holds for Czechoslovakia; it appears also to be valid for the whole of eastern Europe.

The results in Table 3.7 are distorted by the fact that in 1922 the Hungarian Communist party had been outlawed and that the Albanian party did not yet exist. Regardless of these lacunae, however, it seems probable that the three countries nearest Germany would have had, on the average, roughly twice as many Socialist as Communist voters; while the three nearest Turkey would have had four times as many Communist as Socialist voters. Romania, like Slovakia, occupies an intermediate position.

Thus as we proceed south and east into the more agrarian

[20] Calculations based on *Les elections a la chambre des deputes faites en octobre 1929* (hereafter cited as *Chambre des deputes 1929*) (Prague, 1930), pp. 14-33.

TABLE 3.7[21]

Comparison of Communist and Socialist votes

Country and election year	Communist as % of total votes cast	Socialist as % of total votes cast
Czechoslovakia 1925 Poland 1928 Hungary 1922	8.2	13.8
Romania 1922	0.6	1.0
Yugoslavia 1920 Bulgaria 1920 Greece 1926	12.2	2.9

parts of the area, the Communist tends to replace the Socialist vote, and a higher proportion of the (smaller) proletariat is sympathetic to the Communist cause. One further generalization of this sort appears possible: as we move south and east the percentage of women involved in the Communist movement declines (see Table 3.8).

This is partly the result, no doubt, of the fact that women are less exposed to outside (Western) influence. The more backward the society, the smaller the proportion of educated women and the greater the extent to which woman is bound to her family and her locale.

The writer well remembers a conversation with female repentants in the Greek prison for women at Patras. None of the prisoners could have been thought of as even remotely pretty. In clothing and grooming, they were all several cuts below the average of male repentants. Though they were

[21] *Assemblee nationale 1925*, pp. 14*-15*; *Elections a la diete 1928*, pp. xxviii-xxxvii; *Annuaire statistique hongrois. Nouveau cours*, XXXV (Budapest, 1929), p. 245; N. T. Ionescu, "Alegerile legislative din Martie 1922," *Bulletin statistique de la Roumanie. Publie par la direction generale de la statistique du ministere de l'industrie et du commerce* (Bucharest), no. 2 (July-December 1923), pp. 84-118; *Statistichki pregled 1920*, section 56; *Annuaire statistique du royaume de Bulgarie (1913-22)* (hereafter cited as *Annuaire Bulgarie 1913-22*) (Sofia, 1924), part C, p. 60; *Statistique des elections des deputes du 7 novembre 1926* (hereafter cited as *Elections des deputes 1926*) (Athens, 1928), pp. xxii-xxiii.

TABLE 3.8[22]

Females as a percentage of Communist party membership

Party and year		% female
Czechoslovak	1949	33.0
Hungarian	1950	28.9
Soviet	1951	20.7
Yugoslav	1948	20.0
Polish	1951	18.0
Sample of Greek repentants	1952	14.0
Bulgarian	1947	13.1
Slovak	1950	11.7

friendly and even cordial in their behavior, the writer had difficulty in establishing communication. (The majority could neither read nor write and the filling out of the questionnaires had been a long and cumbersome process, involving the employment of amanuenses).

The women prisoners had heard of the United Nations, but they were unable to explain the nature or the function of this organization. They knew that a war was underway in Korea and that the protagonists were Communists on the one side and Americans on the other, but they were not clear as to what nations other than the American were involved. They knew that the Americans had been charged with waging

[22] Korbel, pp. 15-16; I. Revai, *loc.cit.*; *NYT*, 3 May 1951, p. 20, col. 5; Richard F. Staar, *The Political Framework of Communist Poland* (unpublished doctoral dissertation, University of Michigan, 1953), p. 172; Chervenkov, *loc.cit.*; Fred Warner Neal, "The Communist Party of Yugoslavia," *American Political Science Review*, LI (1957), pp. 88-111; Boris Meissner, *Russland unter Chruschtschow* (Munich, 1960), p. 193, gives the percentage of women in the Soviet party as of 1956 as 19.5.

It is worth noting that the returns for the semi-free Hungarian election of 1947 were broken down by sex. Of the Communist electorate 48.5 per cent were female, of the Social Democratic 51.5 per cent, of the Smallholders' 53.0, of the National Democrats' 59.5, and of the National Christian 73.5 per cent. Thus the more radical the party, the lower the proportion of its voting strength which came from women. For the returns see Gyula Mike (ed.), *Magyar statisztikai zsebkonyv. XV Evfolyam 1948. A Magyar kozponti statisztikai hivatel* (Budapest, 1948), pp. 268-69. For the semi-free character of the 1947 Hungarian election see H[ans] E. T[uetsch] in *NZZ, Mittagausgabe 466*, 7 March 1950.

bacteriological warfare, but declared flatly that this charge was a Soviet calumny designed to mislead the masses. Eisenhower was an American general, but what role he had played or where he had served, they could not say. An effort was made to draw them out on some American propaganda films which they had been shown and which, according to the warden, they had enjoyed hugely. But it soon became obvious that the repentants had regarded the films strictly in the light of entertainment.

The women were asked for whom they would vote in the then impending general election, on the (unlikely) supposition that they would be released in time to participate. At this point the writer was talking with a group of eighteen repentants. All eighteen were in favor of Field Marshal Alexander Papagos, chief of the right-wing Greek Rally and principal hero of the recently concluded war against the guerrillas. The writer undertook to explain that the Plastiras coalition, a combination of parties of the center and the left, but excluding the Communists, was in favor of a broad policy of amnesty toward Communist, and particularly ex-Communist, prisoners. The Papagos party was opposed to amnesty.

This line of reasoning failed to budge the ladies of Patras. Papagos was against the Communists, they said. He would deal them deadly blows. General Nicholas Plastiras, on the other hand, was a philo-Communist, whose party was full of "leakages." He would not take serious action against the Communists.

From their experience with Communism, would the prisoners say there was anything at all that was good about the party? Did life in the party present any positive aspects? In their view, the party was pure evil. It had deceived them. It had promised them fine homes and machine-made dresses. Instead, it had brought them struggle, privation, and now suffering. Their lot had been hard enough without the party. Would they enter politics again, once released? Perhaps become active in the cause of the Rally? Once burned, twice shy, came the retort. No, they would never join another political organization!

The interview suggested many things. The prisoners' natural reaction to the world of politics was one of apathy; even though they had been imprisoned for crimes committed in the name of Communism, they still did not possess what might be called political awareness. They could not discuss politics because they knew almost nothing about the subject. By their own account, their motivation in joining the party had been far from ideological. Fine homes and machine-made dresses! Once they broke with the party, they moved off to the extreme right. In their perception there seemed to be no shades of gray.

The declining susceptibility of the female to the Communist appeal as we move into less developed areas may be not only a matter of poorer communication and lower awareness, however. This declining susceptibility may also be related to woman's closer association with the traditional order, the more so the less that order has been disturbed. This affinity is expressed in her close dependence on the church and in her deep religious feeling. She knows that the world must be as it is because the Divine Being has willed that it be so, and His dispositions are not to be changed by the hand of man. In short, woman is not only less aware of the existence of a much more secure and satisfying life elsewhere; she is also more convinced that man-made improvements in her local situation are out of the question.

A non-Marxian hypothesis

We are now in a position to pull together the various causal notions put forward in the present chapter and attempt to shape them into some kind of hypothesis explaining, or helping to explain, why Communism exists in eastern Europe. Essentially, we have come across two kinds of cases: those which are the by-product of a badly disturbed social order, and those which reflect the impact of Western civilization on the more backward east European provinces. In the first category we find the tobacco worker, the cash cropper, and the refugee; in the second, youth and—in a negative sense—women. The two categories are not mutually exclusive, however. The tobacco manipulator, with his conversational trade, has an above average awareness of what goes on in the world.

Let us note, in the second place, that our conglomerate of philo-Communist types has little respect for class lines. The refugees, the women, and the youth represent all social classes. In fact, Communist youths are more likely to be middle class than not, since it is those youngsters whose parents can afford to send them to a higher school who are most likely to fall under the spell of Communism. This, among other things, seems to be clear: it is not usually the poorest and most downtrodden who answer the call.

All our Communist-producing social groups have another trait in common. They combine in an unusual degree personal insecurity and better than average perception of the greater world. This insecurity and this perception are the product of what must appear to the victims as uncontrollable if not demiurgic forces: the failure of the Greek army to capture Ankara, the fluctuation of the prices of tobacco and wheat in the world market, the humiliating contrast between the Balkan and the British ways of life. They are, in short, the kind of forces that from the viewpoint of the individual can be coped with only by religious revisionism.

Finally, there is the matter of the geographic distribution within eastern Europe of the Communist phenomenon. In the interwar period, at any rate, the Socialists were weak and the Communists strong in those countries which were most agrarian, had the lowest standard of living, were religiously Orthodox, and had been for centuries subjected to Turkish rule. Contrariwise, the Socialists were strong and the Communists relatively weak in those parts of the area which were more industrial, enjoyed higher living standards, were predominantly Catholic, and over the centuries had been subjected to strong German influence. This line of change runs generally from the northwest to southeast.

If, by means of the imagination, this line were projected in both directions outside and beyond the area under consideration, there would appear at the northwestern extremity of the line a heavily industrialized society with high living standards, one in which Socialists would be extremely numerous and influential and in which Communists would exist only as a slightly ridiculous sect. At the southeastern extremity of the line would appear an entirely rural society, poverty stricken and ridden with disease, cultivating the soil by antiquated methods, in which Socialists were unknown and Communists constituted a powerful and menacing minority.

In short, a proper explanation of Communism in eastern Europe would begin, not with the industrial proletariat and the class struggle, but with the reaction of economically poorer and less sophisticated cultures to the West, as that contrast affects persons and groups subjected through social disorganization to great personal insecurity. Our hypothesis is less enchanting than the Marxist, with its epic war between classes, and its apocalyptic *finale*. But it seems to us in closer accord with the facts.

CHAPTER IV: IN WHICH WE LOOK AT A MAP

Actually it is possible to examine the complex of forces producing Communism with a degree of sophistication that mere words will not allow. This possibility is due partly to the fact that the government in Prague kept the kind of complex and detailed statistics to which we are accustomed in the West, and partly to the existence of a statistical technique known as multiple correlation.

Simple correlation, which we have employed so far, ignores the existence of causal factors other than the one being treated. Multiple correlation, on the other hand, compares a number of possible causal factors in their effect on a given result. In fact, multiple correlation makes it possible to determine the relative importance of any *one* causal factor, because the effect of the other factors may be subtracted, so to speak, from the total effect. Multiple correlation thus amounts to a statistical substitute for experiment. We can remove one factor or another from the calculation and thus get an idea of which factors count most.

Multiple correlation and Communist adherence

For our statistical experiment we chose a backward part of the Czech state, the province of Slovakia. For our causal factors we chose industrial workers, landless workers, dwarf-holders, and cash croppers. For good measure we threw in an additional factor, an ethnic minority, in this case the Hungarian, or Magyar, population of southern Slovakia.

As far as Tables 4.1 and 4.2 are concerned, the reader need know only that β stands for beta coefficient; it is the multiple correlation equivalent of r, whence $\sigma\beta$, standard error of beta. If β is twice $\sigma\beta$, then the correlation, whether negative or positive, is significant.

Capital R is the coefficient of multiple correlation and states the degree to which the causal factors are related as a group to the Communist vote. R^2 is the coefficient of determination; it indicates the percentage of total variance in the vote which is explained by any factor or combination of factors. R^2 falls as various factors are removed from the computation, the extent of the fall indicating the importance of the factor or factors removed.

Let us, then, peruse Table 4.1.

TABLE 4.1[1]

Multiple correlation analysis of the factors which influence the Communist vote in Slovakia (1929)

$N = 79$

	Indus-trial workers β	Land-less workers β	Dwarf-holders β	Cash crop-pers β	Mag-yars β	R	R^2	Differ-ence
Line								
A	.283	.294	.185	.307	.664	.792	.627	
B		.510	.210	.288	.714		.589	.038
C	.419		.175	.173	.643		.603	.024
D			.213	−.097	.723		.473	.154
E	.366		.242		.735		.592	.035
F			.168		.665		.468	.159
G					.660		.436	.191
H				.420			.176	.451
$\sigma\beta$	(.103)	(.133)	(.087)	(.129)	(.097)			

What we find in the Slovakia of 1929 is that all the causal factors are significantly related to the Communist vote, but that industrial workers, landless workers, dwarfholders, and cash croppers altogether do not produce as much of a change in the Communist vote as does the ethnic factor alone! If we

[1] For the raw data see Appendix B. We isolate the minority factor as the percentage of Magyars to total population of each electoral district and the industrial workers also as a percentage of total population. The concentrations of landless workers we identify by finding the percentage of arable held in estates of 500 hectares (1,235 acres) or more, the concentrations of dwarfholders by the percentage of arable held in farms of 5 hectares (12.4 acres) or less, and the concentrations of cash croppers as percentage of arable put to wheat.

remove every factor except the ethnic (Line G), the R^2 of
.627 falls only .191, but if the ethnic factor is taken out (Line
H) R^2 falls .451 points. In short, the ethnic factor produces
twice as much change in the Communist vote as all the social
and economic factors put together.[2]

Equally interesting results are obtained in Table 4.2, in

TABLE 4.2[3]

Multiple correlation, Socialist and Communist votes
Slovakia (1929)

Vote	Indus-trial workers	Land-less workers	Dwarf-holders	Cash crop-pers	Magyars	R	R^2
Socialist							
β	.353	.380	.336	−.082	−.053	.687	.472
$\sigma\beta$	.124	.159	.104	.161	.117		
Communist							
β	.283	.294	.185	.307	.664	.792	.627
$\sigma\beta$	.103	.133	.087	.129	.097		

which we compare the multiple correlation analysis of the
Communist vote with an analysis, employing identical factors,
of the Socialist vote in the same election.

[2] If we remove industrial workers from the computation (line B)
the fall in the value of R^2 is negligible. This is true if we remove both
landless workers and cash croppers (line E). What happens to R^2 when
both industrial and landless workers are removed (line D) suggests
that here we are not dealing with truly independent variables. Cash-
cropping and Magyarism are also interdependent. The simple correlation between them (r) is .59 while $\sigma r = .11$. Of the two factors, however, minority status is easily the more important. A glance at Table
4.1 will show that the β for Magyars and Communist votes (line G) is
more than 6 times one standard error, while the β for cash croppers
and Communists (line H) is less than three times one standard error.
The fact that under simple correlation landless workers, industrial workers, and dwarfholders produced rr less than two standard errors in size
suggests that, if multiple correlation were applied to other areas, such
as Bohemia-Moravia or Bulgaria, these factors might come into significant relationship with the Communist vote. This result—in case anyone
were willing to undertake the labor involved—would probably not occur,
however, since in Slovakia the rr produced by simple correlation were
so close to two errors, in marked contrast to the situation in the other
provinces mentioned.

[3] For the raw data see Appendix B.

Table 4.2 tells us that three of our factors—industrial workers, landless workers, dwarfholders—correlate significantly with *both* the Socialist and the Communist vote. In the case of cash croppers and Magyars, on the other hand, correlation is with Communism *only*. What is peculiar to Communism is the insecurity-awareness of the cash cropper *and* the liability of belonging to a national minority.

Is this combination an accident? Or is it something peculiar to Slovakia alone? Or does the ethnic factor play a role in east European Communism generally? To find a first answer to these questions we have constructed a map of the Communist electorate in eastern Europe, as that electorate was recorded in the free elections of the 1920's. For purposes of comparison we have added to our map the Socialist electorate, as revealed in those same elections. The technicalities of the construction of the map are given in Appendix A.

The Communist electorate in eastern Europe[4]

From the map certain facts are apparent immediately. The Communist electorate is not concentrated in the more industrial parts of eastern Europe, in provinces like Bohemia, Lodz, and Warsaw; rather, it is the Socialist vote which is concentrated in those areas. The map thus confirms the analysis we made in the last part of Chapter 3.

The Communist electorate is found primarily in Slavic countries. In Bulgaria the comrades got 20.4 per cent of the vote cast; in Czechoslovakia they got 13.2 per cent; in Yugoslavia 12.3 per cent; in Poland 7.9 per cent. This range of electoral strength, from 7.9 to 20.4 per cent, is to be compared with the approximately 25 per cent of the total vote which the Bolsheviks picked up in the election to the Russian constituent assembly in the fall of 1917.[5]

---

[4] See the appropriate countries in Appendix B for the data on the basis of which the map was constructed.

[5] *Annuaire Bulgarie 1913-22*, part C, p. 60; *Assemblee nationale 1925*, pp. 14*-15*; *Statistichki pregled 1920*, section 56; M. K. Dziewanowski, *The Communist Party of Poland. An Outline of History* (Cambridge, Mass., 1959), p. 127; *Shestym kongressom*, p. 239; O. H. Radkey, *The*

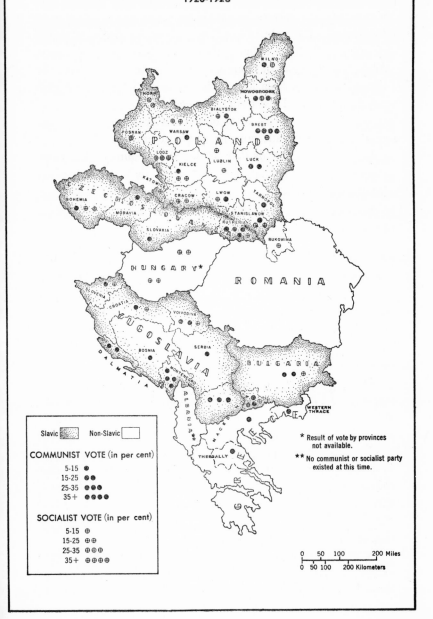

THE COMMUNIST ELECTORATE IN EASTERN EUROPE

1920-1928

Slavic   Non-Slavic

COMMUNIST VOTE (in per cent)
- 5-15
- 15-25
- 25-35
- 35+

SOCIALIST VOTE (in per cent)
- 5-15
- 15-25
- 25-35
- 35+

* Result of vote by provinces not available.

** No communist or socialist party existed at this time.

0   50   100   200 Miles

0   50 100   200 Kilometers

In non-Slavic eastern Europe, on the other hand, the Communist vote in the 1920's was negligible. In Greece the best the Communists did was 4.2 per cent in 1926, but this vote was highly concentrated, so it shows up on our electoral map. In Romania the vote reached a peak of 1.5 per cent in the election of 1926. In Albania no party existed in the twenties. As for the Hungarian Communists, who were outlawed after the overthrow of Bela Kun, it is a reasonable guess that they would have polled less than 5 per cent.[6]

We have thus a rule of thumb: the Communist vote in the 1920's was significant only in Slavic countries.

Our map also reveals that within Slavic countries the Communist vote is concentrated in certain districts. These are listed in Table 4.3.

TABLE 4.3[7]

Slavic districts with the highest
percentage of Communist votes

Province and election	Communist as % of total vote cast
Ruthenia (1924)	42.0
Brest (1928)	37.2
Montenegro (1920)	36.0
Yugoslav Macedonia (1920)	33.0
Nowogrodek (1928)	29.5
Bulgarian Macedonia (1920)	28.2

The Yugoslav Socialists chided their Communist opponents on their electoral strength in Montenegro and Macedonia, two

Election to the Russian Constituent Assembly of 1917 (Cambridge, Mass., 1950), pp. 16-17.

[6] *Elections des deputes 1926*, pp. xxii-xxiii, Ionescu, *loc.cit.*; *Politics and Political Parties in Roumania, with 20 photographs and a genealogical tree* (hereafter cited as *Politics in Roumania*) (London, 1936), p. 55. We have used the Romanian returns of 1922, when the vote was only 0.8 per cent, in the construction of the map, because the breakdown of the 1926 returns by district was not available. In Hungary we have not been able to apply the provincial principle because the only figures given in the official returns available to us were global. Experience with proportional representation suggests that as soon as a party breaks the 5 per cent barrier it has acquired political significance.

[7] For the raw data on which this table is based see the appropriate countries in Appendix B.

provinces where one would have to look for factories with the lamp of Diogenes. None of the provinces listed in Table 4.3 was industrial; on the contrary, there were few areas in eastern Europe more agrarian and isolated.

As for Montenegro, the story is told that a traveller once asked a Montenegrin mountaineer how many people his country had. "Together with the Russians," came the proud reply, "one hundred eighty million." This feeling of identity can be traced back at least to the opening years of the eighteenth century, when the Montenegrin prince-bishop concluded an alliance with the Russian tsar. Perhaps the most recent expression of this sense of identity was the proclamation (1942) of the Partisan-liberated areas of the province as an integral part of the Soviet Union. The size of the Communist electorate in 1920, however, was due not only to the traditional sympathy of Montenegrins for Russia but also to the abstention of the Nationalist party, which advocated autonomy for Montenegro within a federal Yugoslavia.[8]

The Communist vote in Yugoslav Macedonia, on the other hand, has the flavor of a Slavo-Macedonian separatism. In the Yugoslav election of 1920 the Slavo-Macedonians were not permitted to present electoral lists of their own. They therefore tended to vote for the party most clearly in opposition to the new Yugoslav regime, e.g. the Communist. In 1920 the district of Bitolj, in Yugoslav Macedonia directly across the frontier from the Slavic-speaking minority in Greek Macedonia, turned up with a Communist vote of 51.1 per cent. This was the only electoral district in all of eastern Europe to give a straight majority to the Communists before 1945. The

[8] Stephen Clissold, *Whirlwind. An Account of Marshal Tito's Rise to Power* (London, 1949), p. 84; Ante Ciliga, "Ueberblick der Entwicklung der kommunistischen Partei Jugo-Slawiens mit besonderer Beruecksichtigung des nationalen Moments" (hereafter cited as "Ueberblick"), pp. 10-11. This is a typescript of 40 pages prepared by Ciliga at the request of the writer. In the 1920's Ciliga was one of the leaders of the Communist party of Yugoslavia. A most amusing illustration of the Montenegrin affinity for Russia is given in M. B. Petrovich, "Catherine II and a false Peter III in Montenegro," *ASEER*, xiv (1955), pp. 169-94.

fact that the Communist vote in Bulgarian Macedonia was above the Bulgarian national average[9] may have been connected with the expulsion by the Greeks of most of the Slav population of Greek Macedonia. The expellees took refuge in Bulgaria, but the defeated and debt-laden Bulgarian government was unable properly to care for them, and many may have joined the swelling ranks of Communist voters.

Ruthenia, to take another of the Slavic provinces with a high Communist vote, is mainly inhabited by Ukrainians. Until 1919 the province had been part of the Austrian empire; in that year it was given to the newly formed state of Czechoslovakia. Under Czech rule the fate of the Ruthenes was one of neglect rather than forced assimilation. None the less, the Ruthenes voted in large numbers for the Czech Communist party, which was under instructions from the Comintern to work for the transfer of Ruthenia to the Soviet Ukraine.[10]

Brest, like Wilno, is Belorussian in population. These two provinces had belonged to the Russian empire, but had been seized by the Poles in their 1920 war against the Bolsheviks. Nowogrodek, like Wolyn, had been acquired by the Poles in the same war, but was Ukrainian rather than Belorussian in population. Stanislawow, Tarnopol, and Lwow are also Ukrainian-inhabited, but until 1918 they had been part of the Austrian province of Galicia. The peace makers had assigned the three Galician districts to Poland, but there was talk of giving them some kind of special status.

The Polish election of 1922 was the first in which the newly

[9] Ciliga, "Ueberblick," p. 10; Tomasic, p. 16; *Statistichki pregled 1920*, section 56.

[10] *From the Fourth to the Fifth World Congress. Report of the Executive Committee of the Communist International* (hereafter cited as *Fifth World Congress*) (London, 1924), pp. 55, 57; *Piatyi vsemirnyi kongress kommunisticheskogo internationala, 17 iiunia—8 iiulia 1924 g. Stenografischeskii otchiot. Chast' II (prilozheniia)* (hereafter cited as *Piatyi kongress*) (Moscow, 1925), pp. 126-27; Jan Alfred Regula, *Historja komunistycznej partji polski w swietle faktow i dokumentow. Wydanie drugie rozszersone i uzupelnione* (Warsaw, 1934), pp. 98-99. The Fifth Congress also declared that the Lithuanian population of Poland had the right of secession. *Ibid.*

acquired eastern provinces were allowed to participate. In that election the minority populations throughout Poland chose, in the main, to vote for a minorities' bloc. They hoped in this fashion to gain sufficient representation in parliament to prevent the adoption by the Warsaw government of a policy of polonization.

There were some exceptions to the general rule. Ukrainian Socialists in considerable numbers began to join the Communist party of Poland, since this party advocated the principle of ethnic self-determination. Furthermore, the Ukrainian population of the Galician districts abstained from voting, thinking thereby to impress the great powers (who were still considering the ultimate disposition of these districts) with their Ukrainian character. In March 1923 the Council of ambassadors issued its final decision—conditionless incorporation into the Polish state. This decision, together with the introduction of Polish as a language of instruction in the schools of the eastern provinces, produced an atmosphere of violence and revolutionary ferment throughout the area.[11]

In August 1923 the second congress of the Polish Communist party, meeting in Moscow, set up autonomous party organizations for the western Ukraine and western Belorussia and demanded the unification of these territories with the appropriate Soviet republics. For the next several years these autonomous parties trained terrorists and diversionary bands at Kharkov and Minsk, respectively, and infiltrated them into eastern Poland. Such activity contributed substantially to the state of semi-anarchy which prevailed in Poland's eastern provinces. At the third congress of the Communist party of Poland, which convened in 1925 near Minsk, capital of Soviet Belorussia, the Communist party of western Belorussia pressed

[11] M. Felinski, "Les Ukrainiens au parlement de la Pologne restauree," *Questions minoritaires. Revue trimestrielle d'etude et d'information* (hereafter cited as *Questions minoritaires*) (Warsaw) IV (1931), pp. 134-53; Malbone W. Graham, "Polish Politics, 1918-39," in Bernadotte E. Schmitt (ed.), *Poland* (Berkeley, 1945), p. 123-47; Adam Zoltowski, *Border of Europe. A Study of the Polish Eastern Provinces* (London, 1950), p. 313; Dziewanowski, p. 112; Regula, p. 51.

for the development of the Polish disorders into a general insurrection. The Soviet representatives at the congress made it plain that the Red army was not able to intervene in behalf of an insurrection. Terroristic activities continued along the Polish confines until 1931, however.[12]

Meantime the public influence of the Polish Communist party, which had been outlaw from 1919, grew significantly. The CPP proper presented itself at the polls as the Union of workers and peasants while some CPP units, such as the Warsaw committee on unemployment and the Union of Communist youth, were formally turned over to the Independent Socialist labor party. The subparty for western Belorussia appeared before the public both as Hromada and as the Independent peasant party. The subparty for western Ukraine also operated two front organizations, the more widely-known Sel Rob and a group localized in the three Galician districts and known as the Ukrainian party of labor. There also emerged in western Galacia, by way of a split from the Polish Socialist party, a PPS-left; in many localities the local Communist units simply legalized themselves as the PPS-left. Of the seven cover organizations which the CPP had exfoliated, five (Hromada, Independent peasants, Sel Rob, Ukrainian laborite, elements of PPS-left) were active primarily in the eastern provinces.[13]

Simultaneously a Communist club developed in the *sejm*, or lower house of the Polish parliament. The club came into existence largely through secessions from the bloc of national minorities. It included 23 deputies, or 5 per cent of the total *sejm* membership. Six deputies represented the Union of workers and peasants, 7 the Independent peasants, 6 the Hromada, and 4 Sel Rob. This suggests that three-fourths of the Communist deputies came from minority stocks.[14]

[12] *Fifth World Congress*, pp. 55, 57; Dziewanowski, p. 105; Regula, pp. 121, 129-31, 133, 143, 178, 242-43, 257, 266-67.
[13] Dziewanowski, p. 112; Regula, pp. 144-45, 168-69, 177.
[14] Dziewanowski, pp. 105, 112; *Fifth World Congress*, p. 55; *Annuaire statistique de la republique polonaise, VII annee 1929* (Warsaw, nd), p. 459; Zoltowski, pp. 316-20; Regula, pp. 144-45.

In the semi-free general election of 1928, the various front organizations of the Communists together polled 7.9 per cent. This was so even though in 1927 both Belorussian organizations, the Independent peasants and the Hromada, had been outlawed. Indeed, 56 of the Hromada leaders had been tried and imprisoned.[15] Yet the 140,000 ballots cast for the outlawed Hromada in the election of 1928 represented 59.6 per cent of the total vote cast for Belorussian parties.[16] The Communist club in the *sejm* now included 8 representatives of Ukrainian front organizations, 5 of Belorussian, and 7 of Polish.[17] After 1928 there were no more free (or semi-free) elections in Poland, perhaps in part because of the strength of Communism along the sensitive eastern frontier.

It is not unreasonable to guess that, had the elections of 1928 been entirely free, the Communists, through their various front organizations, would have polled as much as 10 per cent of the total vote. It is none the less true that the year 1928 represented a peak in the strength of Communism in Pilsudski Poland. Its subsequent decline was attributable not so much to events in Poland—indeed Communism seemed to thrive in the atmosphere of Pilsudski's military dictatorship—as to developments in the Soviet Union. Already in the election of 1928 Sel Rob had split into two competing organizations; this in turn reflected a schism in the parent body, the Communist party of the western Ukraine.[18]

These divisions had their origins in the quarrel over Shumskyism, a deviation which had come to infect the Communist party of the Soviet Ukraine. Essentially Shumskyism held that the Ukraine, while remaining firmly Communist in its social

---

[15] Graham, *loc.cit.*; Stanislaus Mornik, *Polens Kampf gegen seine nicht polnischen Volksgruppen* (Berlin, 1931), p. 117; Felinski, *loc.cit.*; Regula, p. 199.

[16] "Les minorites de la Pologne et les elections au parlement du 16 XI 1930," *Questions minoritaires*, IV (1931), pp. 33-45. Cf. the results of local elections as summarized in *Shestym kongressom*, p. 239; "Pologne. La representation des minorites nationales au parlement," *Questions minoritaires*, I (1928), pp. 31-35.

[17] Dziewanowski, p. 127.

[18] Regula, pp. 204-06.

and economic orientation, should draw its intellectual and literary inspiration from the West rather than from Russia. The Communist party of the western Ukraine rapidly became the great stronghold of this heresy, whose founder was himself a Ukrainian from Poland. When Soviet authorities condemned the doctrine, virtually the entire central committee of the west Ukrainian party severed relations with the Comintern. In taking this action the committee had the support of the secretaries and the members of the district committee, and of the majority of ordinary activists. The secessionists attacked what they called the Soviet policy of russifying the Ukraine, of undermining the Orthodox church, and of exercising a dictatorship over the Comintern. Moscow countered by calling the secessionist faction a "branch of Polish Fascism."[19]

The development of a campaign of forcible collectivization in the Soviet Union sharply reduced the appeal of Communism to the minority populations of eastern Poland, which were overwhelmingly peasant in character. This was particularly the case in the Ukrainian-inhabited provinces of Poland, since the effects of forcible collectivization were most devastating in the Soviet Ukraine. In the years immediately following collectivization the Bolshevik policy of the russification of the Ukraine was intensified. Leading exponents of what we might today call Ukrainian Communism disappeared from public life. The writer Chvylovy and the commissar of education Skrypnik committed suicide. The historian Hrushevsky was sent into exile. Shumsky and those leaders of the Communist party of the western Ukraine who now resided in the Soviet Ukraine were imprisoned on charges of opportunism and nationalism.[20]

The Communist party of western Belorussia also lost much of its influence. It, too, became infected with nationalist deviation. All the former deputies of Hromada, in residence in

[19] *Ibid.*

[20] *Ibid.*, pp. 263, 294-95; Michael Hrushevsky, *A History of the Ukraine* (O. J. Fredericksen, ed.) (New Haven, 1941), p. 566.

Minsk, were brought to trial on charges of spying for Polish intelligence. Within Poland itself the outlawed Independent peasant party severed relations with the CPP.[21]

The strength of Communism along Poland's eastern frontier thus seems to have waxed and waned in accordance with its national appeal. In the 1920's Communism was powerful in this area because it appeared to promise union with Soviet Ukrainian and Belorussian republics which gave promise of some kind of nationally autonomous existence. In the 1930's Communism lost much of its popularity because it became evident that this expectation would not be realized. A Communist university of the West, which the Soviet government had maintained from the early twenties for the training of Belorussian and Ukrainian activists stemming from Poland and Czechoslovakia, was disbanded in 1935.[22]

Thus the high Communist vote in the eastern provinces of Poland and Czechoslovakia in the 1920's smacks of Belorussian and Ukrainian irredentism. Indeed, our map of the Communist electorate makes clear that, in the 1920's at least, Communism had, in addition to its social and economic drives, a causal connection with the nationalities problem. The Communist vote is sharply concentrated in Slavic countries and, within these countries, in provinces inhabited by some Slavic minority, frequently one with a special relationship to Russia. But before we undertake to examine this relationship, we ought to define the terms "ethnic" and "national."

The terms "ethnic" and "national" defined

The two terms are not interchangeable. An ethnic group may give rise to more than one nation, as in the case of the English-speaking, Shakespeare-worshipping, common-law practicing Protestants who have formed the core of such different nations as the American, the Canadian, and the Australian.

---

[21] Regula, pp. 206, 296-97.
[22] Guenther Nollau, *Die Internationale. Wurzeln und Erscheinungsformen des proletarischen Internationalismus* (Koeln, 1959), p. 140.

Several ethnic groups may combine to make one nation, as, for example, the Germans, French, Italians, and Romansh who together make up the Swiss nation. Neither an ethnic group nor a nation need inhabit the same territory. The wandering Gypsies are an ethnic group and the Greeks, whether those dwelling in Egypt, Cyprus, or the Hellenic kingdom, are a nation.

To put the matter succinctly, ethnic groups are the building blocks of which nations are made. An ethnic group, simply defined, is a population great or small sharing many of the same traits—language, law, religion, custom, tradition—as a matter of social inheritance. A nation, on the other hand, is a population composed of part of an ethnic group, a single such group, or several such groups, which has developed a political consciousness, a will to be master of its own destiny. A nation, to use a very colorful German term, is a *Schicksalgemeinschaft*, a common sharing of human destiny. As an example we may point out that the Austrians of Austria proper thought of themselves as German—which indeed they were in an ethnic sense—after 1918, and wished to be joined to the German Reich, whereas after 1945 they thought of themselves as Austrians and desired (for reasons not altogether obscure) to preserve a distinct national identity.

Part II of this book will be devoted to an examination of the ethnic factor in Communist adherence in eastern Europe. This emphasis is not the result of any tendency on our part to minimize the importance of social and economic factors in producing Communism, but rather results from a desire to explore a relationship which hitherto has been little treated and little understood in the literature of Communism. Our approach will be more historical than was the case in Part I, since the ethnic factor is best handled that way. The national consciousness which transforms peoples into nations is not a static entity; it is emergent and evolving.

We shall begin our analysis of the ethnic factor with one of the Slavic minorities, the Slavo-Macedonian, and attempt to show the relationship between Communism and Slavo-Macedonian nationalism. We then shall broaden our frame of reference to include, not a minority, but a Slavic nation, the Yugoslav, in its relation to the Communist faith. Extending our purview still further, we shall, in the third place, undertake an examination of the relationships between Communism and Slavs, on the one hand, and anti-Communism and non-Slavic peoples like the Turks and the Germans, on the other. Finally, we shall deal with the non-Slavic peoples —minorities, both of them—who in the east European area harbor a penchant for Communism: the Magyars cut off from Hungary by the Treaty of Trianon, and the Jews.

PART II: THE POLITICS OF PEOPLES

CHAPTER V: THE CASE OF THE SLAVO-MACEDONIANS

NUMERICALLY the Slavo-Macedonians are not a very important people. Approximately .8 million live in southernmost Yugoslavia. Another quarter of a million inhabit the southwestern corner of Bulgaria. A further hundred thousand or so live in Greece, adjacent to the juncture of the Yugoslav and the Albanian frontiers. The total Slavo-Macedonian population is thus something more than a million.

The homeland of the Slavo-Macedonians is divided. Approximately 40 per cent of their territory constitutes the Yugoslav republic of Macedonia. With Skopie as its chief city, this section is often referred to as Vardar Macedonia. The Bulgarian part of Macedonia, about 10 per cent of the total, is more or less contiguous with the Gorno Djumaiski district. Its principal town in the interwar period was Petrich. Frequently the Bulgarian part is referred to as Pirin Macedonia. The Greek section of Macedonia is different from the other two sections in that its population is overwhelmingly Greek, that is to say, non-Slavic. It also has a littoral on the Aegean sea (whence the term Aegean Macedonia) and its main city is the port of Salonika.

The mere listing of these territories and towns suggests the rugged complexity of the Slavo-Macedonian problem. What is more, the Slavo-Macedonians are a primitive and backward people. Until very recently their land was innocent of industry; they tilled the valley floors or pastured sheep high in the mountains of their divided homeland. It was only recently, moreover, that they acquired a written language. The dialects which they speak lie somewhere in between the Serbo-Croatian which is spoken to the north of them and the Bulgarian which is spoken to the east.

91

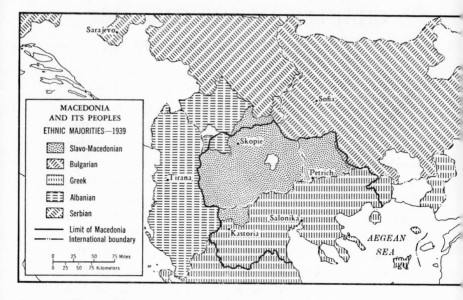

MACEDONIA
AND ITS PEOPLES

ETHNIC MAJORITIES—1939

▦ Slavo-Macedonian
▨ Bulgarian
▥ Greek
▤ Albanian
▧ Serbian

── Limit of Macedonia
─··─ International boundary

0   25   50   75 Miles
0 25 50 75 Kilometers

The problem of national identification

Prior to World War II the Yugoslav government insisted that the Slavo-Macedonians were a species of Serb. Belgrad authorities referred to their Macedonia somewhat contemptuously as South Serbia. The Bulgarian government, on the other hand, contended that all Slavo-Macedonians were Bulgars, and entered World War II (as it had entered World War I) on the German side in the hope of bringing all these unredeemed souls within the confines of the Bulgarian motherland.

The Greeks, of course, regarded their portion of Macedonia as indubitably and perpetually Greek. Their small Slavo-Macedonian minority they referred to as "Slavophones," implying by the use of this term that these were Slavic-speaking Greeks. In fact, Slavophone children went to Greek schools. Their parents could find only Greek newspapers to read. Even the word of God was dispensed to the Slavophones in Greek, since they were automatically members of the Greek Orthodox church. Under dictator Ioannis Metaxas (1936-1941) it became a legal offense to speak Slavo-Macedonian in public places.[1]

No one bothered to ask the Slavo-Macedonians their own views in the matter, whether they preferred to be Serbs, Bulgars, or Slavic-speaking Greeks. There is reason to believe, however, that at least some Slavo-Macedonians held strong views on the subject. Back before World War I, when all of Macedonia was Turkish territory, there had emerged a secret Slavo-Macedonian nationalist society, similar to the Serbian Black Hand, which assassinated the Austrian archduke, or to the Turkish Committee of union and progress, which produced Kemal Ataturk. This society was known as the Internal Macedonian Revolutionary Organization (IMRO). It was a body of terrorists and revolutionaries whose aim was to liberate Macedonia from Turkish rule.

By the time of World War I the Turkish army had been driven out of Macedonia by the Greeks, the Serbs, and the Bulgars, who promptly proceeded to divide that territory among themselves. After 1922 the Macedonian scene was disturbed by forcible exchanges of population. The Turkish population was driven out of Greek Macedonia and replaced with Greeks expelled from Asia Minor and from Russia. Similarly, much of the Slavic-speaking population of Aegean Macedonia was forced to leave Greek Macedonia for Bulgaria and its place taken by Greeks who had long been resident in such Bulgarian towns as Varna and Plovdiv. All told, perhaps 150,000 Slavs were expelled from Greek Macedonia and adjacent Greek Thrace after 1918.[2]

---

[1] The Greek point of view is presented in Christopher J. Christides, *The Macedonian Camouflage in the Light of Facts and Figures* (Athens, 1949). The Greek police carried the Slavophone population as of 1940 at 141,000, of whom 53,000 were credited with "Greek national consciousness." Elizabeth Barker, *Macedonia. Its Place in Balkan Power Politics* (London, 1950), p. 31, maintains that the Slavophones would probably have been peacefully absorbed had it not been for World War II and the foreign occupation.

[2] Ernst Kirsten, Ernst Bucholz, Wolfgang Koellmann, *Raum und*

The government in Sofia, shaken by a disastrous war and laden with debt, was unable to give proper assistance to the refugees. Hungry, unemployed, and embittered, these uprooted peasants must have appeared to the Communist leaders as an army of potential recruits. In 1920 they authorized Haji Dimov, a former schoolteacher and veteran Macedonian nationalist, to found a Union of Communist refugees and to publish a newspaper for them. The position of the Bulgarian party was that the Macedonian problem could best be solved within the framework of a Balkan federation. The three parts of Macedonia should be joined in a single state which in turn should be included in a federal union of Balkan peoples. The Greeks were to be included in this union, and so were the Serbs and the Bulgars.[3]

But Dimov's efforts came to nothing. The newspaper *Osvobozhdenia* was printed in a scant 500 copies and membership in the Union of refugees never came to more than a few hundred. The plain fact was that the vast majority of Macedonians resident in Bulgaria, whether refugees or natives, gave their political allegiance to IMRO. The aims of these terrorists were uncertain. Apparently the majority advocated annexation of Greek and Yugoslav Macedonia to Bulgaria, while a minority sympathized with the notion of unification through federation.

In view of Dimov's failure, the Communists decided that they must strike a bargain with IMRO. Negotiations got underway in 1921. IMRO was hard up for funds; a subsidy it had received under Tsar Ferdinand had been cut off by Alexander Stamboliski, Peasant party premier (1919-1923) and agrarian reformer. IMRO could also expect through such negotiations to gain the support of the Communist inter-

---

Bevoelkerung in der Weltgeschichte. Bevoelkerungs-Ploetz. Band 2. III. Teil: Bevoelkerung und Raum in Neuerer und Neuester Zeit (Wuerzburg, 1955), p. 295; Rothschild, pp. 94, 174.

[3] Barker, p. 48; Kabakchiev, pp. 205-06; L. S. Stavrianos, *Balkan Federation. A History of the Movement toward Balkan Unity in Modern Times* (Northampton, Mass., 1944), p. 205; *Piatyi kongress*, p. 125; Rothschild, p. 176.

national (Comintern) and of Soviet Russia for the liberation of the Yugoslav share of Macedonia. The Communist program actually went much further, proposing the destruction of the Yugoslav state and the incorporation of its peoples into an all-Balkan federation. What the Communists hoped to gain was a major influence in the explosive Macedonian issue.

The negotiations produced a new journal, *La federation balkanique*, published in Vienna from 1924. They also involved a public declaration by IMRO that it favored the unification of Macedonia within the framework of a left-oriented Balkan federation. And they led to a series of gun battles—one on the steps of the opera house in Vienna—between contending IMRO factions, and to the failure of Communist hopes.

One factor in the failure of the negotiations was the overthrow of Stamboliski and the emergence in Sofia of a conservative government headed by Alexander Tsankov. The new government handed over the department of Petrich to IMRO as a virtual fief. IMRO collected a tobacco tax and more or less appointed the Petrich delegation to the sobranje (the Bulgarian parliament). IMRO manipulated financially and in other ways the large Macedonian community spread throughout Bulgaria. In exchange for these privileges, IMRO provided Tsankov and his successors with a corps of assassins and a private army of some 8,000 well-armed *komitadji*. Equally important in IMRO's withdrawal from the negotiations with the Communists was the dawning awareness that any agreement with them meant open warfare with the Tsankov government.

The Communists returned to their earlier policy of putting up a competing organization. This time it was the United IMRO of D. Vlahov, like Dimov a Macedonian nationalist of long standing. But United IMRO was little more than a group of conspirators who frequented Viennese coffee houses. In 1931 *La federation balkanique* ceased publication and

Vlahov and his colleagues drifted off to Moscow.[4] IMRO, left in possession of the field, discredited itself by meaningless raids into Yugoslav Macedonia, and endless assassinations in the streets of Sofia. In the thirties the Macedonian issue was quiescent.

The Axis occupation

The outbreak of World War II, however, gave the issue a new currency. Bulgaria joined the Axis and put Vardar Macedonia under military occupation. The Slavophone country was held by the Italians, but everyone knew that the Slavophones, as well as the Vardarians and perhaps even the Aegean Macedonians, would be joined to Bulgaria if the Axis were victorious.

In the beginning the Slavo-Macedonian population heartily collaborated with the occupying authorities. Characteristic is the behavior of the Vardar Communists. They were instructed by the Yugoslav party leaders to organize armed resistance. They responded by seceding from the Yugoslav and joining the Bulgarian party. When the Yugoslav Communists carried an appeal to Moscow, and the Comintern ruled in favor of the Yugoslavs, both the Bulgarian and the Vardarian Communists *de facto* ignored the ruling. And when Sofia introduced conscription in Vardar Macedonia, the local party organization urged its members to enter the Bulgarian army "in order to keep in touch with the masses."[5]

The situation was not substantially different in the Slavophone area of Greece. The Italians organized a Slavophone gendarmerie to help them police the area, and increasingly employed this force in punitive raids against Greek-inhabited villages which were supporting the Communist-led Greek re-

[4] Barker, pp. 36-40, 41-42, 57, 68-69; Stavrianos, pp. 218, 220-21; Rothschild, pp. 107, 175-77, 179-89, 191-92, 196-97.
[5] Vladimir Dedijer, *Tito* (New York, 1953), p. 173; J. B. Tito, *Relazione politica del comitato centrale del partito Communista della Yugoslavia. Relazione presentata al V congresso del partito communista della Jugoslavia* (Belgrad, 1948), pp. 86, 142-3; Fejto, p. 86; Barker, pp. 85-91, 96-97; Lazitch, *Tito*, p. 129.

sistance to the Axis occupation. The Slavophone gendarmes were not choosey in the methods they employed against Greek villagers.

Such was the situation in the early months of the Second World War. But slowly Slavo-Macedonian sentiment began to shift. The Bulgars ruled Vardar Macedonia with a firm hand: they introduced Bulgarian schools and Bulgarian learning; they decided everything in Sofia; and they treated the natives as somewhat backward Bulgarians.[6] Discontent began to grow. It was not allayed by a steady deterioration of economic conditions, caused basically by the Western blockade of the Axis. Moreover, the prospects of Axis victory began to seem remote. This was especially the case after the raising of the siege of Stalingrad.

While the guns of Stalingrad were still booming, the Yugoslav Partisans (as the Communist guerrilla army was called) made a new effort to organize resistance among the Slavo-Macedonians. They sent a special emissary, the Montenegrin lawyer S. Vukmanovic, known in the underground as Tempo, who spread the word that the Partisans favored Macedonian unification and autonomy. The Vardar Communists now responded to the Partisan appeal. They dropped their connection with the Bulgarian party, purged their pro-Bulgarian leadership, and reentered the Yugoslav party as a separate Macedonian party. Slavo-Macedonian Partisan detachments sprang into action and in October 1943 a newly formed Macedonian general staff issued a ringing proclamation to the Macedonian "people," calling for their unification in a single state and the admission of this state to the new Yugoslav federation.[7]

The Partisans also put pressure on the Communist-led Greek resistance organization, known as EAM, to "permit" the Slavophones to organize resistance units of their own.

[6] Robert Lee Wolff, *The Balkans in Our Time* (Cambridge, Mass., 1956), p. 206; Clissold, p. 138.

[7] Barker, pp. 92-93; Wolff, p. 216; Clissold, pp. 141-42.

The consequence was the development of a Slavophone resistance group called SNOF and of Slavophone guerrilla units under the command of a baker by the name of Gotsi. Relations between EAM and SNOF were strained from the beginning. The bulk of Gotsi's men were former members of the Italian gendarmerie and were regarded by the Greeks as collaborators and traitors. Gotsi, furthermore, openly advocated autonomy for Macedonia. There were armed clashes between Gotsi's bands and ELAS, the fighting arm of EAM. The Slavophone guerrillas shortly withdrew to the safety of Yugoslav Macedonia.[8]

As the Germans evacuated Greece, the Royal Greek gendarmerie moved forward and occupied the country of the Slavophones. This strongly nationalist force took what it regarded as an appropriate vengeance. Witnesses before the United Nations special committee for the Balkans told a sad tale of villages put to the torch, of killings, and of torture. A stream of Slavophone refugees began to make its way northward, swelling Gotsi's bands from some 800 to perhaps 5,000 men, and ultimately totalling some 30,000 persons in all. Gotsi attempted to shield the remaining Slavophones from further Greek terror by periodic raids across the frontier.[9] A war over Macedonian autonomy was in the making.

Meantime the Partisans had also been fishing in Pirin Macedonia. As the war drew to a close, Bulgarian guerrilla units put in their appearance. Usually they emerged in the

[8] McNeill, pp. 262-65; Panteli Vainas, "O dimokratikos stratos kai i Slavomakedones," *Dimokratikos stratos. Miniatiko stratiotiko politiko organo tou genikou archigeiou tou dimokratikou stratou Elladas* (hereafter cited as *Dimokratikos stratos*) (place of publication uncertain), October 1948, pp. 408-11; Vukmanovic, pp. 87-88, 143; Barker, pp. 110, 112; *Apophaseis tis 12's olomeleias tis kentrikis epitropis tou KKE* (Athens, 1946), *passim*; Fejto, p. 87; UNSCOB, Subcommittee 2, "Minorities in Greece." A working paper prepared by the secretariat (hereafter cited as "Minorities in Greece"), 23 April 1948. Gaston Coblentz in the *New York Herald Tribune* (hereafter cited as *NYHT*) (Paris edition), 20 August 1949, declares that Gotsi proclaimed the independence of Greek western Macedonia.

[9] "Minorities in Greece"; Vukmanovic, p. 143; Barker, p. 112; McNeill, pp. 266-67.

neighborhood of the Yugoslav frontier, and drew encouragement and support from the Partisans. Such guerrillas began to operate in Pirin Macedonia also and in December 1944 the Vardar Partisan army began, as a matter of course, to incorporate the Pirin units. While the Pirinians accepted this change without a murmur, the Bulgarian Communists, who had just come to power in Sofia behind the facade of the Fatherland front, strenuously objected.

There were negotiations. The Yugoslavs proposed to solve the problem by making Bulgaria the seventh unit of their new federal state, of which a reunited Macedonia would be the sixth. The Bulgar Communists, such heated advocates of Balkan federation in the years when they had played the dominant role in Balkan Communist politics, stalled for time. They argued that Bulgaria should enter the federation as the equal partner of an already federated Yugoslavia. The matter was referred to Moscow; there a decision was postponed.[10]

The Slavophones and the Greek civil war

Soon, however, negotiations were underway again, among not only Yugoslavs and Bulgars but also Albanians and Greeks. We judge that the Yugoslavs played the principal role in these talks and that they were not always meticulous in keeping the Kremlin informed of what was going on. The storm center of the negotiations was, in all probability, Macedonia. Exactly what was agreed upon may never be known, especially since the enterprise ended in catastrophe. Some of the terms were made public as the Bled agreement (August 1947). Greek anti-Communists claim to know others with certainty, but so far have been unable to provide documentary proof.

Taking everything into consideration—the situation in the three Macedonias in 1944-1946, the terms of the Bled agree-

[10] Dedijer, p. 304; Halperin, pp. 49-51, 78-79; Fejto, pp. 198-99; Clissold, pp. 141-42; Wolff, p. 248; "Moscow and the Southern Slavs," *The Economist*, 11 February 1950, pp. 324-25.

ment, the course and character of the Greek civil war, and the assertions of Greek anti-Communists—we may hypothesize an understanding, or a series of understandings, more or less as follows:

1. The Greek Communist party (KKE) agreed to surrender Aegean Macedonia and the Bulgarian party Pirin Macedonia, thus permitting the creation of a Slavo-Macedonian state. Upon its formation this state would enter a Balkan Communist federation. Meantime Pirin Macedonia would be granted cultural autonomy, so that the gospel of Slavo-Macedonian nationalism could be carried to Pirinia by Vardar Macedonians. Such missionaries actually entered Pirinia in the fall of 1947.

2. Bulgaria, Greece, and Albania would also enter the federation.

3. Bulgaria would be compensated for the loss of Pirin Macedonia by the acquisition of Greek Thrace and an outlet on the Aegean.[11]

4. The Greek party, in return for its cooperation in the unification of Macedonia, would receive extensive support for a new guerrilla war directed against the royal government in Athens and aimed at the seizure of power. This support would include: (a) supplies of arms and equipment; (b) the

[11] One of the elements participating in the Greek guerrilla struggle of 1946-1949 was Organization Thrace. This group was organized on Bulgarian soil sometime in 1944. Its membership was made up from the Slavic speakers who had been expelled from Greek or Turkish Thrace during the exchange of populations which took place in the early 1920's. The headquarters of the Organization were located in Sofia, but local units existed in the Bulgarian villages adjacent to the Greek and Turkish frontiers. Members reportedly regarded themselves as still being the rightful owners of the farms and other properties which they had been forced to surrender a generation earlier. The Organization aimed at the return of Thrace to Bulgaria. It disposed of armed personnel, which was Communist, and which crossed the frontier into Greece and fought in the ranks of the Greek guerrillas. Many of these "Thracians" spoke fluent Greek; some were actually Greeks who had been born in Bulgaria. Members fighting with the guerrillas received their pay from the Organization, which in turn was financed by the government in Sofia. UNSCOB, Observation group no. 6 (Alexandroupolis), witnesses 6W129, 6W130, 6W131, 6W133, 6W123, 6W126, 6W118, 6W119, 6W102.

right of sanctuary in Albania, Yugoslavia, and Bulgaria and the use of hospital facilities in these three countries; (c) the safe-keeping at a special camp in Vardar Macedonia of Greek activists especially vulnerable to arrest;[12] (d) the full cooperation of the Slavophones in support of the military campaign.[13]

The Greek civil war of 1946-1949 was thus in part a war for Macedonian unification. In a larger sense it was a war for Balkan federation, which could not be achieved without first solving the Macedonian problem. The solution of this problem was possible only at the expense of Greece. The fact that less than half the population of the united Macedonia envisioned in this hypothetical agreement would have been Slav was probably of little concern to the negotiators.

As we have said, this grandly conceived enterprise eventuated in disaster. In June 1948 the Yugoslav party was expelled by Moscow from the Communist camp on charges of heresy. Not the least of the Yugoslav sins was the scheme for a Balkan federation, even against the wishes of the Soviet party.

The first effect of the Yugoslav expulsion was the ejection of the Vardar missionaries from Pirin Macedonia. The mis-

[12] After the defeat of the Greek Communists by British forces in the battle of Athens (December 1944 to January 1945), many Greek activists were dispatched to Yugoslavia, where they were put into a camp at Bulkes, Yugoslav Macedonia, and kept in complete isolation from the local Slavic population. Our assassin Zafieris, it will be remembered, served as a police officer in this camp. In due course, the personnel of Bulkes was assigned to the so-called Democratic army, almost always to command positions. The importance of this camp becomes clearer if we compare the number of its inmates, between 4,000 and 5,000, with the 25,000 men and women in the guerrilla army when it was at maximum strength. James Reston in *NYT*, 13 April 1949; S. E. Belikov, *Grecheskii narod i mezhdunarodnaia reaktsiia. Stenogramma publichnoi lektsii, prochitannoi 28 iiulia 1947 goda v lektsionnom zale v Moskve* (Moscow, 1947), p. 26 gives the strength of the guerrilla army in 1947 as 30,000.

[13] Th. F. Papakonstantinou, *Anatomia tis epanastaseos. Theoritiki kai istoriki analysis tis dynamikis tou kommounismou* (Athens, 1952), pp. 184-208. This is a major work, unknown in the West because of the language difficulty. See also Halperin, pp. 51-52; Barker, pp. 116-17; P. E. Mosely, "Soviet Policy and Nationality Conflicts in East Central Europe," in Waldemar Gurian (ed.), *The Soviet Union: Background, Ideology, Reality. A Symposium* (Notre Dame, Indiana, 1951), pp. 67-84.

sionaries had brought with them books and newspapers printed at Skopie in the new Slavo-Macedonian literary language, which now became the language of instruction in the Pirinian schools. The patronymic endings of Pirinian names had been changed from the Bulgarian "ov" to the Slavo-Macedonian "ski." Youngsters from Pirin Macedonia had served in the youth brigades of Vardar Macedonia, or had accepted scholarships at the new university in Skopie. The population of Pirin had welcomed the Vardarian emissaries, but now they were forced to depart and the frontier was closed.[14]

The excommunication of the Yugoslavs also created a real dilemma for the Greek rebel forces. Six months earlier, at the beginning of 1948, the Slavophone component in the so-called Democratic army was reported by an official KKE source as 11,000 men.[15] This was somewhat less than half the strength of the army at that time. If KKE took its stand with the Cominform (Communist information bureau, founded in 1947), it might well forfeit the support of the Slavophones, a crucial loss. If, on the other hand, KKE continued to cooperate with the Yugoslav heretics, it risked the enmity of the Soviet union. Faced with this dilemma, the rebel command split.

At this juncture Gotsi appears to have sent couriers to the Greek rebel headquarters on rugged Mt. Vitsi, proposing the formation of a separate Slavo-Macedonian army, with exclusively Slavo-Macedonian officers. Gotsi also included in his price a KKE amnesty covering all Slavophones who had fled to Yugoslavia. Apparently there was a Greek counterproposal involving the right of KKE to recruit from among the Slavophone refugees in Vardar Macedonia.[16] Meanwhile

[14] "Georgi Dimitrov's Report," *Free Bulgaria. A Fortnightly Review. Special Congress Issue* (Sofia), IV (1949), pp. 3-11; "Moscow and the Southern Slavs," *loc.cit.*; Barker, pp. 104-107.

[15] Vainas, *loc.cit.*; M. Keramidziev in *Novo Makedoniia* (Skopie), 26 April 1950.

[16] Barker, pp. 116, 118-19; A. C. Sedgwick in *NYT*, 2 and 6 February 1949; Coblentz, *loc.cit.*; UNSCOB, Observation group no. 2 (Kastoria), witness 2W306. For the strength of Yugoslav influence among the Slavophones see "Simperasmata tis siskepsis ton slavomakedonikon

the Cominform was insisting that control of the Slavophone resistance organization, now known as NOF, be transferred
from Skopie to Sofia.[17]

The struggle within the Greek party ended in February
1949, with the deposition of M. Vafiades, the rebel commander-in-chief and leader of the pro-Yugoslav faction. The
victorious Cominformists, led by Secretary General N. Zachariades, now made a major effort to retain the loyalty and
support of their Slavophone guerrillas. The rebel radio announced that a congress of NOF would meet shortly to
proclaim "the unification of the Macedonian people into a
single Macedonian state, independent and with equality of
rights, within the framework of a peoples' republican federation of the Balkan peoples."[18] The congress assembled somewhere in the Vitsi area in March 1949 and made clear by its
praise of Dimitrov and its condemnation of Tito that the
Balkan federation it wanted would have Bulgaria and not
Yugoslavia as its center. Two Slavophones were added to the
rebel government and a spokesman for KKE announced that
in the future this government would include Albanian and
Bulgarian elements as well.[19]

The number of Slavophones in the Democratic army now
reached 14,000, perhaps two-thirds of the army's total

---

stelexon tou KKE (eagrithison vassika apo to PG tis KE tou KKE sti
sinethriasi ton tis 12/9/51)," *Neos kosmos*, III (1951), pp. 9-15.

[17] C. L. Sulzberger in *NYT*, 3 April 1949; M. S. Handler in *NYT*,
20 March and 11 April 1949; A. C. Sedgwick in *NYT*, 31 March 1949;
Barker, p. 123.

[18] Cited in Vukmanovic, pp. 91-92. See also A. C. Sedgwick in *NYT*,
3 March 1951.

[19] A. C. Sedgwick in *NYT*, 3 and 11 March 1949; Barker, pp. 122-24.
For the first time since the 1920's KKE had admitted that it counte-
nanced the surrender of Greek territory. The KKE leadership must have
known what such a revelation would cost them within Greece. Among
Communists held in royal Greek prisons the trickle of repentance declarations became a torrent. The Royal Ministry of Public Order even got
out a short form of the standard declaration for those who wished to
renounce the party purely on the grounds of its stand on the Macedonian question. Several thousand formerly recalcitrant Communists
were released from prison. KKE tried to stem the torrent by denying
that it intended to set up an independent Macedonian state, but the
denial had little effect.

strength.[20] In the last engagement of the war, the famed struggle for possession of Mt. Grammos, the rebels fought with a fury which astonished and dismayed the Royalist troops. But the effort to base the rebellion on Bulgaria and Albania alone was from the beginning a hopeless enterprise. In the summer of 1949 the rebels withdrew northward for the last time, Greeks mainly into Albania, Slavophones primarily into Yugoslavia. From Gotsi's retreat in 1944 until the breakup of the Democratic army in 1949, successive withdrawals had reduced Slavophone strength within Greece by a fifth, to perhaps 110,000.[21]

The Vardar republic

With the Cominform split and the failure of the Greek rebellion, the unification of Macedonia had to be put off to the indefinite future. In the interim the Yugoslav Communists continued to bend every effort to make of their Vardar republic a Slavo-Macedonian Piedmont. Slavo-Macedonian was made the official language of the republic, and the language of public instruction. Twenty of the 22 top leaders of the Vardar government were Slavo-Macedonians; none was a Serb. Belgrad introduced industry and poured money into the republic, in the hope of raising living standards. In 1953, according to an unofficial estimate, Macedonia contributed only 9 per cent of the Yugoslav federal budget but was the recipient of 28 per cent of the federal expenditures.

Perhaps most important of all, the CPY backed the Slavo-

[20] *Politiki apofasis tou 2on synethriou tou NOF 25 Martiou 1949* (On the Mountain, 1949), p. 37; V. Koitsev, "Simperasmata ap' to B' sinethriou tou NOF," *Dimokratikos stratos*, May 1949, p. 317 asserts that more than a thousand of the officers of the Democratic army were Slavo-Macedonians. Cf. also Papaconstantinou, pp. 184-208; James Reston in *NYT*, 13 April 1949; UNSCOB, Observation group no. 1 (Joannina), witnesses 1W398 and IW399. In March 1949 President Truman estimated Greek guerrilla strength at 23,000. Felix Belair, Jr. in *NYT*, 13 March 1949. In April, General James Van Fleet, special military adviser to the Royal Greek government, estimated the guerrilla army at 20,000. *NYT*, 30 April 1949, p. 5, col. 5.

[21] *Slobodna Makedoniia* (Skopie), 1 March 1950; Barker, p. 126.

Macedonians in their demand for a national church. The stubborn opposition of the Serbian church, into which Vardar Slavo-Macedonians were automatically born, produced years of negotiation. In 1958 a compromise was reached. A Slavo-Macedonian archbishopric—as distinguished from a patri-archate—was established at Ochrida, a traditional religious center immediately adjacent to Slavophone country. The new archbishop recognized the authority of the Serbian patriarch in Belgrad.[22] In the Orthodox areas of Europe the formation of a separate national church has always been the hallmark of statehood.

The case of the Slavo-Macedonians is of interest to us be-cause it shows how Communism, officially the faith of the industrial proletariat, became the vehicle of the national aspirations of a small, backward, and divided people. From 1924 on, Communism had a virtual monopoly on the idea of Slavo-Macedonian nationalism, the alternative to which was Bulgarian nationhood, as advocated by the annexationist wing of IMRO. The existing evidence suggests that the Slavo-Macedonian preference was for some kind of separate exist-ence. Such indications as we have—the heavy Communist vote in the free election of 1920 (see preceding chapter), the willing audience given the Vardar cultural missionaries by the population of Pirin, the desperate fighting qualities of the Slavophone guerrillas in the Greek civil war, the steady pres-sure of the Slavo-Macedonian Communist party for a separate church—all point in this direction.

If the question be raised whether this connection between Communist ideology and Slavo-Macedonian nationalism was anything more than fortuitous or tactical, we must reply that the answer to this question is not to be found in the Slavo-

[22] Jack Raymond in *NYT*, 27 February and 15 May 1953; M. S. Handler in *NYT*, 30 September 1950, 20 and 22 January 1951; Paul Underwood in *NYT*, 18 November 1959; *NYT*, 6 December 1958, p. 5, col. 2; "Moscow and the Southern Slavs," *loc.cit.*; *NYT* dispatch from Belgrad, 6 October 1955, p. 9.

Macedonian case taken by itself. That case is in fact part of a much larger whole. It is one specific instance of a complex involving Communist ideology on the one hand and the incredibly complicated Yugoslav nationality problem on the other.

CHAPTER VI: THE YUGOSLAV EPIC

ROM its foundation the Yugoslav Communist party (CPY) represented every national group in Yugoslavia and was coextensive with the Yugoslav state. The party was organized in 1919 from a number of previously existing Socialist groups. The Social Democratic party of Serbia, which summoned the founding congress to Belgrad, entered the new movement in a body. The Social Democratic party of Bosnia and Herzegovina, until recently under Austrian rule, also joined up en masse. The Bosnian party was made up primarily of *prechani*, or Serbs not inhabiting Serbia,[1] though it did include as well representatives of the Moslem Serbo-Croatian speaking Bosniaks, and of the German and Czech minorities in Bosnia. Between the Serbian and the Bosnian Socialists, the Serbian element in the CPY was powerful.[2]

But the Croats were also well represented. The Socialist party of the former Austrian province of Dalmatia was composed preeminently of Croats and also entered CPY in a body. Most of the Social Democratic party of the Croat-inhabited former Hungarian provinces of Croatia-Slavonia joined CPY. The two Croatian parties brought with them small admixtures of Serbs and Slovenes.[3]

Other provinces and other peoples were likewise represented in the new party. The Voivodina section of the Hungarian Social Democratic party was preponderantly Magyar. The group

---

[1] Originally *prechani* had been Serbs who, when the Austrian army had to retreat from Serbia in 1690, had fled across the Danube into Habsburg territory. In time, however, the term came to refer to any group of Serbs who did not live in Serbia proper. The Serbian minorities in Bosnia and Croatia were *prechani*, as well as the Serbs of the Banat.

[2] Kabakchiev, pp. 135, 139-40; Sima Markovic, *Der Kommunismus in Jugoslawien* (Hamburg, 1922), pp. 46, 51; Ciliga, "Ueberblick," pp. 1-2. The various depositions which the writer obtained from Ciliga constitute a basic source for the present chapter.

[3] Ciliga, "Ueberblick," pp. 1-2.

from Voivodina known as Pelagic was composed exclusively of Serbs who had been prisoners of war in Russia. There were small Socialist groups from Macedonia and Montenegro.[4]

The left wing of the Yugoslav Social Democratic party of the former Austrian province of Slovenia did not join the CPY until the party's second congress at Vulkovar in 1920. At the same time a rightist faction left the party and, refusing to accept the twenty-one conditions demanded by the Comintern for membership, formed the Yugoslav Social Democratic party, which never offered the Communists serious competition. The effect of the schism was to weaken the Serbian element in the CPY, for the secessionists were almost entirely Serbs.[5]

CPY was thus an all-Yugoslav party. In the election of 1920 —the only free election in the entire history of Yugoslavia— CPY put up candidates and got votes in virtually all 53 electoral districts. Thirty-five parties went to the polls in that election and 32 of these parties represented particular ethnic groups: Croatian peasants, Slovenian clericals, Mohammedan nationals, National Turks, and so on. Even when a party bore an ethnically neutral name—Social Democratic, Republican, Party above Parties—its clientele would be largely restricted to one people or one district.

The other two all-Yugoslav parties besides the Communists were the Radicals and the Democrats. Both were preponderantly Serbian parties standing for Serbian hegemony in the new Yugoslav state. Thirty-eight per cent of the combined national vote of each of these parties came from Serbia proper, and much of the rest from Serbs outside Serbia, the *prechani*.[6]

The Communists, on the other hand, got only a quarter of their national vote in Serbia proper. They were not, moreover, supported by the *prechani*: correlation analysis produces an

[4] *Ibid.*, pp. 2-3.
[5] *Ibid.*, pp. 3-4; *Ezhegodnik kominterna*, p. 989. In the free election of 1920 the Yugoslav Social Democratic party polled 2.9 per cent of the total vote, as contrasted with 12.3 for the CPY.
[6] Based on analysis of the returns found in *Statistichki pregled 1920*, section 56.

r of $-.57$, when $\sigma r = .23$ and $N = 20$.[7] Thus the voting contest in 1920 pitted two all-Yugoslav but preponderantly Serbian parties against the Communists, who were preeminently a non-Serb party.

In 1920 and 1921 a Radical-Democratic coalition government drove the Communists underground. Their party and their trade unions were dissolved, their delegation expelled from parliament, their publications forbidden, their properties turned over to the Socialists. The party, which had boasted 60,000 members in 1920, had only a tenth of that number three years later.[8]

The right versus the left

Once underground, the Communist party broke into two factions. One, the right, was composed primarily of Serbs from Serbia. They belonged to the older, Social Democratic generation, and they were led by S. Markovic, a university *docent* in mathematics, and a god-child of Nikola Pasic, leader of the Radicals and more than any other man the architect of the new Yugoslavia. The attitude of the (Serbian) right toward the anti-Communist decree of the government was one of waiting for the storm to pass, so that the party could resume its activity on a legal basis.[9]

The left, on the other hand, was composed mainly of non-Serbs, although it did include Serbs of the younger generation. The left was more intellectual, less trade-unionist in character. Many of its leaders were not former Socialists at all but ex-terrorists from the days of the Black Hand (which had assassinated the Austrian archduke in 1914) and were already disillusioned with the new Yugoslavia. Typical was R. Colakovic. He had been a member of the pre-1914 student movement known as Young Bosnia, a nationalist group with a Bakunist coloration, made up largely of *prechani*. Young Bosnia had

[7] For the raw data see Appendix B.
[8] Kabakchiev, pp. 144-45; Tito, p. 16.
[9] Ciliga, "Ueberblick," pp. 11-12; Kabakchiev, p. 148; Lazitch, *Tito,* p. 130.

been involved in terrorist activities aimed at the union of Bosnia with Serbia. After this union had been achieved, Colakovic joined the CPY and had a hand in the assassination efforts of 1921. (Years later this worthy was to become Tito's minister of culture.) In Dalmatia and Croatia, Young Bosnia had had sister movements, though here the influence of Bakunin was replaced by that of Mazzini. From these sister movements come such Communist stalwarts as Djuro Cvijic in Croatia and Ivo Baljkas in Dalmatia. The left stressed the importance of developing an illegal apparatus, hoping thereby to halt the demoralization which was now spreading in the ranks.[10]

Despite the difference in their ethnic composition, the left and the right were not at first divided by the national question. The congress of Vulkovar had declared that the party would defend both national unity and the equality of each nationality. By "national unity" the Vulkovar delegates seemed to have meant that Serbs, Croats, and Slovenes constituted a single (Yugoslav) nation; by "nationalities" they apparently meant the non-Slav minorities, whose rights were to be defended against the ruling Yugoslavs.[11]

But if the national question did not divide the two factions at the beginning, it soon became the principal issue between them. As Serbian rule of Yugoslavia became more and more evident, there was an upsurge of restlessness among the non-Serbs. The Croatian peasant party refused outright to cooperate with the Serb-dominated government. IMRO undertook terrorist raids into Yugoslav Macedonia. Among the Albanian minority there emerged the Kossovo committee, a clandestine organization aiming at a greater Albania, that is,

---

[10] Ciliga, "Ueberblick," pp. 12, 18-19; Ante Ciliga to R. V. Burks, 20 May 1949; Ante Ciliga, "Jugoslawischer Kommunismus und der russische Bolschewismus" (hereafter cited as "Jugoslawischer Kommunismus") (typescript in the Library of Congress, dated 1948); A. Ciliga, *Au pays du mensonge deconcertant. Dix ans derriere le rideau de fer* (Paris, 1950), pp. 27-36. Tomasic, pp. 22-24; Markovic, p. 44; Kabakchiev, pp. 144-45; Lazitch, *Tito*, pp. 10-11, 130.

[11] Ciliga, "Ueberblick," pp. 13-14.

the annexation by Albania of the Kossovo-Metohija region of Yugoslavia.[12]

On the Macedonian issue the Bulgarian party seems to have carried an appeal to Moscow. At any rate the Comintern "proposed" to the Yugoslav central committee in May 1923 a party-wide discussion of the national question, and of the party's relation to it. The Comintern pointed to the upsurge of nationalist, primarily peasant-dominated, movements among the non-Serbian elements, and hinted broadly that in these movements was a resource which might be made available for the overthrow of the old regime.[13]

To open the discussion enjoined by Moscow (and also to direct it) party secretary Markovic published a brochure entitled *Marxism and the National Question*. Most of this work was devoted to a general theoretical discussion of the problem; only one chapter was concerned with the situation in Yugoslavia. In this one chapter Markovic ignored the existence of the Macedonians, the Montenegrins, the Bosniaks, and Albanians, but took the position that Slovenians, Croats, and Serbs constituted three separate and distinct peoples. By making concessions to the two most important minorities, Markovic evidently thought to clear the field for what he regarded as the all-important class struggle.[14]

His approach reflected also the predominance of the right, or Serbian wing, in the CPY. A typical politburo—that of 1925 —included four Serbs, two Croats, and one Slovene, although the Serbs constituted only two-fifths of the population.[15]

[12] *Ibid.*, pp. 14-15; Kabakchiev, pp. 149-50; Tomasic, pp. 20-21; Wolff, p. 148.
[13] Ciliga, "Ueberblick," pp. 16-18; *Fifth World Congress*, p. 49.
[14] Ciliga, "Ueberblick," pp. 20-21; Tito, pp. 33-34.
[15] Ante Ciliga to R. V. Burks, 20 May 1949. The politburo of 1925 included the Serbs Trisa Kaclerovic as secretary general, Kosta Novakovic as organizational secretary, Pavle Pavlovic as party responsible for trade unions, and Rajko Jovanovic. The Croats were Ante Ciliga and Zlatko Schneider, the latter being responsible for the Communist youth. The Slovenes were also represented, by a young man whose name Ciliga no longer remembers. Of the seven-man politburo, three were lawyers, one a teacher, one a union organizer, and one a student. The

Markovic was answered by a young Croatian, A. Ciliga, editor of the party newspaper, *Borba*. In the columns of *Borba*, lawyer Ciliga took the position that *all* the nationality problems of Yugoslavia would have to be solved, not merely the Croatian and the Slovenian. There had to come a basic change in the relationship among all the nationalities in Yugoslavia, and the prerequisite of this basic change was the termination of Serbian hegemony.[16]

The bourgeois enemy, Ciliga continued, was incapable of solving the national problem. Even the peasant parties were too narrow in their nationalism to be able to effect a solution, to cross over from the old separatist life of the folk to a new, synthetic way of life common to diverse peoples. Therefore, concluded Ciliga, Communism should spring into the breach, struggle for the overthrow of Serbian hegemony, and employ the liberation of the suppressed peoples as the bridge to social revolution. The two questions, the social and the national, had become inseparable.[17]

Ciliga's theses were promptly and enthusiastically adopted by the left-wing faction of the CPY. Ciliga was himself elevated first to the central committee, and then to the politburo; ultimately he was sent to Moscow in the role of party ambassador. Under Russian pressure an underground party conference was held in December 1923: each Yugoslav people was formally granted the right of self-determination, including the right of secession, and the Slavo-Macedonians were accorded recognition as a nation.[18] The new line was approved by the fifth congress of the Comintern (July 1924), which suggested that it be expressed "in the form of the separation of Croatia, Slovenia, and Macedonia from the body of Yugoslavia and the formation from them of separate republics."[19]

---

profession of the seventh member is not known. According to Lazitch, *Tito*, p. 10, the nine-man politburo of 1919 was composed exclusively of Serbs.

[16] Ciliga, "Ueberblick," pp. 21-23.   [17] *Ibid.*, pp. 23-24.
[18] *Ibid.*, pp. 22, 25-26; Tito, pp. 34-35; Fifth World Congress, p. 49.
[19] *Piatyi kongress*, p. 128. The resolution called upon the Italian party

The right fought back manfully, even at one point announcing in the columns of the principal bourgeois paper, *Politika*, its withdrawal from the party. The right refused to accept the contention of the Comintern that Yugoslav Communists were in duty bound to work for the destruction of the Yugoslav state. Markovic told a royal Yugoslav court, before which he had been haled on charges of sedition, that the CPY would oppose with force armed bands invading Macedonia from Bulgaria. The spokesmen of the right insisted that Croatian, Slovenian, or Macedonian nationalism was no more progressive than Serbian, and that the Serbian revolutionary tradition was at least as honorable as that of any other Balkan people. The union of several nationalities into one large state had, in fact, been a progressive act, and national differences could be resolved by a federalist reform of the highly centralist Vidovdan constitution. Representatives of the right and the left were summoned to Moscow for conversations with such personages as Stalin, Zinoviev, and Manuilsky. To Stalin's exegesis that the right to secession was not equivalent to the act, and that, on the analogy of what occurred in Russia, certain nationalities might not desire to secede from Yugoslavia, Markovic is reported to have retorted that he asked for his country nothing more than the policy Stalin had followed in Russia![20]

Put in bourgeois terms, the issue under dispute is much clearer. The new Yugoslavia was a pillar in the system of alliance which created a French hegemony in eastern Europe. The disruption of the new state was thus a natural Soviet objective, since French hegemony was directed against the USSR and Communism, and the obvious means at hand was the fanning of the smouldering conflict among the divergent Yugoslav nationalities.

---

to advocate the cession of Italy's Slovenian- and Croatian-inhabited territories to the two proposed republics.

[20] Kabakchiev, pp. 150-53; Ciliga, "Ueberblick," pp. 26-27; Tomasic, p. 25; Ciliga to Burks, 20 May 1949; Tito, p. 35-36; Rothschild, pp. 245, 247, 251.

But Comintern policy was not only anti-Yugoslav. It was, at the same time, strongly pro-Bulgarian. Realization of a Comintern-style Balkan federation would not only have broken up Yugoslavia as a separate entity but would also have placed the Bulgarian Communist party in charge of all the Balkan peoples. In a Communist federation, Greece as well as Yugoslavia would have surrendered her part of Macedonia; Turkey and Greece would have given up their portions of Thrace; and Romania, that other Balkan ally of the French imperialists, would have surrendered her share of the Dobrudja. In this way all the territorial claims of the Bulgarian state would have been realized. The agency for implementing this policy of federation, furthermore, was the Balkan Communist federation, a regional organization of the Comintern which had its headquarters in Sofia (until the uprising of 1923). The key roles in the federation were assigned to such Bulgarian comrades as Kolarov and Dimitrov.[21]

In arguing that a federalist reform of the Vidovdan constitution was the proper solution to the Yugoslav nationalities problem, Markovic and the other Serbs in the right wing of the CPY were fighting for the preservation of the Yugoslav state, and *ipso facto* of Serbia's special role therein. In waging this battle, Markovic and his colleagues were not only opposing the separatist claims of the Croats, the Slovenes, and the Macedonians. They were also contending against the chauvinist pretensions of the Bulgarians and the imperial aspirations of the Russian Slavs. When the issue is stated in these terms, it is clear that Markovic and his group of Communist Serbs were engaged in battle on unequal terms. Despite the extent of their support among organized labor within Yugoslavia, their prospects were poor.

Markovic, deposed in 1924, was twice again secretary general, in 1926-1927, and in 1928. Gradually non-Serbian elements got the upper hand in the CPY. *Borba* had been published in Zagreb since 1922. In the mid-twenties a school for Yugoslav

[21] Rothschild, pp. 223-58; *Piatyi kongress*, pp. 125, 128.

Communists was opened in Moscow; most of the students were drawn from the regions outside Serbia, and returned to assume important positions in the party. After 1928 no Serb was ever again secretary general. After Markovic came the Montenegrin J. Malicic, the Croat A. Mavrek, the Czech M. Cizinsky, and the Croat-Slovene J. Broz (Tito).[22]

The anti-faction faction

That same year (1928) Moscow, seeking to put an end to the bitter factional rivalry, installed a new leadership, which was baptized the "anti-faction faction." Among the new leaders Cizinsky was to play a decisive role. Born in Bosnia, where his father had been stationed by the Austro-Hungarian railway administration, Cizinsky was Russian trained and served as effective party leader, whatever his official post, until 1937. Another important member of the anti-faction faction was D. Djakovic, a Croatian labor organizer from Sarajevo. There was also R. Koncar, a *prechanin* and close friend of Tito, who is today a Yugoslav Communist hero. And there was, finally, J. Broz himself, the son of a Croatian father and a Slovenian mother, and married to a Russian wife. A typical politburo in these years included three Croats, two Serbs, and a Bosnian of Czech origin.[23]

The reduction of the influence of the Serbs from Serbia, the *Srbijanci*, was to some extent offset by the growing weight of the Serbs from across the river, the *prechani*. There was not only the influence of the Bosnian terrorists of the Colakovic type, but the key Communist youth organization at the University of Belgrad had a heavy admixture of *prechani* from Bosnia and from the Lika and Cordun areas in Croatia. The abortive Communist rising of 1929 was confined to the Lika.

[22] Ciliga, "Ueberblick," pp. 29-32; Tomasic, p. 26; Lazitch, *Tito*, p. 131; Rothschild, p. 242, 246.
[23] Lazitch, p. 147; Tomasic, pp. 35-37; Fitzroy Maclean, *The Heretic. The Life and Times of Josip Broz-Tito* (New York, 1957), pp. 4-6; Ciliga, "Ueberblick," pp. 29-32; Ciliga to Burks, 20 May 1949. The Croats were Alfred Muk, Ivan Krndelj, and Josip Broz; the Serbs Al Zujovic and Rodoljub Colakovic. The sixth man was, of course, Cizinsky.

Curiously, this rising had been the party's response to the dictatorship of King Alexander, in its turn a last-ditch effort to preserve the hegemony of the Serbs in Yugoslavia. Even more curious, the royal dictator is said to have offered the party a truce, by the terms of which the Communists would be permitted to work in the open if they agreed to drop the touchy nationalities question.[24]

It was only natural that in fighting Alexander's Serbian dictatorship the anti-Serbian character of the Communist underground should have been accentuated. The Slovenes, for example, had in the beginning evinced little interest in Communism. In the election of 1920, Slovenia had ranked fifth among the seven Yugoslav provinces in Communist strength. Since the Slovenian language is distinct from Serbo-Croatian, the Slovenes on practical administrative grounds had to be granted an effective local autonomy. As the cleft between Serbs and Croats deepened, Belgrad sought the alliance and support of the Slovenes, underwriting their national aspirations in Carinthia against Austria and in Trieste against Italy. Although the Slovenes had voted against the centralist Vidovdan constitution of 1921, they ultimately became regular components of every (Serbian-dominated) cabinet.

With the dictatorship of Alexander, however, many Slovenes began to feel that Serbian hegemony offered no sure protection of their national interests. The number of such Slovenes increased when the Slovenian people's party, for which the overwhelming majority of Slovenians voted, deemed it necessary to woo the support of Fascist Italy because Belgrad appeared willing to appease the Nazis. With its promise of Russian support, Communism now seemed to many left-oriented Slovenians as the only force capable of preserving their existence as a nation.[25]

The assassination of Alexander in 1934 was accomplished conjointly by two anti-Serb terrorist organizations, the Croa-

[24] Tito, p. 41; Tomasic, pp. 26-29, 31, 39-40.
[25] Ciliga, "Ueberblick," pp. 6-8.

tian arisers (*Ustashe*) and the Macedonian IMRO. As a consequence of this event, the British and French, who had been the main foreign supporters of the Belgrad regime, advised the Serbs to make concessions to the Croats. The Serbs, under the leadership of Alexander's brother, the Regent Paul, began instead to think of a German alliance as a means of shoring up their threatened rule.

The Yugoslav Communists were thus placed in the fortunate position of being able to identify their anti-Serbian and their anti-German policies. Party membership, which had reached an all-time low of 200 following the Lika uprising and the repressive measures which followed hard upon it, had by 1934 reached 3,000. The party, which had almost been destroyed as an organization, had, by the time of Alexander's assassination, regional committees in every area except the Voivodina. In 1935 the CPY (on Moscow's orders) declared that Hitler's rise to power had made the policy of secession impractical for the time being. Yugoslavia must continue as a single entity, while the state was reorganized peacefully from within. The peoples of Yugoslavia were warned by the party not to lean on foreign imperialism for the realization of their national aspirations.[26] This was an obvious warning to the Croats that they should not be tempted by the resurgence of German power.

This *volte-face* on the part of the Comintern did not seem to affect the party's growing popularity in the non-Serb provinces. No doubt the change in line was taken as a tactical turn produced by the German danger, and was not considered to affect the substance of the anti-Serbian and left-oriented policy of the CPY. The leadership continued in fact to emphasize the principle of autonomy. In 1934 Broz had proposed at a party conference for Slovenia that each nationality or region in Yugoslavia should have its own party, all of which together would constitute the CPY. A year or two later Croatian and Slovenian parties were actually created. In 1940 a CPY con-

[26] Wolff, p. 111.

ference (held secretly in Zagreb) ruled that Bosnia should not be partitioned between the Croatian and Serbian bourgeoisie; reiterated the party's belief in the autonomy of Macedonia, Montenegro, and Slovenia; and formally recognized the national aspirations of the Albanian minority by setting up a regional party organization for the district of Kossovo-Metohija.[27]

Even in Serbia proper Communism achieved a certain popularity again, owing to the growing warmth of official relations between Berlin and Belgrad. This was especially the case after Munich, which brought the break-up of a friendly Slavic state, one also beset with the problems of multi-nationality.[28]

The guerrilla struggle

In the spring of 1941 Yugoslavia came under Axis military occupation. The Royal Yugoslav army made a poor showing against the German invader, partly because it was no match in equipment or training for the German enemy, but also because the non-Serbian elements within its ranks were disaffected, and laid down their arms more or less willingly. (It is said that in the whole of the Royal Yugoslav army there was only one Croatian officer of general rank, and that he was assigned to the quartermaster's corps.)[29]

Under Axis occupation Yugoslavia was dismembered. Slovenia was split up between Greater Germany and lesser Italy, the Kossovo area was given to greater Albania, Macedonia to greater Bulgaria, and portions of the Voivodina to greater Hungary. Croatia was given the much contested province of

[27] Clissold, pp. 27, 54; Fejto, pp. 70-71; Markham, pp. 36-39, 235; "History of the Albanian Communist Party I," *NBIC*, iv (November 1955), pp. 3-10; Ciliga (ed.), "Cinquieme conference 1940," pp. 3, 16, 20, 29. Both in his introduction to "Cinquieme conference 1940" and in his "Ueberblick," pp. 33-40, Ciliga presents the notion that, in adopting the policy of defending the existing (pan-Serb) Yugoslav state, CPY became the defender of Serbian hegemony. Ciliga's *La Yougoslavie sous la menace interieure et exterieure* (Paris, ca. 1951) develops the thesis that the Yugoslav Communist regime represents a continuation of Serb rule over the non-Serb populations. This view of Communist Yugoslavia is widely held among Croatian exiles.

[28] Wolff, p. 111.

[29] Clissold, p. 54; Markham, pp. 36-39; Lazitch, *Tito*, p. 53.

Bosnia, together with her "independence." Montenegro also recovered a separate existence. Serbia was left as a rump state within roughly the same boundaries she had possessed in 1912 before the Balkan wars.

This catastrophe came to the Communists as a godsend for, however small in the number of activists, theirs was the only political party which was trained in the techniques of underground existence and, at the same time, had a following in all parts of the dismembered country. The Communists were, consequently, the only ones capable of setting up a resistance which was national in a Yugoslav sense.[30]

Yugoslavia was overrun in April; Russia was invaded in June. In July there was a guerrilla rising in the hills of Serbia. The Germans were taken by surprise. In this uprising, the joint product of a simmering hatred for the Germans and a stormy outburst of sympathy for the Russians (and a glowing pride in them), there were two guerrilla armies. One was commanded by a Serbian officer of the line, Draza Mihailovic; the other by a professional revolutionary of mixed Croatian and Slovenian ancestry, Josip Broz. In the early weeks of fighting, the guerrillas achieved notable success, but by November they were fighting each other as well as the Germans; when the latter brought up reinforcements both the Partisans of Tito and the Chetniks of Mihailovic were badly beaten.[31]

Draza Mihailovic drew from this defeat the lesson that active resistance against the Axis did not pay. Open acts of resistance led inevitably to German reprisals against the civilian population; the Serbs could easily be decimated and so lose their numerical preponderance and their political hegemony within Yugoslavia. The outcome of the war would not be decided in the backwoods of the Balkans, a minor theatre at best. As time progressed, and Tito began to receive assistance from the Western allies, Mihailovic began to fear

[30] Ciliga (ed.), "Cinquieme conference 1940," p. 24; Fejto, pp. 70-71; Markham, p. 235.
[31] Tito, pp. 98, 101, 105.

that allied victory would mean the triumph of Communism in Yugoslavia and the end of Serb rule. The Serbian leader therefore came to collaborate with the Germans and the Italians, hoping to achieve a local decision which the advancing Russians would not be able to reverse. That in this policy Mihailovic had the tacit assent of the population of Serbia is indicated by the fact that, until the very last months of the war, the Partisan movement in Serbia proper was insignificant.

Upon the defeat of the 1941 uprising in Serbia, Tito withdrew his battered forces into the highlands of Bosnia. His theatre of action from 1941 to 1944 was in fact the zone of the Dinaric Alps, a food deficit area whose population had a long tradition of guerrilla resistance against the Turk. He and his shoeless, ragged, half-starved warriors, only some 20,000 strong during the worst of the fighting, marched from Montenegro to the bleak hills of northwestern Bosnia and back south again, fighting not only the Germans and Italians but the Croatian *Ustashe* and the Serbian Chetniks as well.

In contrast to Mihailovic, who fought for the interests of the Serbs, as he understood those interests, Tito campaigned on a platform of pan-South Slav nationalism. At a time when Yugoslavia had been broken up more or less into her component ethnic parts, the federalist doctrine of the Communists created a haven in which the idea of Yugoslav nationalism could take refuge. Meeting at Jajce (central Bosnia) in November 1943, Tito's Anti-Fascist Council of National Liberation proclaimed:

"1. The peoples of Yugoslavia do not recognize and never have recognized the partition of Yugoslavia by Fascist imperialists, but have proved in the common armed struggle their firm will to remain united in Yugoslavia.

"2. In order to carry out the principle of sovereignty of the nation of Yugoslavia and in order that Yugoslavia may be the true home of all its people, and no longer an arena for the machinations of reactionary influences, Yugoslavia is being built up on a federal principle which will ensure full equality for the nations of Serbia, Croatia, Slovenia, Macedonia, Montenegro, Bosnia, and Herzegovina."[32]

The envoy of Prime Minister Winston Churchill to the Partisans, Fitzroy Maclean, was astonished by the strength of the national feeling which animated these men, by their faith in the rebirth of Yugoslavia. Maclean wondered whether the Communist Tito disguised himself as a nationalist in order to impose his social extremism, or whether his Communism was only an instrument for the realization of a national front dominating all particularisms. The struggle between Tito and Mihailovic, between Partisan and Chetnik, had come to revolve around the alternative of Serbian hegemony versus a Communist Yugoslav nationalism.[33]

The Partisan army

Ethnically speaking, who were the men who fought under Tito's banner? During the 1941 rising, they were primarily *Srbijanci*, Serbs of Serbia, composed mainly of townsfolk from Belgrad. As the defeated Partisans retreated from Serbia into Bosnia, they were met by a stream of *prechani* refugees fleeing the massacres organized by the new Croatian *Poglavnik*, Ante Pavelic, and carried out by a special police bearing the name of Pavelic's old terrorist organization, the *Ustasha*. The object of the massacres was the physical extermination of the Serbian minority in Bosnia and Croatia, so as to make the new enlarged Croatian state Croatian in majority. At the time of the July 1941 rising, the *prechani* of Bosnia and Croatia had put Chetnik units into the field. But the forces of Mihailovic were concentrated in Serbia proper, while the Partisans were in Bosnia. Tito welcomed the surviving *prechani*, fed and armed them. (He also deliberately provoked the Germans to reprisals

[32] Cited in Barker, p. 94.
[33] Halperin, pp. 28-29; Fejto, pp. 72-73; Dinko Tomasic, "Nationality Problems and Partisan Yugoslavia," *JCEA*, vi (1946), pp. 111-125; Clissold, p. 104.

on the civilian population, because the fanaticized survivors sought refuge in his ranks.)[34]

Of the 27 Partisan divisions organized before the end of 1943, approximately 15 appear to have been made up of Serbs, primarily *prechani*. (A Partisan division was little better than a regiment in size and contained approximately 3,500 men.) There were the First and Second proletarian divisions, whose nucleus was the *Srbijanci* of the July 1941 insurrection. The most significant element in these two elite divisions was Communist youth from the University of Belgrad and from provincial lycees. In the capital, the Communist unit at the university had persuaded the Ministry of Defense to provide it with regular military instruction in view of the German threat; now the trainees were to play key roles, not in the Royal but in the Partisan army. The First and Second were cadre divisions, providing officer complements for the newer divisions as these were formed. There were five divisions from the *prechani* area of northwestern Bosnia, where the first fury of the *Ustasha* had been vented, and five from other parts of Bosnia (which may have contained some representation from the Croatian minority in Bosnia). There were two further divisions from Croatian Slavonia, made up primarily from the Serbian minority of that region, and a division from the Voivodina composed of the survivors of Serb massacres perpetrated by the Hungarian occupying forces there. If we add the division of Montenegrin Partisans, we can assert that, up to this point, the composition of Tito's forces was not too different from that of Mihailovic's army. The difference would be that in the Chetnik ranks the *Srbijanci* were the predominant element, whereas among the Partisans the *prechani* were easily the most numerous.[35]

[34] Halperin, pp. 25-26; Clissold, pp. 98-99; Dedijer, p. 174; Maclean, pp. 107-08; Fejto, p. 72; Tomasic, p. 67; Markham, p. 67; Lazitch, *Tito*, p. 73.

[35] Dedijer, p. 174; Fejto, p. 73; Hugh Seton-Watson, *The East European Revolution* (New York, 1951), pp. 124, 130; n. 3; Tito, p. 111; Maclean, p. 157; Clissold, p. 125; Lazitch, *Tito*, pp. 28-33, 37-38, 88-89, 96-97. In the summer of 1942, when Tito's fortunes were at a

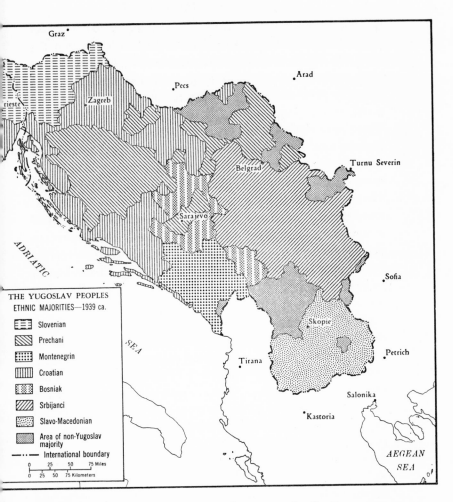

THE YUGOSLAV PEOPLES
ETHNIC MAJORITIES—1939 ca.

- Slovenian
- Prechani
- Montenegrin
- Croatian
- Bosniak
- Srbijanci
- Slavo-Macedonian
- Area of non-Yugoslav majority
- International boundary

0 25 50 75 Miles
0 25 50 75 Kilometers

In contrast with the Chetniks, however, the Partisan army in the days of its greatest trials contained important non-Serb and non-Montenegrin elements. There were, for example, the five Partisan divisions from Dalmatia, composed almost entirely of Croatians. Dalmatia had been annexed by Italy, whom

low point, the Partisan army numbered 3,100 Serbs and Montenegrins, and 2,000 each of Slovenians and Dalmatian Croatians. *Ibid.*, pp. 89-90. The list of Partisan divisions is taken from a plaque which stands in the fortress of Belgrad and commemorates the Partisan army.

the Dalmatians regarded as their hereditary enemy. The fact that the local Serb minority sided with the enemy, that the local Chetniks collaborated with the occupying forces, helped to drive the Croatian majority into the Partisan camp. The Chetniks indiscriminately slaughtered the Croatians in Dalmatia in retaliation for the *Ustasha* massacres in Bosnia. There were also five Slovenian divisions, reflecting perhaps the partition of the country between Italy and Greater Germany, so that even a Yugoslavia organized along Communist federal lines seemed a lesser evil. Finally, there was the Herzegovinian division, one of the last to be organized before the end of 1943, made up of Bosniaks, the Serbo-Croatian-speaking Moslem minority in Bosnia. The Bosniaks had at first tended to sympathize with the Pavelic regime, which treated them as Croatians of Moslem faith. They had even produced an SS division of their own. But now, as the struggle turned, they began to throw in their lot with the Communists.

Thus by a rough calculation, two-fifths of Tito's forces by the end of 1943 represented Slavic elements simply not to be found in Mihailovic's command: Croatians, Slovenians, Bosniaks. This ethnic distribution is also reflected in the composition of the Partisan Anti-Fascist council of national liberation (AVNOJ) at its foundation in November 1942. Of AVNOJ's 70 members, 35 were Serbs, 17 Montenegrins, 13 Croats, 4 Moslems, and 1 was a Jew.[36]

In 1944, as it became clear that ultimate Partisan triumph was certain, a further 27 Partisan divisions were formed. Seven of the new divisions bore familiar names, or came from the old areas; they represented fresh recruitment from the populations who had supported Tito from the beginning. The other 20 were organized in areas where Partisan strength had hitherto been scanty. Who was climbing on the band wagon?

Of the 20 divisions recruited in new territory, 5 came from Croatia proper. By 1943 Tito had brought under his control a goodly section of the new Croatian state. Pavelic's towns

[36] Tomasic, *loc.cit.*; Ciliga, "Jugoslawischer Kommunismus."

were short of food, owing to the disruption of communications. There were as yet no renegades among the *Ustasha*, but the Croatian *Domobran*, or militia, began to desert to the Partisans when it got a chance. By 1944, however, even *Ustasha* units were going over to Tito en masse, under the Partisan policy of amnesty.[37]

Of the 20 divisions formed in 1944 another 9 were organized in Serbia proper. In May 1944 Mihailovic's commander for central and southeast Serbia went over to the Partisans, thus setting the pattern for mass defection. It is worth noting that, at the very last, Mihailovic himself was forced to come out in favor of a federal Yugoslavia. A Chetnik congress at Ba, a little village not far from Belgrad, adopted a resolution in favor of federalism, constitutional monarchy, and economic reform. At the last Mihailovic made overtures to the Croatian peasant party, offered the hand of friendship to those Bosniaks who had survived the Chetnik counter-massacres, and even made a working alliance with the clerical party in Slovenia.[38]

Lastly, in addition to Croatians from Croatia, and Serbians from Serbia, the 20 divisions formed in 1944 included 6 made up of Macedonians. As we have seen, the Macedonians had at first collaborated with the Bulgarian occupiers, and the Macedonian Communists had refused to cooperate with Tito in the development of resistance activities. By 1944 not only had the Macedonians become irked with Bulgarian rule, but it had also become apparent to them that the Bulgars would end up on the losing side.

Thus, by the end of 1944, Tito's army included a representation from each of the Yugoslav peoples, as Table 6.1 shows. According to the table the non-Slavs, the *Srbijanci*, and the Slavo-Macedonians were grossly underrepresented, whereas the Montenegrins and the Bosniaks were heavily overrepresented. None the less, it is clear that the new Yugoslav ruling class (some 92 per cent of Partisan officers were party mem-

---

[37] Tomasic, p. 77; Lazitch, *Tito*, pp. 98-100.
[38] Maclean, p. 163; Markham, pp. 199, 203; Lazitch, *Tito*, p. 121.

bers by 1948) was not what its predecessor had been, primarily a Serbian affair.

Tito's principal party lieutenants were ethnically as many-hued as were his Partisan officers. There was Tito himself,

TABLE 6.1[39]

Ethnic derivation of a sample of Partisan officers

$N = 438$

Ethnic group	% in Yugoslav population 1921	% among Partisan officers
Croats	27.6	27.9
Srbijanci	22.4	13.3
Prechani	16.8	18.5
Non-Slavs	12.5	.0
Slovenes	8.8	12.3
Slavo-Macedonians	5.6	.9
Bosniaks	4.9	10.0
Montenegrins	1.4	17.1
	100.0	100.0

of mixed Croatian and Slovenian descent. There were two Slovenians, E. Kardelj and B. Kidric; two Montenegrins, M. Djilas and S. Vukmanovic-Tempo; two Serbs, S. Zujovic and A. Rankovic; one Croatian, H. Hebrang; and one Jew, M. Pijade.

The new regime

The all-Yugoslav character of the new regime is also confirmed, in a back-handed way, by the unfree Yugoslav election of 1945. In this election the voter could cast his ballot only for the candidates of the Communist-dominated National front. Yet, swayed by the bitter mood of the recent conflict, he could, if he were bold enough, express his opposition to the new regime either by casting an opposition ballot or by staying away from the polls altogether.

[39] According to Rankovic, only 7.7 per cent of Yugoslav army officers did not belong to the party or its youth organization in 1948. Igael Gluckstein, *Stalin's Satellites in Europe* (Boston, 1952), p. 249.

Table 6.2 suggests that the greatest opposition by far was in Serbia. Communist strength was greatest in the south, in the more backward parts, in a red belt beginning with Macedonia, moving northward through Albanian Kossovo, thence northwest to embrace Montenegro and Bosnia. It was roughly in

TABLE 6.2[40]

Yugoslav controlled election of 1945

Republic or autonomous region	Communist as % of total registered voters
Kossovo-Metohija	94.7
Montenegro	94.1
Macedonia	92.7
Bosnia	88.1
Croatia	84.0
Slovenia	79.3
Voivodina	78.7
Serbia	68.3

these same areas that Communist strength had been concentrated at the time of the one free Yugoslav election, that of 1920. While visiting Belgrad in the summer of 1952, the writer was taken to see a collective farm at Stari Pasova, in the Voivodina. On the way out of the capital, the car was held up by a herd of goats driven along by ragged Montenegrin peasants. "*Voila nos nouveaux maitres,*" said the Serb interpreter in evident disdain.

The constitutional arrangements set up by the victorious CPY tell the same story. In the upper house of the new legislature, the assembly of nationalities, each of the federal republics was represented by 25 delegates, autonomous Voivodina by 15, and autonomous Kosmet (Kossovo-Metohija) by 10. Thus Serbia had only 25 votes against 125 for the other 5 republics and the 2 autonomous districts. In a way, Serbia had been partitioned. What Belgrad had been wont to refer

[40] The returns are from *Politika* (Belgrad), 24 November 1945. For an account of the election, see Fejto, p. 83 and Markham, pp. 125-26, 134-37, 178.

to as south Serbia was now the Macedonian republic. Albanian-inhabited Kosmet was autonomous. The territory immediately to the north of Belgrad, although it had never been a
part of the Serbian kingdom, from an ethnic point of view
could have been claimed as well by the Serbs as the Croats;
this territory became autonomous Voivodina. The quarrel over
multi-national Bosnia was "settled" by giving the coveted
province to neither Serbia nor Croatia. Bosnia became a
republic in its own right. The federal organization of Yugoslavia after 1945 is comparable *in form* with the constitution
proposed by the Croatians in 1920. This proposal called for
six provincial governments endowed with wide authority.[41]

In practice, of course, the Yugoslav constitution of 1945 was
even more centralized than the Vidovdan constitution of 1921.
The difference was that government was no longer a preserve
of the Serbs.

To say that the nationalities problem had been solved within
the CPY is not, however, to say that it had been solved in
Yugoslavia generally. Even in 1945, the year of its greatest
triumph, the CPY was probably a minority party. To be sure,
it would have polled much more than the 12.4 per cent of 1920.
If its voting strength had grown at the same rate as that of the
Czech party between the Czech elections of 1925 and 1946,
then the Yugoslav Communist vote in 1945 would have been
something like two-fifths of the total. This would have been
the peak; thereafter the popularity of the CPY would have
fallen off.

What is significant is that the anti-Communist opposition
is not *Yugoslav*. It is Croat, or Serb, or Slovene. Many opposition leaders still think in terms of breaking Yugoslavia up and
making separate states of it. In the late 1950's leaders of the
former Social Democratic party were tried and convicted on
charges that they had secretly agitated for the construction

[41] Tomasic, *loc.cit.*; Halperin, pp. 44-47, 51, argues that while the
constitutional federalism is largely a formality, there is a true federalism among the six Communist parties of Yugoslavia, specifically including patronage.

of a railroad from Belgrad to Bar, on the Adriatic coast of Montenegro. Such a line, though extremely costly to build and to operate, would run entirely through Orthodox-inhabited territory and thus fulfill the Serbian dream of a strictly Serbian outlet to the sea![42]

We do not have to be Communists to recognize that the history of the CPY has about it the excitement and the drama of a Balkan folk epic. If we seek to characterize this epic in political terms, we can say that the struggle within the Yugoslav party paralleled the struggle within the Yugoslav state, except that the outcome was reversed. In both the party and the state there was a basic conflict between the Serbs and the non-Serbs over the question of Serbian hegemony. In the national politics of the interwar period the Serbs won; in the underground politics of the party the non-Serbs were victorious. The German occupation brought the issue to civil war. In this bloody conflict the party became the paladin of a Yugoslav if Communist-formulated nationalism. It defended this Communist nationalism against both the hegemonist nationalism of the *Serbijanci* and the separatist nationalism of the Croats.

If we ask ourselves what provides the operational connection between Communist ideology and Yugoslav nationalism we must answer from the evidence available that it is probably the religious character of Communism. Nationality in the Balkans has long been more definable by the religious than by other differences. This tendency to identify religion and nationality dates back at least to the days of Turkish rule and the millet system of governing subject peoples. The Turks thought of religion and law as inseparable if not identical. Most of what we would today regard as functions of local government they turned over to the alien and heretical clergy. The infidel should be governed by his own (inferior) law. This is

[42] Ernst Halperin in *NZZ, Fernausgabe 320*, 20 December 1952; Victor Meier in *NZZ, Morgenausgabe N. 1762*, 6 June 1959; Paul Underwood in *NYT*, 5 April 1959; Will Lissner in *NYT*, 6 October 1950; Elie Abel in *NYT*, 1 February 1958.

why, until recently, the Moslem peoples of the Balkans tended to think of themselves as Turks, even when this was not ethnically true.

In the Yugoslav case, Serbo-Croatian is a single language. There are neither Serb nor Croat dialects. Dialects exist, but they are spoken by both peoples. It is almost true to say that a Croat may be defined as a Catholic Serb, a Serb as an Orthodox Croat, and a Bosniak as a Moslem Serbo-Croat. During the *Ustasha* massacres—which frequently involved burning down the local Orthodox church with the parish population jammed inside—those who would abjure their Orthodoxy and accept conversion to Catholicism were usually spared.[43]

Thus Communism provided a bridge by which Croats, Serbs, and Bosniaks could all become Yugoslavs in a national sense. Communism replaced the religious faiths which had helped make them different nationalities. It gave them a common faith, a common view of the world and the meaning of existence in it. And if this faith could bridge the gap between Serbs and Croats, it could also serve to bind the Slovenes to the Slavo-Macedonians as parts of the same greater whole.

The Yugoslav Communists were making strict local use of what passed for universal truth. It was in this fashion that Communist doctrine became the midwife of a new and truly Yugoslav nationalism.

[43] Ernst Halperin in *NZZ, Fernausgabe 208*, 30 July 1952.

CHAPTER VII: THE PRINCIPLE
OF ETHNIC PURIFICATION

Insofar as Communism makes Yugoslavs out of Croats, Serbs, Bosniaks, Slovenes, Montenegrins, and Slavo-Macedonians, it tends to reduce in importance the national complexities which for so many centuries have bedeviled the Balkans. The impetus toward assimilation which seemed built into Yugoslav Communism might be characterized as a tendency toward ethnic or national purification.

This tendency also appears in another form. In the Yugoslav epic, the reader will remember, there was little if any place for non-Slavs, for the German, Hungarian, Albanian, Romanian, and Turkish minorities who together made up one-eighth of the total population. None of these minority groups is heard of more than incidentally during the course of the fighting, and none appears in our table of Partisan officers (6.1). At the conclusion of hostilities, moreover, the German minority was expelled in a body from Yugoslavia and the Turks began to migrate to Anatolia. This is also ethnic purification, the rejection by a Communism achieving power of some elements from the ethnic mosaic of eastern Europe, as if they were unassimilable. Such rejection is characteristic not only of Yugoslavia but of eastern Europe generally.

Expulsion of the Germans

A glance at an ethnic map of eastern Europe in 1938 will reveal solid enclaves of Germans scattered all the way from the vicinity of Hitler's Reich to the lower reaches of the Volga river in the Soviet Union. Closer scrutiny of the map will show that within the national territories of both Czechoslovakia and Poland lived masses of Germans who were physically contiguous to the frontier of the Reich. Both the populations of the scattered enclaves and those immediately contiguous

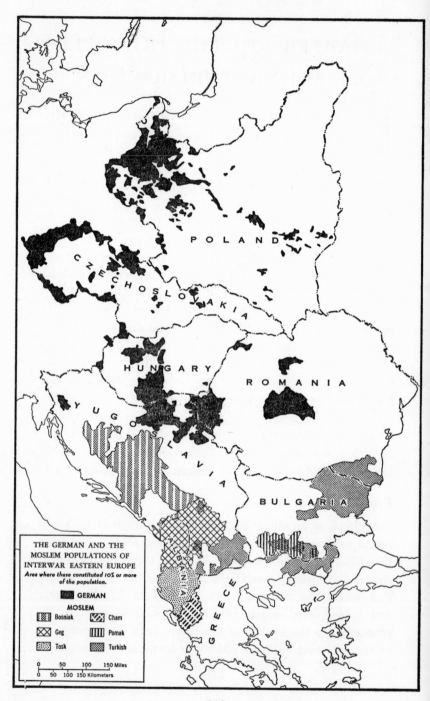

THE GERMAN AND THE
MOSLEM POPULATIONS OF
INTERWAR EASTERN EUROPE
*Area where these constituted 10% or more
of the population.*

GERMAN

MOSLEM

Bosniak   Cham

Geg   Pomak

Tosk   Turkish

0   50   100   150 Miles

0   50   100   150 Kilometers

to the German territorial frontier were known as *Volks-deutschen*, or ethnic Germans, to distinguish them from the citizens of Germany proper, the *Reichsdeutschen*.

The *Volksdeutschen* had been settled in eastern Europe long before the appearance of Communism. For centuries before 1917 they had enjoyed a privileged position there. They had, in general, not intermarried with the local population; they had kept to their own villages or their own quarters; and they had uniformly enjoyed a higher living standard, because their agricultural techniques were more advanced, or because they kept their families small, or because they held a virtual monopoly of some trade or profession. These German-speaking areas and enclaves were, in fact, little Germanies, more sensitive to changes within Germany proper than to those occurring in their immediate environs.

With the collapse of the Austrian, and the defeat of the German, empire in 1918, these ethnic Germans lost much of their privileged position. They were not persecuted, as Hitler claimed, but they did become ordinary (if not second-class) citizens. From what we have said about insecure-aware groups in Chapter III, it would be reasonable to suppose that the *Volksdeutschen* would have reacted in part to their new situation by developing an above average Communist vote. If we take the German population of Bohemia-Moravia—often referred to more simply as the Sudeten Germans—as indicative, quite the contrary was the case.

If, for the Czechoslovak election of 1925, we segregate all electoral districts whose population was 90 per cent or more ethnic German, and those which were 90 per cent or more Czech, we find the following (in Table 7.1, p. 134).

The r for Communist votes and Sudeten Germans in the election of 1935 is —.46 ($N = 23$, $\sigma r = 21$).[1] In this election, which was free by anyone's standards, the Sudeten German Nazi party led by Conrad Henlein[2] received 67.4 per cent

---

[1] For the raw data see Appendix B.
[2] Strictly speaking, Henlein's party was called the Sudeten German party. Its program was, however, thoroughly Nazi.

TABLE 7.1[3]

Distribution of the Communist vote
among Czechs and ethnic Germans (1925)

Province and ethnic group	Communist as % of total vote cast
Bohemia	
62 German districts	9.4
115 Czech districts	13.8
Moravia	
20 German districts	4.5
53 Czech districts	13.6

of the votes cast for German parties.[4] Hitler never received, in any free election held in Germany proper, such a mandate.

The truth is that even the status of equality in a Slavic country like Czechoslovakia was unacceptable to most Germans. The Sudeten Germans turned to the Nazis in part because they identified themselves with the German Reich. This identification not only made it difficult for them to accept membership in a Slavic state (even a democratic one), but it also explains the unusually limited degree of their involvement with a Communist ideology whose world capital was not Berlin but rival Moscow. What was true of the Sudetens was also probably true of the Swabians of Hungary, the Saxons of Romania, and the German minorities in Yugoslavia and Poland, although pertinent electoral data are not available. The Communist appeal was weak among German minorities for the same reason that it was strong among the Slavs.

It is therefore not surprising to find that the advance of the Soviet armies into eastern Europe at the close of World War II had as its accompaniment a drastic reduction in the size and influence of the *Volksdeutschen* populations. It is true that under the Nazis certain of the German enclaves

[3] *Chambre des deputes 1929*, pp. ix, xviii.
[4] *Elections a la chambre des deputes faites en mai 1935* (hereafter cited as *Chambre des deputes 1935*) (Prague, 1936), pp. 14*-15*.

were reduced by migration to the Reich: approximately half a million *Volksdeutschen* were so transferred in the war years 1940-1944, first as a consequence of arrangements made at the time of the Nazi-Soviet pact (*Volksdeutschen* from eastern Poland, Bukovina, Bessarabia, and the Dobrudja); then as a result of evacuation during the final German retreat (*Volksdeutschen* from Galicia and Transylvania). These withdrawals were, however, more than offset by the settlement of 1.5 million Germans in the parts of Poland formally annexed to the Reich.[5] The real reduction in German influence came with the wholesale expulsion of *Volksdeutschen* by the advancing Russians.

Some were stuffed into boxcars and shipped off to the east, but most were forced westward into the territory of the defeated Reich. The advancing Russians not only reduced or eliminated the enclaves, not only expelled the Sudetens en masse and also the Germans who had lived on Polish territory adjacent to the German territorial frontier, but they also deliberately undertook to move both the territorial and the ethnic frontier back to the line of the Oder and (western) Neisse rivers. The Russians handed over to the Poles such territories as German Silesia and the southern half of East Prussia, which had been German for more than six centuries! Approximately 14 million people were expelled, of whom some 12 million actually made their way into what was left of Germany; the others perished along the road.[6]

Prague and Warsaw made haste to settle the newly vacated territories with Slavs. Five million ethnic Poles, transplanted from the predominantly Ukrainian and Belorussian provinces now ceded to the Soviet Union, were settled in the Oder-Neisse area and in the Polish half of East Prussia.[7] Into the empty Sudetenland came approximately 2 million Czechs and Slovaks, particularly those who had participated in the rising

[5] Kirsten, pp. 308-309.
[6] *Ibid.*, pp. 311-12.
[7] "The population of the recovered territories," *Poland of Today. Monthly Bulletin of Information* (Washington), I (1946), p. 15.

at Banska Bystrica (1944), and even a few Gypsies and Magyars. To all these immigrants were given the lands, the houses, and the shops of the departed Germans. The industry and the mines of Silesia and Sudetenland became, of course, the property of the state. The perhaps 1.1 million Germans who remained in Poland and Czechoslovakia were *de facto* treated as second-class citizens.[8]

Even the ethnic integrity of the German rump was subject to attack. In the southeastern corner of the East German republic, adjacent to both the Czech and Polish frontiers, there lived a Slavic enclave, remnant of the Slavic population which a thousand years before had covered the whole area between the Elbe and the Oder rivers. This population, variously referred to as Sorb or Wend, numbered somewhere between 50,000 and 100,000 persons, depending on how the term "Sorb" was defined. Sorb culture was, moreover, slowly dying, especially as the result of the spread of industry to the area.[9]

After 1945 Soviet authorities made an effort to revive this culture. The *Domowina* (homeland) organization, which had been suppressed by the Nazis, was reorganized. Sorb grammars and dictionaries were published, a newspaper in the language appeared, and highway signs were bilingual. Two types of schools were formed in the area. One type employed Sorb as the language of instruction, with German and Russian as secondary languages. In the other type, German was the language of instruction, with Sorb and Russian as secondary. In 1957 there were 9 schools of the first type, which were designed for pupils who spoke Sorb at home, and 110 of the second. Institutes for the study of Sorbian literature and his-

[8] Diamond, pp. 17, 94-96, 98-99, 101; Rudolph Neumann, "Die Lage der Deutschtumsreste im oestlichen Mitteleuropa nach 1945," *Zeitschrift fuer Ostforschung. Laender und Voelker in oestlichen Mitteleuropa* (Marburg/Lahn), I (1952), pp. 427-32.

[9] Guenther Schalich, "Die Sorben in der Nachkriegszeit," 28 pp. A typescript with maps prepared at the request of the writer by a former *Lehrbeauftragte* in Slavic languages who had given up his post at the University of Leipzig and fled to the West.

tory were established at the University of Leipzig, and a Sorb gymnasium was founded in the (German-speaking) town of Bautzen.[10]

The effort to revive Sorb culture, it must be added, did not meet with the unanimous approval of the affected population. Sorb youth seemed reluctant to wear the colorful national dress, which they told outsiders was expensive and cumbersome. The newspaper *Nowa doba* criticized workers who spoke Sorb at the factory gate, but lapsed into German once inside. Some observers felt that the population did not wish to give up being German, in part out of fear that it might someday be exchanged against the German remnants still in Poland.[11]

It is difficult to imagine a German-Slavic frontier better calculated to reduce the influence of Germans, and of Germany, in eastern Europe than that imposed at the close of the second World War. In fact, it has been argued that the new frontiers were so generous as to cast doubt on the ability of the Czechs and the Poles to absorb them. Be that as it may, the frontier settlement was something associated with Russia and Communism. We should compare the 38.0 per cent which the Communists got in the free Czech election of 1946 with the 5.7 per cent which they polled in the free West German election of 1949.[12]

The map on page 138 presents in outline the new frontier arrangement, and suggests that Communism among the Czechs and the Poles had acquired a frontier character. On this map we plot the results of the free Czech election of 1946, the unfree Polish election of 1947, and, for good measure, the free Hungarian election of 1945.[13] In the Polish case we have, for each district, divided the number of valid votes cast by the number of registered voters, thus magnifying the

[10] Schalich; Walter Sullivan in *NYT*, 22 March 1956; F. Lange in *Lausitzer Rundschau* (Cottbus), 27 June 1958.
[11] Schalich; Sullivan, *loc.cit.*
[12] *Sueddeutsche Zeitung* (Muenchen), 16 August 1949, p. 1.
[13] For the raw data see Appendix B.

THE NEW SLAVIC-GERMAN FRONTIER
1945-1947

EAST
GERMANY

WEST

GERMANY

P O L A N D

C Z E C H O S L O V A K I A

AUSTRIA

HUNGARY

 POLISH DISTRICTS WITH ABOVE-MEDIAN PERCENTAGES
OF COMMUNIST VOTERS (UNFREE ELECTION OF 1947)

 CZECH DISTRICTS WITH ABOVE-MEDIAN PERCENTAGES
OF COMMUNIST VOTERS (FREE ELECTION OF 1946)

 HUNGARIAN DISTRICTS WITH ABOVE-MEDIAN PERCENTAGES
OF COMMUNIST VOTERS (FREE ELECTION OF 1945)

 THE "RECOVERED" TERRITORIES

 SORB AREA

0   50   100   200 Miles

0   50 100   200 Kilometers

small differences in the returns of the various districts.[14] In order to employ a uniform cartographic technique we have shaded, in all three countries, only those districts whose rank order of Communist strength placed them in the upper half within the given country.

If the results of the Polish election had simply been invented by some office in Warsaw, or handed down from Moscow beforehand, as is often claimed, the returns would have been arbitrary. The patches of Communist strength revealed by the controlled election would not have made any sense, whether political, economic, or social; certainly they would not have matched the returns of the free election in Czechoslovakia. Our interpretation is reinforced by the fact that the Polish electoral law provided for unequal constituencies, giving disproportionate representation to the so-called recovered territories.[15]

In the course of their medieval *Drang nach Osten* the Germans had thrust forward three salients into Slavic territory. One, along the flats of the Baltic coast, had been established by the hard-fighting knights of the Teutonic order, and had received permanent form as the duchy of East Prussia. A second prong, proceeding down the Oder river valley, had become German Silesia; while a third, moving down the

[14] This step is perhaps the more justified since the Yugoslav Communists in a moment of heresy revealed one of the tricks they employed to secure unanimity among their electorate. Local election officials ascertained the number of eligible voters—those in military service, those confined in hospitals and prisons, those away on official business—who would be absent on election day, then subtracted this figure from the total of those registered. The resultant figure was then published as the actual registration. This device helped to make possible a 98 per cent turn out. See the statement of M. Minic in *NYT*, 11 February 1953, p. 5, cols. 1-2. The Yugoslav confession suggests that the difference between a 99.9 and 97.4 per cent return in a controlled election is not, necessarily, arbitrary.

[15] Richard F. Staar, "Elections in Communist Poland," *Midwest Journal of Political Science*, II (1958), pp. 200-218; Seton-Watson, p. 177. According to Stanislaw Mikolajczyk in *Washington Times Herald*, 29 January 1948, p. 2, cols. 1-2, the western frontier districts were allotted one deputy for each 20,000 inhabitants, while elsewhere each deputy represented 120,000 inhabitants.

Danube, had taken shape as the eastern realm, or *Oesterreich*. Now two of these salients, the Prussian, which had choked off Poland's access to the sea, and the Silesian, which had separated the Poles from the Czechs, were wiped out. In the bargain, the descendants of those medieval German colonists who had pushed their way into the Bohemian forest, the Erzgebirge, and the Sudetes, were now, after six centuries, pushed out again. History had reversed itself.

Looked at in the framework of political geography, the two Slav states now appeared on the map as a compact bloc facing west. Even the rump of Greater Germany, it seemed, had been splintered by the blow from the east. The southern tenth of Hitler's Reich, which caught up Bohemia and Moravia on the south, reassumed a separate existence as the neutralized Austrian republic. After 1949 the eastern fourth came to be organized as a Communist satellite, the German democratic republic, whose existence, guaranteed by the presence of a score of Soviet divisions, in turn guaranteed the new frontier. Furthermore, the small remnant of the huge Slavic population which had inhabited the area between the Elbe and the Oder before the coming of the Germans was now re-slavicized.

The splintering of the German state, the roll-back of the German ethnic frontier, and the accession to power of the east European parties were all part of the same process. All three of these basic changes constituted a reflection of the growth of Russian power and the vast diminution in German influence. All three were covered with the ideological cloak of Communism. To many millions on both sides of the new frontier, the three basic changes appeared inseparable if not irreversible.

Reduction of Turkish influence

Like the German minorities, the Turkish population of eastern Europe manifested little interest in Communism. In the Greek elections of 1928 and 1933, the Turkish minority, located almost entirely in Western Thrace, voted as a separate electoral college. In each election their vote for Communism was less than one per cent, as compared with a Greek vote in that same province of Western Thrace of 4.2 and 8.4 per cent, respectively.[16]

Another sizeable Turkish population was to be found in Bulgaria, particularly in the province of Dobrudja. For this group there is also clear evidence of a substantially below average Communist vote. Three of four correlations in Table 7.2 are significant.

TABLE 7.2[17]

Turkish minority and Communist
votes in Bulgaria (1919-1931)

Election	r	σr	N
1919	−.53	.27	15
1920	−.69	.27	15
1923 (April)	−.67	.26	16
1931	−.36	.26	16

The Turkish case is not dissimilar to the German. The Balkan Turks had been first established as military colonists in a conquered land. For centuries they had belonged to the Balkan ruling race, and had lorded it over the Christian peasants. The gradual deterioration and final destruction of the Ottoman empire in Europe converted these compact bodies of Turks into exposed and vulnerable minorities. In the aftermath of the Graeco-Turkish war of 1920-1922 the Turkish population of Greek Macedonia was expelled bodily. In 1925 Ankara concluded an agreement for the gradual repatriation of the Turks of the Bulgarian Dobrudja,[18] explaining that

[16] *Statistique des elections des deputes du 19 aout 1928* (hereafter cited as *Elections des deputes 1928*) (Athens, 1931), pp. xxiv-xxxi; *Annuaire statistique de la Grece 1933. Annee IV* (hereafter cited as *Annuaire Grece 1933*) (Athens, 1934), pp. 318-321.

[17] For the raw data see Appendix B. The election of 1931 was semi-free.

[18] Wolff, p. 477.

the Turk was unable to live as a slave where previously he had been the master.

The coming of Communism to power naturally accelerated this trend. In 1950-1952 the Bulgarian Communists drove out a quarter of a million Dobrudjan Turks, or 40 per cent of Bulgaria's remaining Turkish population. Turks were also leaving Communist Yugoslavia; in 1954, for example, one-fifth of the 100,000 Turkish-speaking minority returned to their ancient homeland.[19] The limit on the rate of return was the ability of the Turkish economy to absorb the returnees. It was clear, however, that in the not too distant future there would be no Turks left where Communism held sway.

There were, moveover, dwarf Balkan peoples who, because of their Moslem faith, had been identified with the ancient ruling race and for centuries had regarded themselves as Turks. Only with the breakdown of the Ottoman empire had they slowly begun to surrender this identification. The events of World War II and the postwar period tended to push these peoples to an entirely new and non-Turkish identification. For the most part these peoples inhabited the more mountainous and backward regions. In the Rhodope chain, along the frontier between Bulgaria and Greece, lived the Bulgarian-speaking Pomaks; in the Pindus mountains of northwestern Greece were the Greek-speaking Chams; in Bosnia-Herzegovina, the Serbo-Croatian-speaking Bosniaks. The most important case, however, was that of the Albanians.

Under Communist rule the sheep-herding Pomaks, numbering perhaps 100,000, exhibited a tendency to drive their flocks southward into Turkey and Greece. Those on Greek territory petitioned the United Nations special commission for observation in the Balkans in 1949, asking for a plebiscite in the

[19] Joseph B. Schectmann, "Compulsory Transfer of the Turkish Minority from Bulgaria," *JCEA*, xii (1952), pp. 154-69; "The Expulsion of the Turkish Minority from Bulgaria," *The World Today*, vii (1951), pp. 30-35; Reuters dispatch from Belgrad in *NZZ*, *Fernausgabe 64*, 6 March 1955.

Rhodope range, with a view to its unification with Greece.[20] The coming of Communism thus tended to make the Pomaks homeless.

For the Chams the problem of a homeland was even more difficult. At the time of the exchange of populations between Greece and Turkey, Athens undertook to expel the Chams as Turks, while Tirana threatened to expel her Greek minority in reprisal. (The Chams had become converts to Islam in the early nineteenth century, when Epirus has been ruled as a semi-independent duchy by that proud and doughty Albanian adventurer, Ali of Janina.) When the Italians invaded Greece, Chamish guides brought them through the rugged mountain passes. Albanian and Cham formations fought on the side of the invaders. During the Axis occupation of Greece, the Chams terrorized their Orthodox Greek neighbors.[21]

As the occupying forces withdrew from Epirus, non-combatant Chams began to seek safety in Albania. In late 1944 Napoleon Zervas and his royalist and nationalist-minded guerrillas drove 23,000 Chams, the bulk of those who remained, northward across the frontier. The Greeks applied retaliatory terror to the stubborn remnant. In 1946 Tirana appealed to the Council of foreign ministers asking that an end be put to the persecution of the Chams still in Greece, and that the repatriation of those in Albania be provided for. In the last days of the so-called Democratic army (1946-1949), when KKE guerrillas were struggling to keep a foothold on Greek territory, some 1,500 Chams were drafted into the ranks of the guerrilla army by the Albanian government.[22] In

[20] UNSCOB, Observation base no. 5 (Kavalla), witnesses T/212, T/97, T/98, T/242; UNSCOB, Observation base no. 6 (Alexandroupolis), Report for the period 1-15 October 1950; UNSCOB, Resolution de protestation a la commission des Nations unies pour les Balkans en Grece, 30 November 1949. The Pomak population of Greece was about 17,000. Cf. UNSCOB, Subcommittee no. 2, Minorities in Greece, a working paper prepared by the secretariat, 23 April 1948.

[21] *Ibid.*; UNSCOB, Subcommittee no. 2, Study paper on the question of the Cham refugees in Albania, 30 June 1949.

[22] *Ibid.*; UNSCOB, Subcommittee no. 2, Minorities in Greece, a working paper prepared by the secretariat, 23 April 1948; UNSCOB, Ob-

Albania the Chams had to exchange the life of a better-off peasantry for the miseries of a nomad existence or life in camps. The Albanian government did what little it could for them, and they were grateful.

The case of the Bosniaks has already been dealt with in connection with the Partisan war. This people, isolated among a Christian population which worked the land of the Moslem landlords, had been more Turkish than the sultan. In 1848 they had even rebelled against a sultan who had undertaken Westernizing reforms. After 1878, when Bosnia-Herzegovina was occupied by the Austrians, several thousands actually migrated to Turkey. Even in 1951, when Tito ordered Bosniak women to take off the veil, they rioted briefly.[23] But when, despite the personally delivered plea of the Grand Mufti of Jerusalem, they joined the Partisan ranks, they had in fact opted for Yugoslav nationality. The writer remembers a lengthy conversation with the Bosniak director of a Herzegovinian *lycee* who interrupted the discussion of whether Spinoza was to be considered a reactionary or a progressive by detailing each item of clothing he wore and naming the Yugoslav town in which it had been manufactured.

Gegs, Tosks, and Albanians

The case of the Albanians is more complicated. Not all Albanians are Moslem. In the north of the country there is a small Catholic minority, and in the south a somewhat stronger Orthodox minority. Moreover, the Albanian language, mother tongue of perhaps 2 million persons, is broken into two principal dialects. The rough dividing line between these dialects is the Shkumbini river, which traverses the

---

servation base no. 5 [*sic*; the correct number was probably 4] (Florina), witness T/176; UNSCOB, Observation group no. 1 (Joannina), witnesses 1W409, 1W404, 1W408, 1W394, 1W377, 1W383, 1W385, 1W395, 1W403, UNSCOB, Report of observation group no. 2 (Kastoria), witnesses 2W445, 2W566.

[23] UP dispatch from Belgrad in *NYT*, 24 February 1951, p. 4, cols. 2-3; "Albania," *Enciclopedia italiano di scienze, lettere ed arte. Publicato sotto l'alto patronato di s.m. it re d'Italia*, ii, 97-128.

tiny country from east to west perhaps 25 kilometers south of Tirana. North of the Shkumbini the dialect is Geg; south of that river it is Tosk.

Among the Gegs, tribal organization and tribal loyalty have remained important. The blood feud was still practiced in the interwar period, and the population dwelt in isolated homesteads. In northern Albania, where livelihood depended primarily upon the herding of sheep, no one thought of doing anything so outlandish as sending a boy abroad to study.

South of the Shkumbini, tribal loyalties had become attenuated, people lived in agglutinated villages, agriculture was the chief occupation, while socially the population tended to be divided into two classes, a small group of great landlords and a mass of landless peasants. The standard of living was higher than in the north, literacy more widespread, and the populace more sensitive to material deprivation. Most of the Albanians who migrated to America were Tosks.[24]

There were thus two Albanias, and over the centuries the more primitive had been the political master of the more advanced. Skanderbeg himself, the Albanian national hero, had been a Geg chieftain. The movement for Albanian independence (formally achieved in 1913) centered in the Geg towns of Przren and Djakova, presently situated in Yugoslav territory.[25] Tirana, the new capital, was located on the Geg side of the line.

The first break with the tradition of Geg domination was the revolutionary government of the Orthodox Bishop Fan Noli which existed for some months in 1924. Much impressed by what they chose to regard as the Great October revolu-

[24] Skendi (ed.), pp. 57, 148-51; Franz Borkenau, *Der europaeische Kommunismus. Seine Geschichte von 1917 bis zur Gegenwart* (Bern, 1952), p. 371.

[25] Victor Meier, "Politische und ideologische Wurzeln des albanischen Kommunismus" (hereafter cited as "Politische Wurzeln"), *NZZ Morgenausgabe 1073*, 13 April 1957; Victor Meier, "Die Mazedonienfrage als historische Erbe des Tito-Regimes" (hereafter cited as "Mazedonienfrage"), *NZZ, Morgenausgabe 3099*, 25 October 1958; I. G. Senkevic, "Natsional'no-osvoboditel'naia bor'ba albanskogo naroda v 1911-1912 godakh," *Novaia i noveishaia istorii*, no. 5, 1957, pp. 43-67.

tion, Fan Noli and his Tosk followers proclaimed a drastic land reform and startled the Western powers by extending diplomatic recognition to the Soviet government. In turn, Moscow was the only government to recognize the Noli regime. The revolutionary government was overthrown by a rising in the north, headed by the Geg chieftain Ahmet bey Zogu and supported by the Yugoslav monarchy.[26]

Some of Noli's followers made their way to Moscow. Among these was the bishop's secretary, Dr. Sejfulla Malleshova, who became the *lame kodra*, the red poet, the Albanian Maxim Gorki. Others went to Vienna, and organized a *Komiteti nacional revolucionar*. There were close ties between this committee and one for Balkan federation which the Slavo-Macedonians of United-IMRO had organized in the Austrian capital. Under the staunchly anti-Communist regime of King Zog (1925-1939), Communism existed only in the form of isolated discussion groups, the most important of which was located in the Tosk town of Korca in southeastern Albania.[27]

The Albanian Communist party did not come into existence until Zog's regime had been overthrown by Italian Fascist invaders, and then only as an adjunct of the Yugoslav Communist resistance movement. During the days of the Axis occupation the strength of Communist resistance was to be found in the south, while the anti-Communist resistance forces, such as the *Legalitet* of Abas Kupi, were strong in the north. The members of the quizling government set up by the Germans in 1943 were mostly Gegs from the Albanian-inhabited Kossovo area of Yugoslavia.[28]

In Zog's time the intention had been to make the middle-of-the-road dialect of Elbasan the literary language, but, with the advent of Communism, Tosk became both the literary

[26] "History of the Albanian Communist Party I," *loc.cit.*; Skendi (ed.), p. 14.
[27] Stavro Skendi, "Albania within the Slav Orbit; Advent to Power of the Communist Party," *PSQ*, LXIII (1948), pp. 257-74; Skendi (ed.), pp. 19, 76-77, 312; Meier, "Politische Wurzeln," *loc.cit.*
[28] "History of the Albanian Communist Party I," *loc.cit.*; Wolff, p. 221; Meier, "Politische Wurzeln," *loc.cit.* and "Mazedonienfrage," *loc.cit.*

and the official language. Radio Tirana broadcasts in Tosk. Only in Scutari does there still appear a newspaper in the Geg dialect. Of 27 key Communist leaders of the postwar period some 19, or two-thirds, came from south of the Shkumbini. Although the Orthodox (all of whom are Tosks) constitute only one-fifth of the Albanian population, within the leadership sample they are nearly a third.[29] Today such Geg territories as the mixed Catholic and Moslem district of Scutari, and the entirely Catholic Mirdite region, have almost the appearance of occupied territory, where the Tosk policeman rules with an iron hand.

Viewed in ethnic terms, Communism came to Albania as a revolt of the more advanced Tosks against the political domination of the more backward Gegs. Viewed internationally, however, the Albanian Communist party was the handiwork of the Yugoslavs. The Albanian party had itself been founded by Yugoslav emissaries who had merged several isolated groups of Communist believers. After the party had come to power a Yugoslav comrade, as a member of the Albanian central committee, wielded commanding power. Under his aegis, the economic plans of the two capitals were coordinated, the two countries were joined in a custom's union, the Albanian army was reorganized by a Yugoslav military mission, and the study of Serbo-Croat made compulsory in the Albanian schools.[30] In short, Albania was being prepared for membership in the Yugoslav federation.

When in 1948 the Yugoslavs were expelled from the Cominform, the Albanians, after a sharp intraparty struggle, seized upon the occasion to make themselves independent of Yugoslav domination. The economic agreements which had threatened to engulf Albania were denounced.[31] The host of Yugoslav "advisors," military and otherwise, was sent scurrying.

[29] Meier, "Politische Wurzeln," *loc.cit.*; Skendi (ed.), pp. 301-02, 323-45.
[30] Skendi, *loc.cit.*; Skendi (ed.), pp. 24, 230; Fejto, p. 239.
[31] M. S. Handler in *NYT*, 10 December 1948.

When the Partisan regime began to show signs of heresy, Tirana emphasized its rigid Stalinist posture, maintained regardless of any changes elsewhere in the Communist world.[32]

It was, of course, perfectly true that in order to achieve independence from Belgrad, Tirana had to become a dependency of Moscow. But the fact that the Albanian state was not viable, and had to be subsidized by one or another foreign power, was not the fault of the Albanian Communist party. Moscow was more distant than Belgrad, more important in the world, and more able to help (although Belgrad had subsidized the Albanian budget to the tune of 56 per cent). Politics is always a choice between evils. If the year 1948 is to be regarded as the year in which Communist Yugoslavia acquired its independence from Soviet Russia, it can also be viewed as the year in which Communist Albania escaped from the clutches of the Yugoslav federation. Perhaps it is too much to say that in 1948 the Tosks decided they were Albanians and not a species of Yugoslav, but the year is certainly an important one in the history of Albanian nationalism.

The process of ethnic purification had begun in eastern Europe even in the early years of the nineteenth century. We may date its beginning from the massacres of their Turkish fellow denizens by the Greek rebels of 1821-1829, or from the silent migration of Hungarian peasants to Budapest which began shortly after the emancipation of the serfs in 1848 and would eventually transform that city from a German-Jewish into a Magyar town. In one sense, east European Communism with its principle of ethnic purification only represented a continuation of a long-established trend.

But Communist ethnic purification was different because it had a Slavic bias. The Germans and the Turks had in common that they had at one time built up empires (Hapsburg and Ottoman) which had ruled large areas of eastern Europe,

[32] Skendi (ed.), pp. 239-40; "History of the Albanian Communist Party II," *NBIC*, v (January 1956), pp. 22-30.

and their chief competitors for the control of this area had been first the Slavic Poles and then the Slavic Russians. Reduced to its political protoplasm, Communism, in its overall east European context, was the ideological instrument for a new and more inclusive Russian and Slavic hegemony. In this context, the remnants of the former ruling peoples had to go.

CHAPTER VIII: REJECTED
PEOPLES: JEWS AND MAGYARS

W E HAVE considered the case of the Slavic peoples, such as the Bulgars and the Czechs, who have shown a predilection for Communism. We have also dealt with the case of the non-Slavic Turks and Germans who seem to be natural enemies of Communism. Our analysis of the politics of east European peoples will not be rounded out, however, until we have examined the extreme case, that of the non-Slavic peoples who have shown a special interest in Communism. In this last category we have the Hungarians, or (as they call themselves) Magyars, and the Jews, both the German-speaking Ashkenazic Jews who lived to the north of the Danube and the Spanish-speaking Sephardim who inhabited the territory to the south of that river.

The kingdom of St. Stephen

We have already noted the high positive correlation between Communist votes and Magyar voters in the Slovak election of 1929 (Table 4.1). This positive relationship also holds for the elections of 1925 and 1935 ($r = .52$ and $.56$ respectively, where N is 23 and σr .21).[1] Furthermore, Table 8.1 provides direct evidence that the Communist vote of the Magyar minority was substantially higher than that of the Slavic peoples inhabiting interwar Czechoslovakia.

The Slavic vote is high, but the Magyar vote is twice that of the Slavs. For comparison we may point out that the east European average in the twenties was 6.3 per cent.[2] This kind of voting behavior for non-Slavs is astonishing. How is it to be explained?

---

[1] For the raw data see Appendix B.
[2] Calculated from the returns of the Bulgarian and Yugoslav elections of 1920, the Hungarian and Romanian elections of 1922, the Czechoslovak election of 1925, the Greek election of 1926, and the Polish election of 1928. For the sources, see the proper footnotes in Appendix B.

TABLE 8.1[3]

Distribution of the Communist
vote among various ethnic groups
in Czechoslovakia (1929)

Province and ethnic group	Communist as % of total vote cast
Bohemia	
115 Czech districts	9.6
Moravia	
53 Czech districts	10.5
Slovakia	
27 Slovak districts	7.6
6 Hungarian districts	22.5
Ruthenia	
5 Ukrainian districts	11.5

Communism made a dramatic entry into Hungary in the spring of 1919, shortly after the collapse of the Austro-Hungarian empire. It arrived in the form of the dictatorship of the bank clerk, Bela Kun. But it would not be entirely correct to say that the Hungarian Bolsheviks *seized* power. The tottering Karolyi government had held office on the basis of the widespread supposition that Count Michael Karolyi's personal connections with the Allied leaders, together with his liberal, Wilson-like, political views, would mitigate the terms to be imposed upon a defeated Hungary. When it became apparent that the count could exercise no such influence and that the victorious Allies intended to hand over Transylvania to the despised Romanians, and some purely Magyar territory as well, the Karolyi government released the Communist leaders from prison, and in effect turned Hungary over to the dictatorship of the proletariat. The initial proclamation of Red dictator Kun is worth noting:

"The Hungarian revolution was created by two forces: one of these was the resolve of the industrial workers, the agri-

[3] *Chambre des deputes 1929*, pp. ix, xviii. Except for Ruthenia, the inhabitants of each set of districts were 90 per cent or more of the given ethnic group. The Ukrainian districts were only 80 per cent of that national group, there being no districts 90 per cent or more Ukrainian.

cultural proletariat, and the soldiers no longer to endure the yoke of Capital; the other is the imperialism of the Entente, whose intention was and is to rob Hungary of its food supply, its industrial raw material, and all the [pre]conditions of existence, by dismembering its territory. To the ultimatum of the Entente [concerning Transylvania] . . . the answer of the Hungarian people is the creation of the Dictatorship of the proletariat."[4]

At the moment of this proclamation a Soviet army was reported to be advancing in the western Ukraine, near the borders of Romania. "In the future," said one Communist leader, "we shall receive from the East what the West has denied to us."[5]

As the Romanian army advanced toward the river Tisza in central Hungary, the new Communist regime in Budapest was busy organizing a Red army. Like its Bolshevik counterpart, this army was equipped with proletarian regiments, soldiers' soviets, and wide-ranging political commissars. But the core of its rank and file was made up of demobilized peasants, many (if not most) of them unable to return to their villages because of foreign military occupation. The core of the officer class was composed of professionals and reservists, representatives of the landowning and professional classes. As in the Russian case, the officers were probably motivated almost entirely by a desire to prevent the dismemberment of the fatherland. In essence, Kun's dictatorship was a government of national defense in alliance with a Bolshevik Russia. Bolshevik ideology might not be the most palatable dish in all the world, but the essential thing was to save the thousand-year-old kingdom of St. Stephen.[6]

The Romanians had scarcely been driven back over the Tisza than a new danger appeared. The Czechs, under French commanders, were pushing forward through Slovakia toward

[4] Cited in Albert Kaas and Fedor de Lazarovics, *Bolshevism in Hungary. The Bela Kun Period* (London, 1931), p. 327.
[5] Cited in *ibid.*, p. 81.
[6] *Ibid.*, pp. 193, 197, 200, 204-06, 209-15, 358-61.

Budapest. Kun's Red army wheeled, drove deep into Slovakia —since A.D. 906 an Hungarian province—and, in June 1919, the Red dictator proclaimed a Slovak soviet republic at Presov.[7] This act should be viewed in the light of the first two paragraphs of Kun's decree on nationalities:

"1. The Hungarian soviet republic desires to do away with all forms of the oppression of the proletariat produced by the capitalist system of production and social order. One form of such oppression is represented by nationalist oppression of the population of non-Hungarian mother tongue. The Hungarian soviet republic, which is based on a federation of peoples speaking various languages but possessing equal rights and which does not face a nationalities question in the usual sense of that term, brings this situation to an end.

"2. Until such time as the Soviet government has finally determined upon the constitution of the Hungarian soviet republic, the revolutionary Soviet government directs the election of German and Ruthenian soviets. . . ."[8]

As the fighting progressed, the working class element tended to melt away, and the Hungarian Red army came more and more to be run by nationalists, particularly by Magyars whose homes were in enemy-occupied territory.

The Allies called upon Kun to evacuate the Slovakian territory he had conquered and promised, in exchange, that the Romanians would withdraw from the Hungarian territory they still held. Kun wavered and then pulled back from Slovakia. This proved to be a disastrous blunder, the effect of which was compounded when the Romanians refused to live up to the Allied promise and remained on ethnically Hungarian soil. Some of Kun's officers, believing the cause was lost, entertained secret negotiations with the leaders of a counter-revolutionary Hungarian army which had begun to form in the south on Hungarian territory occupied by an Allied army under French command. Kun attempted to re-

[7] *Ibid.*, p. 190.
[8] Cited in Pavel Reimann, *Geschichte der kommunistischen Partei der Tschechoslovakei* (Hamburg, 1931), p. 140.

vive morale by ordering a new assault on the Romanians, but half his army now refused to obey orders, and the Romanians broke through to Budapest.[9] The Bolshevik regime was shortly replaced by a right-wing dictatorship under Admiral Miklos Horthy which, in the two decades that followed, subordinated all else to the aim of recovering Hungary's lost provinces. It was this rightist dictatorship which cooperated with the Nazis in order to recover, between 1939 and 1941, the southern part of Slovakia, all of Ruthenia, the northern half of Transylvania, and a part of the territories lost to Yugoslavia.

Communism and Magyar irredentism

The impact of Kun's dictatorship was also felt in Slovakia. Hundreds of his followers, fleeing the Horthy terror, sought refuge among the Hungarian minority there. The first newspaper in all of Czechoslovakia to publish a Comintern appeal was the Magyar *Kassai munkacs*,[10] and the earliest pressure for the organization of a Communist party came from the Hungarian minority.

It seems reasonable to believe that the interest of this minority in Communism was an expression of irredentist feeling. Certainly the aim of Comintern policy in the twenties was to break up Czechoslovakia into its constituent parts. According to the fifth Comintern congress (1924):

"1. The nationality situation in Czechoslovakia is entirely comparable to the nationality situation in Yugoslavia. The congress affirms that in Czechoslovakia there does not exist a single Czechoslovak nation and that the Czechoslovak state, in addition to the Czech nationality, consists of the following

[9] Kaas, pp. 192-98.

[10] Reimann, pp. 144, 146-49, 153. In January 1921 a conference of the Marxist left met at Lubochna, founded a party of its own, and accepted the 21 points. Of the 153 delegates to the conference, 36, or 23.5 per cent, were said to be Magyars. H. Gordon Skilling, "The Formation of a Communist Party in Czechoslovakia," *ASEER*, XIV (1955), pp. 346-58. According to the Czech statistics, Magyars constituted only 17.2 per cent of the population of Slovakia and Ruthenia in those years.

nationalities: Slovak, German, Hungarian, Ukrainian and Polish.

"2. The congress considers it necessary for the CPCz, in connection with these national minorities, to proclaim and to follow the slogan of the right of nations to self-determination, including the right to secession. . . ."[11]

Comintern policy in this matter was undoubtedly influenced by the fact that the new Czechoslovak state had become an outpost of Western, particularly French, influence in eastern Europe. Whatever the Comintern's reasons, the Magyar minority would feel a strong attraction for a policy advocating the breakup of the new state. For a thousand years, as the advance guard of the main body of Hungarians, this minority had dominated the whole of Slovakia. Now, under the arrangements of Trianon, it had become a suspect minority in a foreign land.

It is probably for the same reasons that Communism developed a strong following among the Szeklers, the Hungarian outpost in Transylvania, a population completely surrounded by Romanians and the more intransigeant in its nationalism because it was physically cut off from the main body of Hungarians. Until 1918 the province of Transylvania had been part of the empire of St. Stephen, although the population was in majority Romanian. Under instructions from the Comintern, the Romanian Communist party advocated the creation of a special regime in Transylvania.[12] Sometime in the 1930's there appeared in the province an organization known as the Magyar workers' alliance, MADOSZ for short, which was composed largely of Szeklers and in elections tended to ally with the Romanian Communist party.[13]

[11] *Piatyi kongress,* p. 129.
[12] *Fifth World Congress,* p. 50; *Piatyi kongress,* pp. 126-27; "Romanian Party and Congress. I. Short History of the Romanian Communist Party," *NBIC,* v (February 1956), pp. 3-21; Henry L. Roberts, *Rumania: Political Problems of an Agrarian State* (New Haven, 1951), p. 253.
[13] *Politics in Roumania,* pp. 267, 277. *VII kongressom,* p. 345, refers to the organization in Transylvania ca. 1934 of an independent national-

In 1940, as a consequence of a Nazi decision, the northern half of Transylvania, including the Szekler enclave, was returned to Hungary by the so-called Vienna award. When the advancing Soviet and Romanian armies recovered the territory some three years later, there emerged in Kolosvar, or Kluj, the capital of northern Transylvania, a Hungarian-dominated proto-Communist government, which took the view that northern Transylvania should acquire an independent status, and even laid claim to the part of Transylvania which had remained Romanian by the terms of the Vienna award.[14]

The driving force in this north Transylvanian regime was provided by the Magyar workers' alliance, now renamed the Magyar people's alliance. The MADOSZ regime, as we shall call it, established a Central advisory board or parliament. It laid the foundation of a people's court, set up "purification" committees to cleanse its territory of reactionary and fascist elements, lowered the voting age to 18 years, enfranchised those who had migrated to northern Transylvania from Hungary since 1940, and enacted a land reform whose provisions foreshadowed with astonishing prescience the law later enacted for all Romania by the Communist-dominated Groza government.[15]

Meantime the coalition government in Bucharest repeatedly petitioned Moscow for the return of northern Transylvania to Romanian administration.[16] The Russians seemed to have difficulty deciding. In the course of their military operations in Hungary they took prisoner Count Istvan Bethlen, whose ancestors had ruled a flourishing and independent Transylvania in the seventeenth century. They are reported to have suggested to Bethlen that he assume the governorship of a new

---

revolutionary organization of workers and the toiling masses. It had 3,000 members and some legal newspapers and journals.

[14] "The Situation of the Hungarians in Transylvania since Romania Changed Sides on August 23rd, 1944" (mimeographed memorandum of the Hungarian government, in possession of Count Geza Teleki, formerly Hungarian minister of education), pp. 43, 50, 56-59, 75.

[15] *Ibid.*, pp. 63-65, 60-63, 65-68.

[16] P. E. Mosely, *loc.cit.*

"independent" Transylvanian state. Bethlen is said to have refused to have anything to do with the scheme.[17] Whatever the truth of these reports, a delegation of Romanian Communist leaders, upon their return from a visit to Moscow in January 1945, made clear by their pronouncements that if the coalition government in Bucharest were replaced with a Communist-dominated one, northern Transylvania would be returned to Romanian administration.[18] With the installation of the Groza cabinet in March 1945, the MADOSZ administration was brought to an end, and all hope for an "independent" Transylvania was terminated.

Thus in the end the Magyars got very little for their interest in Communism. The boundaries of Hungary in 1945 were identical with those imposed by the Treaty of Trianon. There was only one gain, and that was negative. In 1945 the Slovaks, with the consent of Prague and under the leadership of the principal Slovak Communist, the Bratislava lawyer V. Clementis, attempted to expel the Hungarian minority. This action would have been parallel to the ejection of the Sudeten German population from the Czech lands. It is said that the Hungarian Communist party carried an appeal to the Kremlin, and that the Kremlin ruled in favor of the status quo. In any case the Slovak plans were frustrated, and Soviet troops in Hungary were employed to turn the expellees back.[19] Hungary could retain her territorial claim to southern Slovakia.

There was another sop. In 1952 the Szekler-inhabited part of Transylvania, a territory perhaps one-third of that which MADOSZ had ruled, was made an autonomous region. In

[17] Count Istvan was reportedly taken prisoner in February 1945 and brought to Kecskemet, some distance southeast of Budapest, where high-ranking Soviet officers attempted to persuade him that he should play a leading role in an "independent" Transylvanian state. The Soviet officials declared their readiness to introduce a new fundamental law, based on the Transylvanian constitution of 1863. Bethlen refused the offer.

[18] Roberts, p. 262.

[19] Istvan D. Kertesz, "Minority Population Exchanges: Czechoslovakia and Hungary," *American Perspective*, June 1948, pp. 138-44.

this region there were Hungarian newspapers, schools, theaters, and radio.[20] This was not Hungarian rule of Transylvania, but it was better than nothing.

Even had Bela Kun been victorious, even had he, by some miracle, been able to establish a multi-national Union of Soviet Danubian republics—to reestablish in Communist dress, that is, the sacred empire of St. Stephen—it seems doubtful that in the long run Communism and Magyar nationalism could have worked out a durable alliance. Kun's Communist Danubian state would have been heavily dependent upon the support of Soviet Russia. Its essential Magyar component would have been for many reasons a weak buckle on which to pivot Russian domination of eastern Europe. There would also have existed deep conflicts of interest between Kun's Communist Danubia and such Slavic peoples as the Slovaks, Croats, and Serbs. The union of Magyar irredentism and Communist ideology was basically a political *mesalliance*.

Extent of Jewish participation

Persons of Jewish background played a major role in the history of every east European Communist party except the Yugoslav, the Albanian, and the Bulgarian. The reason for these three exceptions is probably to be found in the small size and restricted influence of the Jewish populations of the three countries named.

On the score of Jewish participation there is some statistical evidence. The r for Jewish population and Communist votes in the free Polish election of 1922 is .77, three times the standard error. ($N = 17$; $\sigma r = .25$.)[21] This correlation is supported by the results of the 1927 election to the Warsaw municipal council. In that election the Communists more than doubled the vote they had received in the general election of 1922. This accretion came primarily at the cost of the Jewish parties, though to a lesser extent it was at the cost of the right

[20] Paul Underwood in *NYT*, 10 June 1959.
[21] For the raw data see Appendix B.

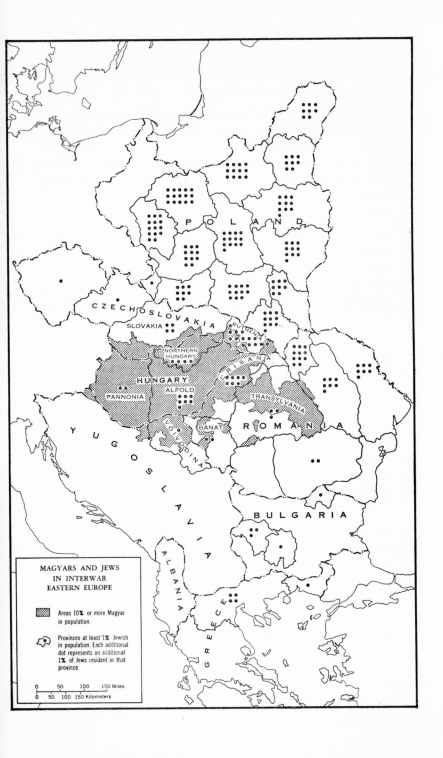

MAGYARS AND JEWS
IN INTERWAR
EASTERN EUROPE

Areas 10% or more Magyar
in population.

Provinces at least 1% Jewish
in population. Each additional
dot represents an additional
1% of Jews resident in that
province.

0   50   100   150 Miles
0   50   100 150 Kilometers

POLAND

CZECHOSLOVAKIA

SLOVAKIA

RUTHENIA

NORTHERN
HUNGARY

HUNGARY

PANNONIA

ALFOLD

CRISANA

TRANSYLVANIA

VOIVODINA

BANAT

ROMANIA

YUGOSLAVIA

BULGARIA

ALBANIA

GREECE

wing National Democrats. The strength of the Polish Socialist party was not at all affected. Incidentally, more than one observer of Polish Communism in the interwar period reports that Communist demonstrations were largely carried out by Jewish youngsters.[22]

In the Greek elections of 1928 and 1933 the Israelites voted in a separate electoral college. Their Communist vote was 15.7 and 15.4 per cent in these two elections. These figures are to be compared—since almost the whole of Greek Jewry was resident in the city of Salonika—with the Communist vote cast in those same elections by the non-Jewish residents of Salonika district: 1.3 per cent in 1928 and 7.2 per cent in 1933.[23]

As for the hard core, we have a certain amount of data from the Polish party. According to an official Communist source, in 1933 some 26 per cent of party members were Jewish.[24] This figure seems on the low side. Perhaps it covers only those activists who were willing to admit that they came from Jewish families. An anti-Communist source estimates the proportion of Jews in the party in 1931 at about half and there are indications that in 1940 the percentage of Jews in the Communist party of neighboring Lithuania was 53.8. In any case, it is clear that the bulk of the Communist youth organization was Jewish.[25] In the Polish population as a whole Jews amounted to 10.5 per cent (in 1924).[26]

The proportion of Jewish activists in the Polish party varied with time and place. During the middle twenties, when the party was at its apogee, the proportion declined notably, owing to the vast (if largely temporary) influx of Ukrainian and Belorussian peasants. Geographically, Jewish activists tended to

[22] Regula, pp. 199, 239.
[23] Election des deputes 1928, pp. xxiv-xxxi; Annuaire Grece 1933, pp. 318-21.
[24] Polityka (Warsaw), 29 November 1958.
[25] Regula, p. 259; VII kongressom, p. 539; Fifth World Congress, p. 55.
[26] Annuaire statistique de la republique polonaise, III annee, 1924 (Warsaw, 1925), pp. 12-17.

concentrate in congress Poland—the part which had belonged to tsarist Russia—and Galicia. This distribution conformed to that of the Jewish population as a whole. The revolutionary committees which the Red army installed in 1920 as local government were in majority made up of Jews from the smaller towns. Many came from the non-Communist Jewish parties, such as the Bund and the left-wing *Poalei Sion*. In such western territories as Posnan and Pomerania, on the other hand, the Jewish minority population tended to be replaced by the German, and the CPP barely existed.[27]

The influence of Jews on party life, moreover, was generally greater than the percentages would suggest. Jewish activists were probably better educated than the average, and more likely to achieve the level of leading cadre. Many Jewish members of the Polish party were former rabbinical students. Many came from well-to-do and well-known merchant families, such as those of Eiger, Teich, Jachweta, Cukier-Kolski, and Jaszunski, to take the city of Lodz as an example.[28] To further document the extent of Jewish influence in the *apparat*, let us draw upon the histories of the Greek and Hungarian parties.

As early as 1909 a group known as *Federacion* had developed among the Sephardic (Spanish-speaking) Jewish population of Salonika. *Federacion* spread Socialist ideas in Greece and advocated a Balkan federation in which Salonika, with its many nationalities, would be a free city. The founder of *Federacion* was a Bulgarian Jewish printer, Abraham Benaroya, and its most militant supporter was the society of Jewish tobacco workers. The 60,000 members of *Federacion* became one of the constituent elements of the Greek Socialist Labor party at its founding in 1918. The two deputies of *Federacion* in the Greek national assembly became the first parliamentary delegation of this party, which joined the Communist Inter-

[27] Regula, pp. 42, 251, 259-60.
[28] *Ibid.*, pp. 88-89, 252, 259-60.

national in 1920 and formally took the name KKE in 1924.[29] The new party published weekly newspapers in the two languages employed by the Salonika Jews, Spaniole and Hebrew. During the dictatorship of Metaxas, Solomon Tsaltiel, a Sephardic Jew, published clandestinely and at great risk to himself the party's Greek language organ *Risospastis*.[30]

Salonika Jewry thus played a major role in the foundation of the Greek Communist movement. With the passage of time, however, the Jews became less and less prominent in KKE. By the thirties they were no longer represented in the top leadership. In the early forties the Jewish population either fled the country or was physically exterminated by the Nazis. In the postwar KKE the Jewish element had almost disappeared.

Jews also played a prominent role in the history of the Hungarian party, to take an illustration from the area of the Ashkenazim, or German-speaking Jewry. Bela Kun was, of course, Jewish and so were two of his colleagues destined to play a major role in international Communism; Eugene Varga, the Soviet economist, and Matyas Rakosi, the Stalinist dictator of Hungary. In fact, during Kun's brief regime most of the commissars, the managers of the new state farms, the bureau chiefs in the central administration, and the leading police officers were Jewish. Of 203 higher officials in the Kun government, 161 were Jewish.[31]

New recruitment was made during the Horthy dictatorship (1920-1944). Many Jews were prevented by a *numerus clausus* from attending university at home. Those inadmissible on this ground often had the means for study abroad, where they became infected with the Communist bacillus, as did so many non-Jewish east Europeans. E. Gero, Rakosi's alter ego, is merely the most prominent example of this process. When

[29] Stavrianos, p. 201; Kabakchiev, pp. 176-78; *Ezhegodnik kominterna*, p. 660; Rothschild, pp. 213-14.

[30] *Ibid.; Shestym kongressom*, p. 216; *I organotiki politiki tou KKE 1918-1950* (? Bucharest, nd), 22 pp.

[31] Werner Sombart, *Der proletarische Sozialismus* ("*Marxismus*") (Jena, 1924), II, pp. 299-300.

Radio Kossuth, a Soviet station broadcasting in Hungarian, called for the organization of an Hungarian resistance movement in 1943, the appeal was heard first and foremost by the Jewish students abroad. Of the 22 members of the Swiss branch of the new resistance organization (*Magyar nemzeti fuggetlensegi moszgalom*) 20 were Jewish. The most prominent member of the Swiss group was the physician T. Szonyi, hanged with Laszlo Rajk in 1949 on charges of nationalist deviation. So heavily Jewish was the Hungarian politburo under Rakosi that the wags of Budapest explained the presence of the lone gentile in that august body on the ground that there must be someone available to sign decrees on Saturday!

The problem of motivation

In terms of basic attitudes, the Jewish population of eastern Europe tended to divide into those who wished to forget their Jewish backgrounds and become indistinguishable from the people among whom they lived, and those who with grave determination held to the faith and the customs of their ancestors. Jews who believed that assimilation was the answer to the Jewish problem tended to espouse radical causes. Usually they were Socialists or Communists.[32] Their position was not altogether bereft of logic.

In large parts of eastern Europe anti-Semitism is endemic. It appeared to many to be inherent in the existing social order. Assimilationist Jews, therefore, tended to believe that genuine assimilation would become possible only if and when the existing society underwent some fundamental change. Marxism preached that basic social change, whether achieved

[32] A good discussion of the Jewish problem in eastern Europe is to be found in Hugh Seton-Watson, *Eastern Europe between the Wars 1918-1941* (Cambridge, England, 1945), pp. 288-96. What existed would more properly be called a gentile than a Jewish problem, for the gentiles engaged in the persecution of the Jews as a way of relieving tensions existing within gentile society. These tensions had almost nothing to do with the Jews as such, except that the Jews, being defenseless, were a safe target.

by parliamentary methods, as with the Socialists, or by revolutionary Communism, was not only necessary but inevitable. The founder of "scientific" Socialism, himself a Jew, held that Jewishness was destined to disappear along with those feudal and capitalist relationships of which it was a by-product. Judaism was merely one of the forms of social alienation which Socialism, in completing the process of social leveling begun by capitalism, would abolish for good. Judaism was bound to disappear in the same way as its gentile counterpart, anti-Semitism.[33]

At a less "scientific" level we may point out that Marxists believed in a proletariat which, like Jewry, was persecuted (exploited) and homeless (without a fatherland) and chosen, e.g., the nucleus of a perfect society. Revolutionary Marxists viewed the historical process as eschatological in character; for assimilationist Jews it could serve as a new (if secular) orthodoxy. We do not mean to assert that all assimilationist Jews were either Communists or Socialists, but rather to explain the route travelled by those who arrived at the Communist portal.[34]

Those Jews who did not favor assimilation, or who did not believe assimilation possible, tended in the long run to become Zionist. This shift also had a kind of inner logic. If the environment were hostile, and would always remain so, then the Jewish community would have to draw upon the resources of the millenary Jewish tradition and execute a spiritual withdrawal from the land of the gentiles. This turning-in upon itself of the Jewish community could have, as a logical extension, a physical withdrawal from eastern Europe and the setting up in the original Jewish homeland of a Jewish national state. Jews who shared this point of view we may refer to as

[33] F. F., "The USSR, the Soviet Jews, and Israel," *The World Today*, XIV (1958), pp. 41-49. In 1924 the central committee of the Polish party called for a struggle against Jewish separatism inside the party. This appeal camouflaged the real problem, which was that of persuading the ethnic Poles to cooperate with the Jewish element. Regula, p. 120.
[34] Gehrlich, pp. 227-28.

orthodox, though in this usage the term does not have a strictly religious connotation.

The relative strength of assimilationists and orthodox among the Jews of eastern Europe we have no means of knowing. We must emphasize, however, that the Jewish Communist represents only one brand of assimilationist, just as the Jewish Zionist is only one type of orthodox. Between these two extremes there were many intermediate positions, some reasonable, some confused.

The great Jewish purge

The seizure of power by the Communists in 1945-1948 brought large numbers of Jews to high places for the first time in the history of eastern Europe. To be more accurate, this was true of that part of eastern Europe which lay north of the Danube river, which was where the vast bulk of the Jewish population had been concentrated before the advent of Hitler.

North of the Danube the influence of the Jews in the Communist *apparat* was by far and away greatest in the two non-Slavic countries, Hungary and Romania. In Budapest all basic decisions were taken by the Jews Rakosi, Gero, and Farkas. In Bucharest decisive influence was wielded by Pauker, Chisinevski, and Luca, though significant authority also rested with the gentile Gheorghiu-Dej. The extent of minority participation in the Romanian regime is suggested by two decrees issued in 1949. These made it legally possible to change the given name, as well as the surname, and provided that it was no longer necessary for the official documents to indicate the original names.[35]

In Czechoslovakia and Poland, Jewish influence was less extensive, though still potent. In Czechoslovakia the power of Slansky and Geminder, who controlled the party *apparat*, was offset by that of the gentiles Gottwald and Zapotocky, who

[35] *Monitorul oficial. Partea 1-a; Legis decrete. Anul CXVII* (Bucharest), nr. xxxiv, 10 February 1949, p. 1,177.

had the firm allegiance of the state bureaucracy.[36] In Poland there was also a balance. Berman, who controlled the secret police, and Minc, who ran the economy, shared power with the gentiles Beirut, who was liaison with Moscow, and Gomulka, who dominated both the recovered lands and the cadre office.

Just below the summit of power, the party Jews tended to concentrate in certain ministries and functions. They congregated in the foreign ministry and the ministry of foreign trade, because they were almost the only ones whom the party could trust who had the requisite knowledge of foreign languages and high finance. They also flooded into the central committee and the security police, perhaps because they felt safer near the centers of decision-making. In Bucharest, Budapest, and Warsaw virtually every important police official was Jewish; and in the Hungarian secret police the bulk of the rank and file was Jewish. Often these police officials were survivors of Nazi extermination camps, and they did not let mercy or other humanitarian considerations stand in their way when it came to dealing with the class enemy.[37] Indeed, many Jews were publicly associated with the extremist policy followed by the Satellite regimes in the years between the formation of the Cominform (1947) and the death of Stalin (1953).

In these years the satellite regimes attempted to develop basic industry at a rapid pace. To acquire the necessary capital they forced down the standard of living. They forced compliance with their draconian economic measures by an extensive use of the secret police and a systematic application of political terror. They sought to reduce the influence of the West among their populations by setting up an iron curtain against Western ideas, broadcasts, goods, and visitors. The

[36] See particularly the last chapter of Dana Adams Schmidt, *Anatomy of a Satellite* (Boston, 1952).

[37] For the role of the Jews in the officer corps of the Communist armies see Ithiel de Sola Pool (ed.), *Satellite Generals. A Study of Military Elites in the Soviet Sphere* (Stanford, nd).

lives of the satellite populations were steeped in terror and miserable with fatigue.

In eastern Europe, particularly in Poland and Romania, it was an old trick to turn the discontented masses on the Jews. The Jews were unpopular because their ways were different and because many people owed them money. Besides, they were helpless. The new Communist anti-Semitism was disguised as anti-Zionism. There was a difference. Anti-Zionism implied that Jews who were either party members or Communist sympathizers—in short, assimilationists—were acceptable members of the new society. But the difference was reduced to nearly nothing by the party past of the activists who were purged.

Early in 1949 the Hungarian and Romanian governments, on whose territories 90 per cent of surviving east European Jewry was domiciled, outlawed Zionist organizations and deported Zionist missions. Local Zionist leaders were secretly tried and given long prison terms. Israeli diplomats were accused of espionage and expelled.

In September 1949, on the occasion of the trial of L. Rajk, the leader of the nationalist wing in the Hungarian party, almost the entire body of Hungarian Jewish Communists who had spent the war years in Switzerland was executed. In the summer of 1952, three top-drawer Romanian Communists of Jewish origin—Pauker, Georgescu, and Luca—were purged. In December 1952, the *emminence grise* of the Czech party, R. Slansky, was placed in the dock, along with a dozen other Jewish leading cadres.[38]

According to Slansky and his "accomplices" there had taken place in Washington, sometime in 1947, a secret conference of high American and Israeli officials, including Truman, Acheson, Ben Gurion, Morgenthau, and Sharet. The conferees agreed that the Zionist organizations existing in the People's

[38] Harrison E. Salisbury in *NYT*, 7 March 1956; Franz Borkenau, "Was Malenkov behind the Anti-Semitic Plot?" *Commentary*, xv (1953), 438-46; Halperin, pp. 229, 238-44, 249-51; Schapiro, p. 538.

Democracies should be employed as centers for anti-Communist espionage and sabotage. In exchange, the United States would undertake to support the new state of Israel. Everyone knew that neither Slansky, nor Geminder, nor Katz, nor any of their colleagues were or ever had been Zionists. What linked them together was their Jewishness, and the fact that they were also accused, on Zionist orders of course, of sabotaging the Czechoslovak economy and depriving the masses of badly needed consumer goods. The Jewish component of the east European *apparat* was now under suspicion. It stood accused of holding a higher allegiance than that it owed to Communism.

Slansky and his fellow accused were condemned in December 1952. In January 1953, the Soviet government officially announced that the physicians who treated the men in the Kremlin, the physicians to the court, as it were, had been arrested on charges of murdering two politburo members through false medication and of having planned to murder leading Soviet military figures. Most of the doctors arrested were Jews, and the official statement declared that they had acted on instructions from Zionist organizations, which in turn were working for the American intelligence service. It seemed clear that the whole Soviet bloc was moving toward a general purge of Jewish cadres, comparable in extent to the great Stalinist purges of 1937-1938.

On March 3, 1953, Stalin died. Hardly had he been buried in the huge tomb hard by the Kremlin wall than the nine doctors were exonerated and released.[39] Throughout the bloc, imprisoned Zionist leaders and Jewish leading cadres were also given their freedom. Some of the Jewish Communists who had been executed were now exonerated.

None the less, it must have been clear to activists that there had been a breach of faith. Jews could no longer trust a party which, despite its doctrine, was capable of anti-Semitic out-

[39] *Ibid.*, pp. 155-57, 197-204, 214-15.

rages. What had happened once could more easily happen again. After severe rioting broke out in Posnan in June 1956, the Soviet politburo suggested to the Polish politburo, through N. Bulganin, that the Poles try Berman and Minc as scapegoats for the parlous state of the Polish economy. The suggestion was rejected, but the fact that it was made became generally known. Increasingly Jewish party members sought to escape to the West or to emigrate to Israel.

Many important Jewish Communists, moreover, had become so closely identified with the extremist policy of 1947-1953 that, in the aftermath of Stalin's death, they were forced into retirement. Rakosi had to withdraw from public life in July 1956; Gero and Farkas were overthrown in the October upheaval. Minc had gone to the Soviet Union for medical treatment many months before the return of Gomulka to power; Berman's withdrawal followed that dramatic event. The trend is clearly illustrated by comparison of the ethnic composition of the Polish politburo in 1945, at the moment of German withdrawal, and that of 1956, just after Gomulka's return to power (Table 8.2). In 1945 more than half the politburo was Jewish; in 1956 the proportion was 2 out of 9.

TABLE 8.2[40]
Ethnic composition of the Polish politburo

1945		1956	
Name	*Ethnic derivation*	*Name*	*Ethnic derivation*
Berman	Jewish	Cyrankiewicz	Polish
Gomulka	Polish	Gomulka	Polish
Minc	Jewish	Jedrychowski	Polish
Spychalski	Polish	Loga-Sowinski	Polish
Zambrowski	Jewish	Morawski	Jewish
		Ochab	Polish
		Rapacki	Polish
		Zambrowski	Jewish
		Zawadski	Polish

[40] Richard F. Staar, "The Political Bureau of the United Polish Workers' Party," *ASEER*, xv (1956), pp. 206-15. However, five members of the 1956 politburo had Jewish wives, to wit, Cyrankiewicz, Gomulka, Loga-Sowinski, Ochab, and Zawadski.

There were still Jews in high places—Chisinevski in Romania, Zambrowski in Poland, Muennich in Hungary—but they were many fewer, as were Jewish activists generally. The time seemed not far off when the Jewish influence in the east European parties would be reduced to nothing.

Not even the Communists could rule eastern Europe without recourse to anti-Semitism. For all its revolutionary doctrine and its terroristic policies, or perhaps because of them, Communism could not provide a bridge to assimilation. Insofar as the argument between the Communist assimilationists and the Zionists was concerned, the latter had been right.

CHAPTER IX: THE COMMUNIST MOVEMENT IN OTHER AREAS

O BVIOUSLY, the composition and character of the Communist movements of other areas must vary from that which we have discovered in eastern Europe. But there must also be significant similarities. What insights will these differences and these similarities provide with respect to the dynamics of Communism in the European east? Before we attempt to synthesize our own results, it will be useful to take note of the data available concerning the ethnic and social composition of the Communist movements in other quarters of the globe. Unfortunately, this data concerns primarily the hard core and does not deal except incidentally with the composition of the soft periphery. It will be easiest to begin with the movement ancestral to them all, the party of the Russian Bolsheviks.

The Communist party of the Soviet Union

No one has as yet attempted a systematic study of the social and ethnic composition of the Russian Bolsheviks. In fact, a serious non-partisan history of that party has only recently become available. On the basis of material presented in Leonard Schapiro's wide-ranging and scholarly *The Communist Party of the Soviet Union*[1] we may make some pertinent generalizations.

As of 1918, the Bolsheviks claimed that 57 per cent of party members had originally been employed as industrial workers. Since, however, many members were expelled in the 1920's for having concealed their true social origin, and since also many others must have succeeded in hiding their "improper" backgrounds, it seems reasonable to suppose that even in 1918

[1] London, 1960. Cf. Alex Inkeles, "Soviet Nationality Policy in Perspective," *Problems of Communism*, IX (1960), no. 3, 25-34.

171

workers probably did not constitute a majority. In any case, the percentage of workers gradually declined, despite recruitment and purge policies which were biased in favor of the proletariat. After 1928, figures on social composition for the whole party were no longer published. Under pressure of the requirements of the five year plans the policy of favoring workers was quietly dropped, and by 1939 more than 70 per cent of recruits came from the intelligentsia. In the Ukraine in 1958, workers formed but 22.5 per cent of party membership. One of Schapiro's associates estimated the middle class elements in the Soviet party (as of 1957) as no less than 68 per cent.

Aside from those openly of bourgeois origin, a significant proportion of party members were workers making their way into the middle class. An analysis made in the 1927 party census revealed that about one-third of those who had joined as workers were already either employed as administrators or were studying in preparation for such employment. Partly as a consequence of this training, and partly as a result of the change in recruitment policies, the percentage of party members with either a higher or a secondary education rose from less than nine per cent in 1927 to nearly 40 per cent in 1956. The remainder, insofar as they held responsible positions, must have been self-tutored.

On the ethnic side, one fact stands out with great force: from beginning to end the Soviet party has been a Great Russian party. Even at the 1907 congress of the Russian Social Democratic workers party, the Bolshevik faction was preponderantly Great Russian, while the more moderate Menshevik delegates were in the majority of minority stocks, principally Georgian and Jewish. In 1922 Great Russians formed 72 per cent of the party membership, although they were only 52.9 per cent of the total population.[2] Thirty-five years later the story was the same: 4.4 per cent of the population of the Russian republic belonged to the party whereas in the

2 Kirsten, p. 331.

non-Russian republics the percentage was 2.6.[3] The non-Russian representation in the non-Russian areas was somewhat lower than even this figure implies, since Great Russian, Jewish, and other minorities in the republics were proportionately overrepresented. In the Belorussian party the percentage of Belorussian members in 1930 was 55.5. In the Moldavian party the percentage of "Moldavian" or Romanian members in 1952 was 24.7. In the Ukrainian party in 1958 the percentage of ethnic Ukrainians was 60.3.

While it is in general true that in the Soviet party the minorities have been sharply underrepresented, there are three prominent exceptions to this rule. A fourth minority, the Latvian, was heavily involved at the time of the revolution but thereafter gradually crossed over to the anti-Communist camp. It is probably also true that the Jewish contingent has been substantially reduced as a result of the great cosmopolite purge which began in 1948. In 1922 Jews had formed 5.2 per cent of the party members, though they were only some two per cent of the population. As late as 1940 Jews formed 13.4 per cent of the Ukrainian party membership but they constituted only about five per cent of the population of the Ukraine. In addition to the Jews the other minorities allied with the Great Russians are the Armenians and the Georgians. At the sixteenth party congress in 1930, the Armenians, who formed 1.1 per cent of the Soviet population, and the Georgians, who formed another 1.2 per cent, together comprised 4.1 per cent of the delegates.

To this line-up of Great Russians, Jews, Armenians, and Georgians we must contrapose the Soviet populations with substantially below-average proclivity for Communism.

It is evident that the relatively anti-Communist minorities can be classified in three groups. There are the Slavic minorities, e.g., the Ukrainians and Belorussians; the non-Slavic Christians ("Moldavians," Lithuanians) for the most part located on the Western frontiers; and, finally the Turkic-

[3] Meissner, pp. 191-92.

speaking Moslems who spread geographically from the Crimean peninsula in the west to the Tian Shan range on the border of China. To the second group must be added the Volga Germans, whose party was only a third German in its membership, and who were deported *en masse* to the east during the Nazi invasion. To the Moslem peoples listed in Table 9.1 we

TABLE 9.1[4]

Percentile party membership
in various Soviet republics

Republic	Party membership as percentage of total population
Georgian	4.6
Russian	4.4
Armenian	4.3
Aserbaijanian	3.5
Esthonian	3.2
Turkmen	3.2
Kasakh	3.0
Latvian	3.0
Kirgis	2.9
Ukrainian	2.5
Tadzhik	2.2
Uzbek	2.0
Belorussian	1.8
Lithuanian	1.4
Moldavian	1.4

may add the Tatars, the Kalmyks, the Chechens, the Ingushi, the Karachai, and the Balkars, all of whom were deported during the Nazi war.

The parties of the Middle East

Another pioneering study makes it possible to generalize in a broad way about the social and ethnic composition of some Communist parties of the Middle East. Based on original sources in Turkish, Arabic, Hebrew, and Russian, Walter Z. Laqueur's *Communism and Nationalism in the Middle East*[5]

[4] *Ibid.*

will probably remain a standard work for many years to come.

Laqueur asserts that in the Moslem countries of the Middle East a tie between Communism and the proletariat just barely exists. Communist activists are, on the contrary, primarily lawyers, students, teachers, physicians, and poets. In the higher echelons of the Syrian-Lebanese party Laqueur found that somewhere between half and three-quarters were lawyers. Worker members were to be found only on occasion, and peasants (*fellahin*) not at all. Where trade unions existed, Communist leaders were under compulsion to penetrate and control them, but that was the extent of the connection. The carrier of Communism in the Middle East was the class most largely under Western influence, an intelligentsia which, when not educated in the physical West, had gone to school in the spiritual West, and which had also developed a marked indifference to the religion of Islam.

It is not surprising, therefore, that Communism appeared to be strongest in those Middle Eastern countries where Western influence had been most potent. These were Syria, the Lebanon, and Palestine. Aside from its strategic location for trade between East and West, each of these countries boasts important institutions of Western learning (as, for example, the American university of Beirut) and each has migratory bonds with the West. There are significant Syrian, Lebanese, and Jewish colonies in the new world, not to speak of Western migration to Palestine. In these countries there is also a sizeable Arab-speaking Christian population, principally Maronite and Orthodox, with traditional European ties.

Precisely the parties of the Syrian-Lebanese-Palestinian area had the longest histories and the greatest influence. The Syrian-Lebanese party functioned as guide and arbiter for the other Arab states, intervening in their quarrels and serving as liaison with distant Moscow. The Palestinian party, on orders from the Kremlin, transformed itself into a Jewish-led Palestinian Arab entity which, when the right bank of the

[5] New York, 1956.

river Jordan went to the Hashemite kingdom, spawned the Jordanian Communist party.

The influence of the ethnic factor in Middle Eastern Communism may be illustrated by the story of the Turks and of their relationship to the Kurds and Armenians. Marxism made its entry into Turkey by way of the Jewish, Bulgar, and Greek colonies of Salonika and Istanbul. During the resistance against the Greek invader (1920-1922), the Turks received both supplies and advice from the new Bolshevik government in Moscow (just as the advancing Greeks were encouraged and subsidized by the powers of the Entente). Within the Turkish resistance movement there developed in the highlands of central Anatolia a Communist guerrilla force known as the Green Apple. This force, led by a Young Turk, proclaimed Communism as "an instrument to serve the welfare of the Turkish nation,"[6] to promote its strength and unity.

In due course, Kemal Ataturk, chief of Turkish resistance forces turned on the Green Apple guerrillas, attacked, defeated, and dispersed them. When a new Communist leadership was dispatched from Moscow, it was set upon by a mob at Trebizond and drowned in the sea. From this time on, the Turkish Communist party withered on the vine. The modernizing reforms of Ataturk, and the patronage offered him and his successors by the United States, seemed to deprive the party of any *raison d'etre*, and it remained the weakest of the Middle Eastern parties, without prospect for the foreseeable future.

By contrast, Communism was a vital force among two small peoples who live adjacent to the Turks in scattered groups: the Armenians and the Kurds. The history of the Armenian populations of the late Ottoman empire, especially under Abdul Hamid II (1876-1909), had been tragic. In contrast, the new Soviet regime permitted its Armenian population a republic of its own and revived Moscow's claim to Ardahan and Kars, thus backing Armenian territorial aspira-

[6] Laqueur, p. 209.

tions. Laqueur is of the opinion that in 1917 the percentage of Communist adherence in Soviet Armenia was higher than in Russia proper. The all-important Syrian-Lebanese party was, in its beginnings, made up mainly of local Armenians. In the years 1946-1948, the Soviet Union conducted a repatriation campaign among the Armenians of Greece and the Middle East and persuaded 100 thousand (perhaps one-fourth of the total) to migrate to Soviet Armenia. Of all the Soviet repatriation movements in the postwar period this is the only one which may properly be described as voluntary.

Some four million Kurds lead a semi-nomadic existence in Syria, southeastern Turkey, northern Iraq, northern Iran, and the Soviet Trans-Caucasus. A sheep-herding people, in contrast to the city-dwelling and shop-keeping Armenians, the Kurds have supplied the leadership of the Syrian party, and up to 40 per cent of Iraqi party members. In 1945, while the Soviet army still occupied northern Iran, Moscow created an autonomous Kurdish republic at Mehabad. This republic was short-lived, but the Kurds continued to harbor aspirations for unification and independence, and they continued to look to Moscow for help and succor.

Southeast Asia: the Malayan party

An American student (Schapiro and Laqueur are British scholars) has made a study of the Malayan Communist party by means of on-the-spot depth interviews of some 60 defecting activists. Lucien Pye's *Guerrilla Communism in Malaya*[7] is both a very sophisticated and a very exciting book; it is, moreover, directly concerned with the problem of Communist dynamics.

Of Pye's respondents the largest single element (40 per

[7] Princeton, 1956. Despite its title, Pye's work does not deal so much with rank and file guerrillas as with an *apparat* which was, at the time of the investigation, engaged in conducting a guerrilla campaign. His SEPs (Surrendered Enemy Personnel) were for the most part *apparatchiki* who had given themselves up and had agreed to cooperate with the British authorities.

cent) consisted of skilled workers, rubber tappers and tin miners in particular. Pye found that the Malayan party (MCP) did not set great store by its proletarian element, however. The leadership of the MCP tended to the view that in colonial areas all social classes are weak and undeveloped. As a consequence all classes manifest unstable attitudes and are unable to act in a manner consistent with their ultimate role in history. Thus each class has its revolutionary potentiality, and each its counter-revolutionary qualities. To judge from Pye's sample, all social classes were represented in the Malayan Communist party.

The SEPs (Surrendered Enemy Personnel) with whom Pye talked shared a conception of politics which does much to explain their adherence to Communism. They conceived of public life as shot through with violence and struggle. Those who rule have always triumphed through the use of force. All of the contending groups have virtues and vices, but the group which wins power is the one with the biggest army. Authority, furthermore, is arbitrary, personal, and unpredictable. The small fellow has no rights against the powerful, though he may be able to protect his interests through resort to corruption or through personal contacts.

The SEPs also thought of politics as a monopoly of elites. It is unrealistic, they asserted, for a political grouping to seek popular support, since the man in the street has no influence on the decision-making process. Propaganda is not so much an appeal to the population as a smoke-screen to cover the party's tactical intentions, or to recruit new members of the elite by creating an impression of strength and vitality.

It was also the view of Pye's respondents that the play of politics is thoroughly personal. Since authority is personal, it follows that loyalty is also. The solution of personal career problems seemed to them more or less identical with the resolution of public issues. The success of any party or clique is measured by the pelf and the place which it can procure for its individual members.

178

In joining the Malayan Communist party, the SEPs consciously and voluntarily applied for membership in an elite group. The MCP had a private army and an articulated hierarchy of dedicated careerists; it operated a whole series of front organizations; it produced an extensive and impressive propaganda. It could extract monetary payments, apply sanctions, even inflict the death penalty. Finally, the MCP was allied with Soviet Russia, in the view of the SEPs the greatest power on earth.

In addition to their authoritarian outlook, which smacked as much of Orientalism as of Marxism-Leninism, the SEPs were favorably disposed toward Communism by their reaction to Western influences. The Malayan peninsula possesses resources in tin and rubber of world-wide significance. The exploitation of this wealth led to the modernization of one segment of the Malayan economy: the introduction of Western engineering, of Western technology, above all of an impersonal and competitive labor market. The Malayan standard of living became one of the highest in southeast Asia. At the same time, employment in the mines and on the plantations varied sharply with changes in the international price structure. These changes affected, of course, not only those who worked as miners and as rubber tappers, but also those employed as clerks and schoolteachers, and those who owned their own shops.

The people drawn into the Westernized segment of the Malayan economy were, for the most part, migrants. They, or their parents, had migrated from abroad. Approximately half of Pye's respondents had been born outside Malaya. They were, so to speak, uprooted. They had come from a primitive, peasant-dominated culture in which face-to-face relations were paramount (e.g., their conception of political loyalty) and had been plunged into the impersonal relationships characteristic of modern industry.

The result was a deep feeling of uncertainty and isolation. This was typically followed by a rejection of the parents and the parental culture, a process accelerated by the younger generation of schoolteachers, who had only disdain for the ancestral tradition (and who frequently spread Western Marxist ideas). The migrant sought the approval of his peers rather than the guidance of his elders. The patriarchal family of tradition collapsed almost overnight. Bored with the monotony of his work, and faced with the unwonted problem of filling leisure hours, the migrant sought entertainment and instruction in constant gossip. In prolonged conversations the migrants compared their grievances and elaborated upon them.

What is more, the migrant developed an almost compulsive orientation to whatever was new and modern. Whatever came from the West was necessarily superior. At the same time the migrant knew that he was not the equal of an Englishman, even of an English laborer or house servant. There was something about Western culture that he, the ignorant and backward Oriental, could not comprehend. This made him ashamed and bitter.

To the complex of problems associated with Westernization, Communism provided an excellent antidote. To begin with, the party was highly structured. It afforded comradeship and demanded discipline and thus was a kind of substitute for the face-to-face relationships of the traditional society. Within the party, the migrant could predict with assurance the consequence of any action. Adherence to Communism also helped to resolve the feeling of ambivalence toward the West. Marxism-Leninism was a Western body of knowledge; it made possible the prediction of future developments; it could also be used as a weapon against the West. Yet Marxism-Leninism was not too difficult to be mastered by an untutored Oriental. As an Oriental the West might look down upon him, but as a Communist the West would fear him.

To the impact of Western civilization, and the authoritarian view of politics held by the Orientals, Pye adds a third basic driving force in the development of Malayan Communism: the ethnic. The Malayan Communist party was in fact Chinese.

180

Its language of command was Chinese and 90 per cent of its casualties during the guerrilla war which began in 1948 were Chinese.

In Malaya there are three ethnic groups: Indians, Malays, and Chinese. The Indians, mostly Tamils, comprise the smallest group (around 10 per cent of the total population); they were brought to Malaya as contract laborers. Transported by the British government of Malaya, paid by that government, and returned to their native land when their labors were no longer needed, their attitude toward the government was friendly. Nor were they hostile to the Japanese occupation authorities. Many Tamils worked for the Japanese; few joined the anti-Japanese resistance. In the guerrilla war of 1948 and after, 10,000 Indian troops (Gurkhas) campaigned on the government side.

The Malays constitute perhaps 45 per cent of the total population of Malaya. They inhabit the rural areas, have the lowest living standard of the three peoples, remain strong in their Moslem faith. Like the Tamils, their attitude toward the British is amicable. They made careers in the British-run civil service and the British-organized militia. Very few are rubber tappers. They also tended to collaborate with the Japanese during the occupation. In the guerrilla war they contributed five battalions of regulars and 100,000 militiamen to the government side.

The Chinese (another 45 per cent of the total population) migrated to Malaya as common laborers. They became not only the tin miners and the rubber tappers but also the commercial element in the towns. Singapore is predominantly Chinese. Their attitude toward the government was hostile. The government was British and the British had—the opium war is a case in point—humiliated the Chinese. The government in turn neglected the Chinese, who had to maintain their own school system. The teachers were underpaid and insecure, and played an important role in spreading Communist doctrine in the Chinese community.

When the Japanese invaded Malaya, the Communist party organized the resistance against them, arguing that such resistance would help the Chinese motherland. By the time the Japanese withdrew, the Communist party was the dominant force in the Chinese community of Malaya, and it instigated bloody massacres of Indians and Malays who had collaborated with the Japanese. The guerrilla war which began in 1948 may properly be described as a war of Chinese guerrillas against British and Indian regulars and Malay militiamen. A few Malays and Tamils were enrolled with the guerrillas, but they were regarded as outcasts by their respective ethnic communities and despised by their Chinese comrades in arms.

Pye found that Communism proved particularly attractive to Chinese who had strong prejudices against the physical and cultural characteristics of non-Chinese. Communism and being Chinese were so closely identified that the expression "racial bad character" was employed by activists to denote those Chinese who opposed Communism. The British government stood for interracial cooperation, and hence was to be distrusted. To Malayan Communism the theme of Chinese racial unity was of paramount importance.

Thus, for a good part of the Chinese community of Malaya, international Communism became the vehicle of Chinese nationalism. By belonging to an organization that played a major role in international affairs, these Chinese had also become actors in the drama of world history, along with Wall Street and the Kremlin. The October revolution symbolized for them a miraculous historical transformation, a social mutation in which one of the poorest, most downtrodden, and most backward of peoples became a great, modern, industrial power. The MCP was the channel to the wisdom, power, and success of the men who had effected this miracle, and support of this party was the duty of all good Chinese.

The Western parties

The forces motivating Western Communism have been subjected to detailed and penetrating analysis by another American scholar, Gabriel Almond. Assisted by a sizeable research staff, Almond undertook depth interviews and psychiatric study of more than 200 former Communists, drawn in roughly equal numbers from the Italian, French, British, and American parties. His *Appeals of Communism*[8] is an important work. His findings are systematically arranged; his respondents are dealt with in terms of motivation, echelon, class origin, and party type.

Two sets of motives pushed the Western respondents into the arms of the party. Some were suffering from "situational damage." That is to say, they had joined the party in order to resist a foreign military occupation, or because of personal suffering, such as the immigrant's difficulty in adjusting to a new land and a strange society. Such people came to the Western parties for objective reasons.

There were also those who joined the party in response to the pressure of internal and subjective needs. The unconscious hostility which resulted from an unhappy childhood, for example, could find in the party an instrument through which hatred could be impersonalized and morally justified. Those suffering neurotic isolation might find in the party the comradeship of aggressive people. To the Jew or the blind man who suffered from self-rejection, the party offered dignity. This second group of motives may be termed "neurotic."

It would, however, be incorrect to say that all emotionally maladjusted persons are susceptible to Communism, or that a particular type of maladjustment is congruent with the Communist appeal. Joining the party cannot properly be described as a specific act in time, but rather as a series of decisions. In addition to the presence of neurotic or situational motivation, there must be a specific and massive exposure to the Communist bacillus.

[8] Princeton, 1954.

Within the party Almond defined three types of Communists: high echelon, low echelon, and rank and file. Trait-wise, the low echelon was transitional. Between the high echelon and the rank and filer there was significant contrast. The rank and filer typically came to the party before becoming Communist. Once in, he remained unindoctrinated and re-tained outside commitments and loyalties. He was never really aware of the true nature of the party, which he thought of primarily as a militant opponent of such immediate evils as Fascism, racial discrimination, imperialism, or as a pro-ponent of the good, of social reform and world peace.

The high echelon Communist, on the other hand, was politically active at an early age and was exposed to the sacred literature before actually joining. He had an abiding faith in the party, which could do no wrong. For him, the world was unambiguously evil. The party was the one means of coping with such a world. The only meaningful goal was power and the only possible outcome the total destruction of the antagonist. The high echelon Communist was thus above all a power-oriented tactician.

The middle class members of Almond's sample of 221 former Communists were more frequently neurotic in their motivation and were more often defying their parents and their social background by joining. Their rate of defection was higher and, after defection, they more often relapsed into indifference and political inactivity. Middle class people tended to cluster at the level of the rank and file.

The working class membership, on the other hand, more often suffered from situational damage. Less exposed to the esoteric doctrine at the time of joining, working class mem-bers tended to leave doctrine to others and to regard the party as fundamentally concerned with humanitarian objec-tives. At the same time, the workers provided a larger pro-portion of the higher echelon leadership.

All these differences of motivation, echelon, and social class also possessed a cultural pattern. The British and American parties were high in the proportion of members who satisfied neurotic needs by the profession of Communism. These parties also had a high proportion of foreign-born. CPUSA, according to Almond's sample, was only 20 per cent native-born white, of native-born parents. The British and American parties were small and insignificant, incapable of acquiring mass followings. They were not so much parties as deviant sects.

The French and Italian parties, on the other hand, were mass operations. They were laden with the situationally damaged and with those whose family background was one of revolutionary extremism. In France and in Italy the working classes have been historically alienated from their national communities and were revolutionary long before Communism arrived upon the scene. The Communist workers have been joined by large numbers of middle class intelligentsia who cannot tolerate political systems unable to cope with pressing social problems, and who see in the working class the only hope for morality and progress. Far from being deviational, the Latin parties, with their mass membership, their huge electorates, their social and athletic organizations, their own media of communication, in fact constitute subcultures.

A suggested typology

This brief and superficial review of the composition of Communist parties in various parts of the world suggests that certain features or characteristics are common to several parties and that it is possible to classify them according to type. There are sectarian or deviational parties, mass proletarian parties, and national, anti-Western parties.

The sectarian party is found in the most advanced industrial countries of the West. It is made up essentially of middle class neurotics and ethnic outcasts. It is minuscule in size and has almost no influence on the course of events (except to provide an occasional spy for a foreign power). Since violence is not required to bring about reform in these advanced Western countries, and since the living standards and the industrial installations of these countries are the envy of the rest of the world, the Communism of these sects remains an impotent act of protest.

The second type of party, the mass proletarian, is found in Western countries where industrialization has gone far but has failed to produce living standards equal to those prevailing in the most advanced industrial countries. In these semi-affluent Western countries a situationally damaged urban proletariat has an interest in drastic reform which seems realizable only through the use of force. Through the instrumentality of the party, this dissident and secessionist proletarian mass develops its own newspapers, athletic organizations, festive days, even mores. It becomes a kind of subculture and in some ways leads a life of its own.

The third type of party, the national and anti-Western, flourishes in countries which are poor and backward. Such a party is comprised mainly of professional people, formally trained or self-taught, with some large element of Western education or influence. It is so comprised because the intelligentsia is the conductor through which Western influences penetrate non-Western cultures and because this party, to win and hold power, must provide a ruling class capable of governing in the conditions of that rapid industrialization and cultural metamorphosis which we call Westernization. Such a party is a national party because its basic aim is national power through the development of modern industry.

CONCLUSION: THE DYNAMICS OF COMMUNISM IN EASTERN EUROPE

THE Communist movements of eastern Europe do not fit exactly any of the three types outlined in the preceding chapter. But on the whole they fit the deviant and proletarian types less well than they do the national. This will become clear as we summarize the findings of the present work.

The Communist masses in eastern Europe are not in any real sense of the term proletarian in character. In fact, all social classes are involved, and the single most important element, at least numerically, is not the proletariat but the peasantry. Of all the types of Communists it was, curiously enough, the opportunists flooding into the parties after the seizure of power who had the most proletarian complexion. Communist guerrillas and insurgents were overwhelmingly peasant and mountaineer in their composition. Communist voters were located largely in rural constituencies and industrial workers voted for the extreme right as well as for the center and the left. In an industrialized area like Bohemia-Moravia the workers voted primarily for the Socialists.

The hard core of the east European Communist movements represents a cross section of the class structure of the area, but with a strong urban bias. Both the middle class and the city workers are overrepresented among activists, while at the leading cadre level middle class professionals squeeze out the peasants altogether and leave only a small minority representation to the proletariat. Since worker cadres in effect receive on-the-job professional training, it would be accurate to say that at least the cutting edge of the movement consists of a professional elite group (what Djilas calls the "new class").

Communism in eastern Europe has many causes, but the notion that it represents, or is led by, the suffering proletariat is largely fictional. Those interested in the dynamics of the movement should study, not the distress of the proletariat, but two other less dramatic factors: the proclivity of certain ethnic groups for the Communist cause and the impact of the highly industrialized countries of the West on the more backward regions of eastern Europe.

The ethnic factor

We may erect almost as a principle the proposition that in eastern Europe numerically weak ethnic groups produce above-average numbers of Communists, providing these groups have a traditional or an ethnic tie to Russia. Other factors being equal, the weaker the ethnic group, the greater the proclivity. On the other hand, if there has been a strong traditional enmity toward Russia, a weak ethnic group reveals a lower than average susceptibility to the Communist appeal, and the traditional enmity can offset even an ethnic bond.

The most obvious and important instance of this principle is the typical distribution of Communist strength among the Slavic peoples. Within the multi-national Soviet union it is the approximately 100 million Great Russians who are the paladin of Communism. The three Slavic peoples immediately adjacent to the Great Russians—40 million Ukrainians, 8 million Belorussians, and 25 million Poles—all have Communist movements substantially below-average in strength. At least two of these peoples, the Ukrainians and the Poles, have centuries-old traditions of bitter conflict with the Russians. In the inter-war period, however, oppressed Ukrainian and Belorussian minorities trapped in Pilsudski Poland produced remarkably strong and virile Communist parties. Moreover, among the 12 million Czechs and Slovaks (particularly the Czechs, who were virtually surrounded by German enemies), and among the 24 million Slovenes, Croats, Serbs, Montenegrins, Slavo-Macedonians, and Bulgars, supporters of Communism were very much more numerous than in eastern Europe generally.

The greater proclivity of the Slavs is matched by the greater immunity of the non-Slavic populations of the area. Of these the German minorities are a good example. Scattered in crazy-quilt fashion over eastern Europe, even as far to the east as the lower reaches of the Russian Volga, these German colonists persisted in looking to the German *Reich* for both political protection and ideological inspiration. As a kind of counter-point to their low Communist response we have the relative philocommunism of the Czech and Polish countercolonists settled in the territories from which German populations have been ejected.

The Turkish (Moslem) case was essentially the same as the German, but more complex. Not all Moslems were Turks and any prospect of protection from the Ottoman empire had long since vanished. Nonetheless, the Turkish area, which stretched in a great crescent-like arc from the Bosniaks and the Albanians of the Dinaric Alps, through the Ottoman Turks in the high-lands of Anatolia, to the Kasakhs in the shadow of the Tian Shan and the Bashkirs in the foothills of the Urals, was an area of far below average Communist activity. The Turkish Green Apple flourished only so long as the Greek invader clung to the rugged coasts of Anatolia, so long (that is) as Russian help was required. Even the Green Apple was, from its very inception, a movement of national deviation. And all along the Turkish confines there are peoples with both a tra-ditional enmity for the Turks and a strong Communist move-ment: Bulgars and Greeks to the west, Syrians and Kurds to the south, Armenians and Georgians in the Caucasus, Great Russians to the Siberian north. Through conversion to Commu-nism such non-Turkic Moslems as the Bosniaks tended to lose their Turkish identification and become Yugoslav.

A few non-Slavic peoples have a high susceptibility to Com-munism. The most prominent case in eastern Europe (and in Russia as well) is that of the Jews. But the Jewish story has its analogue in the history of the Armenians. The two peoples had much in common. Both were small in number. Both lived scattered over a wide territory among sovereignties frequently in conflict. Both were essentially commercial peoples. If the Jew lived in fear of the Russian pogrom, the Armenian dreaded the Turkish massacre. From the Bolsheviks the Armenians received a kind of homeland in the Armenian Socialist Soviet republic. The Jews were offered, somewhat disdainfully, the autonomous territory of Birobidjan, half ethnic experiment, half prison colony. The foundation of a Jewish state in Palestine set off a persecution of Jews in the Soviet bloc precisely because it created an alternative to both conformity and assimilation and hence brought into question the basic loyalty, not only of Orthodox Jews, but even of Jewish cadres.

Thus there appear to be non-ideological communities of peoples—Slavic, Moslem-Turkish, Germanic—whose presence strongly affects the distribution of Communist strength in eastern Europe. This notion is not so startling if we consider the fact that Lutheranism in its spread was largely confined to the Germanic-speaking peoples, or that liberal Democracy has developed its most stable institutions among speakers of English. Language is, to be sure, only the most apparent common trait in such a complex of peoples.

The cultural factor

The ethnic factor thus does much to explain who in eastern Europe is a Communist and who is not. A second important factor is the impact of the influence of the most industrialized countries of the West. This impact is transmitted in two ways, through the mechanism of international prices and through the cross-cultural education of the young.

Interwar eastern Europe was an exporter of raw materials—coal, copper, wheat, pork, oil, and tobacco. In exchange for these exports eastern Europe obtained manufactured goods produced in the West. (The Czech lands, with their exports of shoes, porcelain, and beer, constituted an exception to the general rule.) The prices of the commodities eastern Europe exported shifted sharply, sending economic shock waves throughout the area. The rhythmic alternation of prosperity and poverty, especially when it affected conversational trades or migrant groups, created deep-going discontent. Communist votes and Communist ideas tended to concentrate where the impact of these price changes was greatest, among, say, the wheat growers of Slovakia or the tobacco workers of Macedonia. The most backward areas and the poorest—e.g., those which continued to practice a more or less self-sufficient agriculture—were not really involved. It was the valley floors and their transportation hubs, not the isolated highlands, which became strongholds of Communism in the interwar period. The contrast between the Communism of southern Albania, a wheat-growing plain, and the anti-Communism of northern Albania, which was much poorer, but mountainous and economically self-sufficient, is characteristic.

While within any given area it was likely to be the economically more advanced parts which were affected, in the east European area as a whole it was the more backward provinces, those which had lived long under Turkish rule, which in general developed the stronger Communist movements. As one moved east and south, the proportion of the total Marxist vote which went to the Communists increased sharply. As one moved east and south, the strength of trade unions dropped off, but the influence of Communism in trade unions increased. This progression we inferred to be the result of the contrast between conditions in eastern Europe and those prevailing in the most industrial nations of the West. This contrast achieved its social imprint through students and teachers who had received a Western education, either in schools of the area or abroad, and who found themselves overtrained and perhaps even unemployable in their native environment. From this situation followed the decisive role in the party of what the Russians would call the intelligentsia, the lawyers, teachers, doctors, and other professionals who provided three-fourths of the Communist leadership.

Thus we add a cultural factor to the ethnic. At times the two operated together, as when the Tosks of the south Albanian plain used Communism to overthrow the rule of the northern mountaineering Gegs, or when the cash-cropping Magyar minority of southern Slovakia turned to a Communism which stood for the reconstruction of the Hungarian empire. At other times, the two factors ran counter to each other, as when the Montenegrin mountaineers, just north of the Gegs, produced a high Communist vote as early as 1920, or when Romanian peasant plain-dwelling growers of wheat proved almost impervious to the appeal of Communism because it was associated with a traditional enemy. In general, we are inclined to believe that the ethnic factor takes precedence over the cultural factor, as these last two examples suggest. This precedence was also indicated by the multiple correlation exercize, which measured the weight of the two factors when their influence ran parallel.

Communism and the construction of states

Both factors, the ethnic and the cultural, have an obvious influence on the formulation of Communist policy. The cultural factor is evidently connected with the marked tendency of east European Communist parties to industrialize their respective countries under forced draft and to modernize their agriculture; to create, so to speak, a society in which overtrained surplus professionals can find appropriate employment. The ethnic factor is certainly not unrelated to the powerful penchant of the Communists to push for the development of what, for want of a better term, we may call supranational states. Both policies are understandable in terms either of national interest or of Communist power. Since Communist industrialization has been widely studied we may confine our attention here to summarizing our findings concerning the supranational state.

The first instance of this empire-building proclivity of the Communists of eastern Europe is provided by the Bela Kun regime, which showed signs of transforming Stephen's holy kingdom into a Union of Socialist Danubian republics. The political vertebrae of this union would have been a Jewish-led, Magyar-dominated, multinational Communist party.

A second example is provided by the scheme for Balkan federation advanced interwar by the Bulgarian party. At that time, as we now can see, such a proposal was bound to remain a political chimera. But if the Bulgarian comrades could have had their way, the existing Balkan states would have been dissolved into smaller components and then all brought together again in a Balkan-wide state under the federal principle. The whole arrangement would have been held together by a multinational Communist party in which the Bulgarian element, backed by the might of Soviet Russia, would have predominated.

While both the Danubian and the Balkan federation schemes fizzled out, something analogous to them did take place within wartime Yugoslavia. Broken up more or less into its component ethnic parts by the Axis occupiers, the country was reconstituted on a federal basis by a multinational Communist party which was imbued with a true Yugoslav nationalism and in which all the Slavic nationalities of prewar Yugoslavia were represented. In the course of the civil war it was the *prechani* members of the traditional Serb ruling nation who played the decisive role in keeping Tito's cause afloat.

Toward the close of World War II, the Yugoslavs sought to extend the Communist principle of federation to the whole Balkan area, and create thus a constellation of Communist power second only to that represented by the USSR. In the years 1945-1948 the Yugoslavs came within an ace of absorbing Albania, whose Communist party they had founded and controlled. The Yugoslavs were probably the moving spirit in the second Greek civil war (1946-1949), one object of which was to solve the Macedonian problem at the expense of Greece and thus make possible the federation of Communist

Yugoslavia and Communist Bulgaria. The Yugoslavs also had designs on Greece, Romania, and even Hungary. Needless to say, the Bulgarian party now *de facto* opposed federation, and in this it had the powerful, if covert, support of Moscow. In all probability these differences over federation constituted a major factor in producing the breach in the Cominform.

This brings to mind the concrete historical nexus between imperial and Soviet Russia. As a consequence of defeat in war the Russian empire was on the verge of disintegration. Independent Ukrainias, Polonias, Siberias, and Georgias were threatening to emerge on the peripheries of the empire. It was the Communist party under Lenin and Trotsky, operating from the Great Russian center, which, at the cost of a bloody civil war, put the tsarist humpty-dumpty back together again. The new Soviet Russia was a federation of many and diverse national units, held together by a monolithic multinational ruling party whose language, tradition, and outlook were Russian.

Nor is the Chinese population of Malaya, which produced the Malayan CP, unique. There are overseas Chinese in large numbers in other parts of southeast Asia, in Indonesia, Indochina, the Philippines, and so on. There are also indigenous populations—Burmese, Thais, Laotians, Vietnamese, and in the far north, Koreans—whose languages and cultures are closely related to those of China. It is not inconceivable that Communist elements in this complex of minorities and nations will someday become basic components in a reconstitution of the Chinese imperium in Asia.

It may of course be mere coincidence that so far only those supranational Communist entities which were predominantly Slavic in population have succeeded in establishing themselves on a more or less permanent basis. What is significant here is not that there are Croats or Ukrainians in opposition, or that Belorussians or Tadzhiks are greatly underrepresented in the party, but that Communism is able to assemble and retain Croatian, Ukrainian, Belorussian, and Tadzhik cadres. The key development is the ability of Communism to produce within its own ranks something akin to a Yugoslav or Soviet nationalism. Within its own ranks it produces new arrangements of ideology, ethnic group, and national awareness. In so doing, Communism demonstrates that an international ideology can serve as a fundamental component of national consciousness.

Comparison with other areas

We are now ready to deal with the question of how the east European parties may fit into the typology developed in Chapter IX. Could it, for example, be argued that the interwar Romanian Communist party should be classified with the American and British parties as sectarian and deviational?

It is true that the interwar Romanian party was comparable in size and make-up to, let us say, the American Communist party. Throughout the interwar period the Romanian party remained a political absurdity, minuscule in size and torn by factionalism. Like the American party also, its make-up was heavily exogenous: Jewish, Magyar, Ukrainian, Bulgar.

But these parallels are misleading. The American party had no future because in time the Negro population would acquire equal rights, while the Jews and the other immigrants from eastern Europe would be culturally absorbed. This granting of equal rights and this cultural assimilation were, in the last analysis, made possible by the free institutions and the growing wealth of the United States. The Romanian party, on the other hand, stood condemned to a sectarian existence because it advocated the cession of national territory to traditional enemies, e.g., the retrocession of Bessarabia to the Russia of the Soviets. There could be little expectation that, with time, the minorities could be Romanized. Except for the Jews, they tended to live in compact bodies near the frontiers, and could hope someday that a turn in the political wheel of fortune would bring union with the mother country. It was not the absence of the characteristic social and economic problems which produced Communism elsewhere in the Balkans that accounts for the weakness of the Romanian party. It was rather the fact that it was impossible to identify the national interests of ethnic Romanians with Soviet Communism.

Similarly, there were mass parties in interwar eastern Europe, but they are not truly comparable to the mass parties of France and Italy. The largest east European party interwar, at least if we speak in terms of party membership, was that of Czechoslovakia. But the Czech party was not predominantly a formation of workers. The bulk of the Czech workers gave their support to the two Social Democratic parties, which together had a larger electoral following than the Communists did. Furthermore, the interwar Czech party contained important minority elements, located mostly in backward and rural areas, Magyar, Jewish, Ruthene, Slovak, whose adherence affected both the party's program and its tactics. In Italy and France there were no minorities comparable in size and significance to those of the Slav state, and such minorities as there were, Germans of Bolzano and Alsace, Basques and Bretons in France, tended to support Catholic and conservative parties.[1] Ethnically speaking, the French and Italian parties were of purest *souche*. The dynamics of the Czech mass party were not to be found so much in the secession of the Czech working class from Czech society as in pro-Russian tradition, minority status, and cash-cropping.

The deviational and mass party types characteristic of the West are not really relevant to the Communism of eastern Europe. The national party of the underdeveloped areas appears to be a closer, but by no means exact, fit. Both the ethnic and the cultural factors which operate in eastern Europe find parallels in Russia and Asia.

In such parties as the Malayan, Soviet, and Kurdish there is a note of national rebirth and affirmation. The Malayan party was literally permeated with Chinese nationalism. The

---

[1] Burks, "Catholic Parties in Latin Europe," *loc.cit.*

Soviet party is preeminently Great Russian in composition, language, and outlook. The Kurdish party seeks the union in independence of the Kurdish lands. The Turkish party, on the other hand, is almost a *contradictio in adjecto*, while among Turkey's enemies Communism is a vital force.

As for the cultural factor, there is the dependence of the Malayan economy upon the export of rubber and tin, of the Middle Eastern countries upon the export of oil, cotton, and chrome, and of tsarist Russia upon the export of wheat, lumber, and furs. There is the concentration of Communist influence at the geographic points where the impact of the West is greatest, near the mines and on the plantations of Malaya, and along the trade routes of Syria-Palestine. And together with this come the rejection of the traditional culture and the eager grasping for anything Western which Pye found among his respondents, the overwhelming importance of Western-trained or Western-influenced intellectuals which Laqueur found in the parties of the Middle East, and the overpowering predominance of middle class professionals which Schapiro says characterizes the Soviet party. It is probably true that in Asia the crucial problem is not so much industrialization and modernization as it is the absence of a class capable of governing in the new circumstances. The Communist party, along with the army officers' corps and Western universities, are competitive if interlocking schools for the training of such a class.

But the many similarities between the national parties of the underdeveloped areas and the Communist movements in eastern Europe should not be allowed to obscure a real and substantial difference. For the Russian and Asian cultures there is, in the realm of government, virtually no alternative to political despotism. Historically, government in these areas has been both autocratic and theocratic (or at least caesaropapistic). Pye is very clear on this point. His respondents thought of politics in terms of violence and struggle. Authority was arbitrary, personal, and unpredictable. The small fellow could protect his interests only through bribery or personal contacts. The choice in the Chinese community of Malaya seems to have been between the MCP and a hardly less authoritarian Kuomintang.

It is of course true that eastern Europe has a lengthy tradition of political authoritarianism. Prior to 1815 the area had been ruled for centuries by great empires—Austrian, Russian, and Turkish—whose political processes Pye's respondents would not have had great difficulty in understanding. Furthermore, swollen and corrupt bureaucracies, palace revolutions, fixed elections, and oppressive taxation had not been unknown even in the parliamentary era of the nineteenth and twentieth centuries. In fact, many east European states had returned to authoritarian rule before the occupation of the area by Nazi and Communist powers. Hungary acquired an authoritarian regime in 1919, Albania in 1924, Poland in 1926, Yugoslavia in 1931, etc.

Nonetheless, the liberal tradition was present in eastern Europe, and its force should not be underestimated. Hungary had had a parliamentary system, largely restricted to Magyars of upper class origin, since the middle ages. In the early years of the nineteenth century, other east European states had begun to experiment with parliamentary systems and liberal suffrage. Russian Poland was granted a constitution in 1815 and liberated Greece adopted her first in 1822; the others followed in time. By the opening years of the twentieth century most east European states had both universal manhood suffrage and a set of political parties. Socialism was known in the area, as well as Communism, and there were also Liberal parties, peasant parties, and Catholic parties. At the time of the Versailles settlement, written constitutions, parliamentary government, and broad suffrage became well-nigh universal.

The peoples of eastern Europe, in contrast to those of Russia and Asia, were therefore well aware of alternatives to authoritarian government, and never more aware than after a generation of rule by authoritarian outsiders, first Nazis, then Communists. The activities of Western propaganda have served, no doubt, to keep alive this awareness. The short-lived Hungarian rebel government of 1956 made only too obvious its intention to hold free elections. Widespread consciousness of parliamentary government and democratic rule constitutes one of the most enduring and important weaknesses of the Communist satellite regimes.

The state of our knowledge

The first man to investigate the hypothesis that Communism might be a force which Marxism did not adequately describe was Werner Sombart (1863-1941). In 1924 this German sociologist, former Marxist and future Nazi, published a finished version of his two-volumed *Der proletarische Sozialismus* (*"Marxismus"*).[2] In this work Sombart asserted that Communism was not really a proletarian movement. It was rather, he said, "a variegated structure from the most diverse social classes."[3] By analyzing election returns, Sombart showed that a high proportion of industrial labor in western Europe did not vote for the extreme Marxist left. The British labor party, he observed, was by no means thoroughly Marxist, and in highly industrial America, Communism was an insignificant force. Sombart regretted that it was impossible to obtain a clear and precise picture of the social composition of the Communist movement. "Because of the difficulties of establishing the facts," he predicted, "we may have to forego the acquisition of such a picture for all time."[4]

Sombart distinguished between three types of Communist adherents. There were the true proletarians, whose recruitment he regarded as entirely normal; the proletaroids (small shop-keepers, dwarfholders), who were restrained from joining the party only by idealist traditions such as nationalism or religion; and, finally, persons of bourgeois origin who were

[2] Jena, 1924.   [3] Sombart, II, 120.   [4] *Ibid.*, p. 113.

attracted by the Messianic ideal or who had some resentment against the world at large.

The German professor was especially concerned to explain the (unnatural) adherence of persons of bourgeois origin. He found that it was always certain types of individuals from this class who became involved: the physically handicapped, those who had moved downward in the social scale, emancipated women, youth, the socially uprooted. One of Sombart's students made a study of the Bela Kun regime and showed that a high proportion of key positions was held by persons of Jewish background 23 years of age or less. Communism in the United States, Sombart pointed out, was almost entirely a matter of the foreign-born.

As of 1924 Sombart's analysis was penetrating, even brilliant. Many of his key generalizations have been confirmed by recent research. Yet there are grave weaknesses in his analysis, both substantive and methodological. A brief listing of these weaknesses will serve to highlight the present state of our knowledge of Communist dynamics.

To begin with, Sombart had not really broken with the Marxist tradition. He was concerned with explaining how persons of bourgeois origin became Communists, and to do so he developed what is essentially a pathology of the middle class. It is scarcely the fault of honest proletarians that the middle class produces so much dross! Furthermore, he remained almost unaware of the ethnic factor, or of the role of Western influence in producing Communism in underdeveloped areas. In his time, to be sure, Communism had hardly begun to penetrate these areas, except for Russia.

The more sophisticated views of contemporary scholars are pivoted on a much broader informational base, which in turn is a reflection of the greater refinement of their methods of study. Sombart, for illustration, was unaware of the area approach to the analysis of social phenomena; he dealt with Communism on a world-wide basis as if cultural differences could be ignored. He realized that the internal composition of the movement was of decisive importance, but with the techniques then available he doubted if a clear picture of this composition would ever be possible. As we have seen, since Sombart's day students of Communism have learned to make use of the interview in depth, the background question-naire, the public opinion poll,[5] comparative ecological analy-sis,[6] and the statistical technique of correlation analysis.

[5] Especially by Hadley Cantril, *The Politics of Despair* (New York, 1958) which is based on an elaborate polling of party members in France and Italy.

[6] For this see Braga's *Il comunismo fra gli italiani,* which presents a very detailed ecology based on election returns.

APPENDICES

APPENDIX A: EAST EUROPEAN
ELECTIONS

THE free elections which have been held in eastern Europe since 1917 are relatively few in number. In some instances these elections are of little interest to us, because no Communist party had yet been organized (Czechoslovak election of 1920, Albanian elections of 1920 and 1921)[1] or because the party refused to campaign for reasons of its own (Poland 1919). Nor are the free elections well distributed in time and place: they tend to cluster in the 1920's and in Greece. For one country, Albania, there has never been a free election in which the Communists participated. In two countries (Yugoslavia 1920 and Hungary 1945) only one such election has taken place, though in this connection we must mention the free elections in Trieste (1949).

The Czechoslovaks, however, held four free elections in which the Communists participated, and these were regularly spaced in time (1925, 1929, 1935, 1946). The 1946 election cannot be considered as free as the others, because two important prewar parties were outlawed, the Agrarian because it was ready to compromise with the Sudeten Germans, and the Hlinka Populist because it had supported Father Tiso's Slovak Fascist regime. But in 1946 the electors were free to vote for parties other than the Communist, and did so.

In addition to the number and spacing of the free Czech elections, two other factors made Czechoslovakia methodologically the most important country in the present study. These are Czech statistics, which in detail and accuracy compare with those of the West, and the fact that the Czech provinces differed so widely in ethnic composition, historical tradition, and living standards. Bohemia and Moravia in the west were peopled by Czechs and Germans and were highly industrialized; the Czechs had lived for centuries under Ger-

[1] Skendi (ed.), pp. 74-75.

205

man influence or domination. Slovakia, on the other hand, had traditionally been ruled by the Magyars; it contained Hungarian and Jewish minorities and was overwhelmingly rural and agrarian. Ruthenia, the easternmost tip of the cigar-like country, was preponderantly Ukrainian in population, and was among the poorest and most neglected districts in eastern Europe.

The free elections of eastern Europe have been multiparty elections based on proportional representation. This made it possible to apply the technique of statistical correlation to the problem of the Communist constituency. In the biparty system, which tends to prevail in English-speaking countries, the voters are presented with a single choice; everyone must line up on one side or the other, so that it becomes most difficult to isolate special groups by correlation analysis. But in eastern Europe it was different. In the Czechoslovak election of 1929, for example, 19 parties participated, the largest of which polled 15.0 per cent of the total vote. These parties not only divided along ideological lines—Socialist, Communist, Catholic, and the like—but they could also to a considerable extent be classified according to ethnic affiliation. There was a German as well as a Czech Social Democratic party, and Czech, Slovak, and German Catholic parties. The choices offered the voter were so numerous that the identification of the specific groups which supported particular parties becomes much easier.

There is another sense in which east European electoral practice facilitates ecological research. The choices put before the voter were not only of method, they were also heavily ideological in content. When the American voter chooses between Democrat and Republican, he is choosing between two democratic parties, whose differences concern not the system of government but the means of achieving commonly accepted goals. In eastern Europe, on the other hand, there were major parties which aimed at overthrowing or subverting the existing system of government, not only Communist parties, but also Fascist parties and, from the viewpoint of anticlericals, Catholic parties as well. Thus the east European voter could express a choice between *systems* of government as well as sets of policies, and each free election was, in a sense, an ideological plebiscite. This served to clarify the issues and helps to account for the very high rate of voter participation in east European elections.

The technique which we have applied to the study of these free elections, in the attempt to isolate the Communist electorate, is described by the statisticians as correlation analysis. It is based on the notion that if in every instance in which we find an increase in phenomenon X we also find a roughly proportionate increase in phenomenon Y, there may be some necessary connection between the two phenomena. Which of the two is to be regarded as cause and which as effect, is a question to be answered on the basis of our general knowledge of the phenomena involved.

If for every increase in the percentage of industrial workers to total population there is (as we move from one electoral district to the next) an increase in the percentage of Communist to total votes cast, we may believe there is some kind of connection between Communist votes and industrial workers. If the connection were necessary, that is to say causal, we would incline to the view that industrial workers were voting Communist and in this way account for the correlation between workers and Communist votes.

This is probably, but not necessarily, the case, especially since the Communist vote is usually only a fraction of the total cast. Theoretically, middle class people, emotionally affected by the sufferings of the proletariat, could have cast these Communist votes; the greater the concentration of workers, the more middle class people so affected.

On the other hand, absence of a correlation between two phenomena, such as industrial labor and the Communist vote, is final and definitive. It is clear proof that there is no relationship between the variables under examination.

In so complex a matter as an election, the existence or non-existence of a correlation cannot be established simply by inspection. It can be done only by careful statistical measurement. To this end the statisticians have a formula:

$$r = \frac{N \Sigma XY - \Sigma X \ \Sigma Y}{\sqrt{N \Sigma X^2 - (\Sigma X)^2} \ \sqrt{N \Sigma Y^2 - (\Sigma Y)^2}}$$

The letter r stands for coefficient of correlation, N for the number of cases, Σ for "the sum of," X for the variable which is thought to be causal, and Y for the other variable.

The application of this formula to any particular case produces an r always varying from -1.00 to 1.00. If there is a perfect correlation between the two variables, if for every increase in workers there is a corresponding and proportional increase in votes, then $r = 1.00$. If, on the other hand, for every increase in workers there is a corresponding and proportional *decrease* in votes, then $r = -1.00$. If there is no correlation whatever, $r = .00$.

Of course, perfect correlations, whether negative or positive, do not exist, at least in social science. If the r for the relationship between Communist votes and industrial workers is .46 or $-.23$, what then? Does such an r have any meaning? Is it anything more than a chance result?

The statisticians have a gadget here, too. This gadget is called the standard error of the coefficient of correlation, written as σr. The standard error is nothing mysterious; it merely defines the degree of correlation which might have occurred by chance. The standard error of r is reached by a second statistical formula which, in turn, is based on the laws of probability. In fact, σr varies with the size of the sample, in the present instance the number of electoral districts. The bigger the sample (represented symbolically by the letter N) the smaller σr will be and, conversely, the smaller the sample, the greater σr. We may be sure that an r of .46 or $-.23$ is significant (not merely the result of chance) if it is substantially greater than σr for the particular N. If, for example, r is at least twice σr, then the probability of r

occurring by chance alone is only one in twenty; or, to put it in other words, the risk of an accidental correlation is five in a hundred. If r is 2.6 times the size of σr, the chances of accidental relationship will be only one in a hundred, and so on. In the present work those r's which are twice their standard errors have been taken as significant.

It must be stated, however, that this method of evaluating r can be rigorously applied only to large samples, where N is more than thirty. Most of the samples presented in the preceding pages are, perforce, less than thirty. This does not mean that significant correlations based on smaller samples are not, in fact, significant. It means rather that the conclusions of smaller sample tests tend to be overstated and that border line cases will be more border line, so to speak, less clearly one thing or the other, than if the sample were large. It is quite possible for a large sample test to show significance where a small sample test would not. Fortunately, as the reader will remember, there were very few border line correlations in the preceding pages. Most of them were either extremely significant or altogether insignificant.

Multiple correlation is a much more complicated business. We have used it only once, in Tables 4.1 and 4.2, which are crucial to the argument. The calculations in these tables were carried out by the electronic computer at Wayne State University. This computer accomplished in approximately two minutes calculations which would have taken the writer and his students several weeks of full-time labor. Concerning the technique of multiple correlation we will say nothing in addition to what we have already said in Chapter IV, except that β is, more specifically defined, a measure of the extent to which variations in the Communist vote are the product of changes in the particular factor (say cash-cropping) when the influence of some of the other factors listed (e.g., in line B of Table 4.1, landless workers, dwarfholders, and Magyars) has first been subtracted from the variations in the vote. As in the case of simple correlation, the minimum requirement for statistical significance at the .05 level (one out of twenty chances) is a β which is at least twice the size of $\sigma\beta$.

A final word concerning the map of the Communist electorate in the 1920's. Where there was a choice, e.g. Poland, we chose to plot the election in which the Communists had achieved their maximum success. We did so on the hypothesis that the more symptoms there were to look at, the easier the diagnosis. In this election the CPP campaigned under the name of Peasant and Workers Union. It had various Ukrainian and Belorussian affiliates or front organizations. The vote of its Belorussian front organization, Hromada, has had to be interpolated, since that party's vote was lumped with the other ballots under the rubric "votes obtained by lists not adhering to state lists." We know that the total vote cast for Hromada was approximately 140,000, and that the districts of Bialyztok, Brest, Nowogrodek, and Wilno contained (according to the Polish census of 1931) 99 per cent of the Belorussian population living in interwar Poland. The votes cast for non-adherent lists in these districts in 1928 totaled 196,476, or 28.6 per cent more than those cast for Hromada. The estimates by district of the Hromada vote have been reached by reducing the non-adherent vote in each district by 28.6 per cent.[2]

As the border of significance we took five per cent, and we applied this limit to historic provinces, election districts, or meaningful sections of the country concerned, whichever seemed likely to produce a more comparable spread. Thus if either the Communists or the Socialists got five per cent or more of the vote cast in a given province, the province was outlined on the map and the vote recorded, even though, nationally, the party in question may not have broken the five per cent barrier. In the case of Hungary, election returns were not given by district. In an effort to keep a proper balance, we have recorded the Socialist vote on both sides of the Danube.

[2] For details, see "Poland" in Appendix B.

APPENDIX B: STATISTICAL DATA

BULGARIA

District	% of Communist to total vote				% of Socialist to total vote		
	1919[1]	1920[2]	April 1923[3]	1931[4]	1919	1920	April 1923
Burgas	32.5	30.1	24.8	20.4	2.8	5.7	2.5
Varna	15.7	23.3	21.5	10.6	12.0	4.6	9.0
Vidin	26.9	22.7	28.0	7.5	7.9	3.5	.8
Vratsa	22.9	25.1	23.8	13.1	18.8	8.2	14.1
Gumerdjina	7.9				29.4		
Kyustendil	14.6	17.7	16.7	11.4	7.4	4.4	3.8
Mastanly		.0	1.7	.0		13.4	.0
Odrin	5.8				27.8		
Pashmakly		5.3	2.7	3.3		5.0	.0
Petrich		28.1	23.7	60.3		4.9	6.1
Plovdiv	18.5	17.3	19.5	15.9	14.2	5.4	3.3
Pleven	25.0	24.9	24.8	13.5	8.7	4.8	2.8
Ruse	7.2	12.6	10.0	10.3	8.4	4.6	1.4
Sofia	15.5	19.4	17.3	11.0	11.0	5.7	4.5
Stara Zagora	18.6	18.6	23.1	17.7	13.8	8.3	14.5
Strumitsa	18.9				16.1		
Tirnovo	17.2	20.2	19.5	13.4	15.4	8.4	8.8
Khaskovo			12.6	18.9			9.3
Shumen	14.1	14.8	12.4	10.7	10.1	5.8	2.2

Province	% of Communist to total vote, 1920	% of Socialist to total vote, 1920
Bulgarian Macedonia (Petrich)	28.2	4.9
Remainder of Bulgaria	20.2	6.1

[1] *Annuaire Bulgarie 1913-22*, part C, p. 59.

[2] *Ibid.*, p. 60.

[3] *Elections pour la xxeme assemblee*, pp. 3-16.

[4] *Annuaire statistique du royaume de Bulgarie 1932* (Sofia, 1932), pp. 370-73.

District	% of industrial workers to total population, 1926[5]	% of holdings 60 dekars and less to total area held, 1926[6]	% of total arable planted to wheat, 1925[7]	% of Moslem to total population, 1926[8]
Burgas	2.8	17.7	31.6	10.9
Varna	3.7	27.7	39.7	21.9
Vidin	1.6	19.7	35.7	3.8
Vratsa	1.3	24.0	32.7	2.8
Gumerdjina	1.2			75.0
Kyustendil	2.4	34.4	6.6	.8
Mastanly		81.3	19.5	
Odrin				
Pashmakly	3.1	59.0	5.6	11.8
Petrich	1.4	58.4	9.9	3.9
Plovdiv	3.8	32.7	19.4	6.3
Pleven	1.9	25.5	28.7	4.3
Ruse	2.5	29.4	23.7	34.8
Sofia	6.1	30.1	4.4	1.2
Stara Zagora	2.6(2.5)	22.1	38.9	7.7(6.4)
Strumitsa				
Tirnovo	4.0	33.0	27.8	6.6
Khaskovo	2.7	32.8	27.8	9.3
Shumen	1.7	39.7	42.2	43.9

[5] *Resultats generaux du recensement de la population dans le royaume de Bulgarie au 31 decembre 1926. Tome III: Statistique des professions* (*d'apres la profession principale*) (Sofia, 1932), pp. 94-97; *Tome IV: Population active* (*d'apres la profession principale exercee personellement*) (Sofia, 1933), pp. 140-47. Gumerdjina and Mastanly are identical, as are Odrin and Pashmakly. In the returns for 1923 and 1931 Khaskovo was separated out from Stara Zagora, thus reducing industrial workers from 2.6 to 2.5 per cent and Moslems from 7.7 to 6.4 per cent, in the case of the parent district.

[6] *Annuaire statistique du royaume de Bulgarie 1928, XX annee* (Sofia, 1929), pp. 114-17.

[7] *Annuaire Bulgarie 1926*, pp. 112-13.

[8] *Resultats generaux du recensement de la population dans le royaume de Bulgarie au 31 decembre 1926. Tome I: Principes et methodes du recensement. Menages, population legale, et population presente. Sexe, lieu de naissance, nationalite ethnique, sujetion, religion, langue maternelle et degree d'instruction de la population presente. Infirmes, absents de leur residence* (hereafter cited as *Recensement Bulgarie religion*) (Sofia, 1931), pp. 242-49.

STATISTICAL DATA

CZECHOSLOVAKIA

District	% of Communist to total vote			% of Socialist to total vote		
	1925[9]	1929[10]	1935[11]	1925	1929	1935
Prague	15.5	11.4	12.9	12.5	17.0	15.9
Prague A			13.2			
Prague B			12.5			
Pardubice	8.8	6.0	6.6	14.8	22.0	19.5
Hradec Kralove	8.4	6.2	6.4	16.9	21.8	16.4
Mlada Boleslav	15.4	12.8	10.2	11.8	15.4	12.5
Ceska Lipa	12.1	12.0	6.4	24.8	28.7	15.9
Louny	21.2	15.9	13.7	22.6	27.1	20.7
Karlovy Vary	9.4	12.0	5.9	29.9	35.3	17.7
Plzen	5.2	4.4	3.2	33.4	38.4	29.0
C. Budejovice	8.6	6.1	4.9	14.3	20.0	16.4
Jihlava	9.4	6.9	5.0	10.3	15.4	12.2
Brno	13.8	9.8	8.9	11.2	18.8	16.1
Olomouc	7.0	6.5	6.3	18.8	24.1	18.2
U. Hradiste	16.0	11.3	9.3	6.3	14.0	14.0
M. Ostrava	12.4	10.1	11.4	19.6	25.7	20.1
Trnava	13.7	11.3	12.2	6.2	12.1	12.8
Nove Zamky	20.0	16.8	17.1	5.6	11.0	11.1
T. S. Martin	9.5	6.2	7.8	3.0	9.9	12.3
B. Bystrica	11.0	7.6	11.7	7.5	14.1	12.5
S. Mikulas	1.4	7.9	16.3	4.4	11.4	13.9
Kosice	20.9	15.6	17.8	3.7	7.3	11.7
Presov	6.2	4.6	7.4	1.4	3.3	8.6
Uzhorod	31.2	15.2	25.6	7.4	8.6	10.0

Province	% of Communist to total vote, 1925	% of Socialist to total vote, 1925
Bohemia	12.4	20.2
Moravia	11.1	14.1
Slovakia	13.0	4.4
Ruthenia[12]	42.0	9.6

[9] *Assemblee nationale 1925*, pp. 14*-15*.
[10] *Chambre des deputes 1929*, pp. 14*-15*.
[11] *Chambre des deputes 1935*, pp 14*-15*.
[12] *Piatyi kongress*, p. 232.

CZECHOSLOVAKIA, CONTINUED

District	% of industrial workers to total population, 1930[13]	% of Magyars to total population, 1930[14]	% of Germans to total population, 1930[15]
Prague	12.4		
Prague A		.2	3.1
Prague B		.1	2.6
Pardubice	13.9	.2	11.8
Hradec Kralove	18.9	.3	27.2
Mlada Boleslav	18.6	.1	31.7
Ceska Lipa	21.2	.2	85.9
Louny	17.6	.1	39.4
Karlovy Vary	20.0	.0	94.7
Plzen	12.2	.0	32.4
C. Budejovice	10.3	.0	27.6
Jihlava	9.3	.0	28.4
Brno	13.6	.0	16.4
Olomouc	13.1	.2	36.4
U. Hradiste	10.4	.1	1.0
M. Ostrava	18.2	.0	23.2
Trnava	5.4	1.6	1.8
Nove Zamky	3.1	54.2	6.5
T. S. Martin	4.9	.3	4.9
B. Bystrica	6.6	1.7	5.0
S. Mikulas	7.8	.8	1.5
Kosice	4.7	38.6	9.5
Presov	1.3	1.4	.6
Uzhorod	2.8	15.2	1.9

[13] *Recensement de la population dans la republique tchecoslovaque du 1er decembre 1930. Volume CIV. Tome II. Profession de la population. Ier partie: sous-groupes, groupes et classes de professions principales, rapport a la profession et repartition sociale, classes de professions accessoires* (hereafter cited as *Recensement tchecoslovaque 1930. Profession de la population*) (Prague, 1934), pp. 108-25, 228, 246, 264, 282, 300, 318, 336, 354, 360.

[14] *Recensement de la population de la republique tchecoslovaque, effectue le 1er decembre 1930. Volume XCVIII. Tome I: accroissement, concentration et densite de la population, sex, repartition par age, etat matrimonial, nationalite ethnique, religion* (hereafter cited as *Recensement tchecoslovaque 1930: nationalite ethnique*) (Prague, 1934), p. 47.

[15] *Ibid.*

CZECHOSLOVAKIA, CONTINUED

District	% of Communist to total vote, 1946[16]	District	% of Communist to total vote, 1946
Usti nad Labem	56.4	Praha	36.1
Kladno	53.6	Pardubice	35.7
Karlovy Vary	52.2	Trencin	34.0
Liberec	48.3	Brno	33.8
Praha Venkov Jih	47.2	Zilina	33.8
Plzen	44.9	Opava	33.1
Mlada Boleslav	43.4	Trnava	33.0
Ceske Budejovici	42.7	Olomouc	32.4
Havlikuv Brod	41.3	Zlin	30.9
Tabor	39.7	Bratislava	30.2
Hradec Kralove	39.5	Nitra	29.0
Banska Bystrica	39.3	Presov	28.1
Jihlava	38.6	L. S. Mikulas	27.2
Moravska Ostrava	37.9	Kosice	20.0

[16] *Mlada fronta* (Prague), 28 May 1946 and *Pravo lidu* (Prague), of the same date.

CZECHOSLOVAKIA, CONTINUED

Slovak district by number and name	% of industrial workers to total population, 1930[17]	% of area in holdings 500 ha plus to total arable, 1930[18]	% of area in holdings 5 ha minus to total arable, 1930[19]
332. Piestany	5.9	18.4	22.1
333. Hlohovec	4.1	20.6	19.4
334. Trnava	7.5	27.5	13.4
335. Galanta	4.7	14.1	16.6
336. Sala	2.9	14.5	29.7
337. Nitra	3.9	13.5	19.9
338. Nove Zamky	6.7	11.4	23.3
339. Vrable	2.1	3.0	22.7
340. Levice	5.9	20.8	15.2
341. Zeliezovce	4.8	12.7	13.4
342. Banovce nad Bebravou	4.0	34.9	13.4
343. Topolcany	4.7	30.3	16.3
344. Zlate Moravce	4.7	46.5	15.8
345. Ilava	9.1	30.6	18.4
346. Trencin	9.7	33.9	16.2
347. Nove Mesto nad Vahom	5.3	21.6	22.5
348. Senica	6.0	17.0	13.1
349. Skalica	6.3	22.4	24.4
350. Modra	4.3	35.5	19.3
351. Bratislava vonkov	7.2	34.8	21.9
352. Bratislava mesto	20.2	61.7	9.9
353. Samorin	3.1	9.6	10.0
354. Dunajska Streda	3.5	7.4	10.9
355. Komarno	5.8	15.3	14.3
356. Stara Dala	1.9	22.7	12.6
357. Parkan	4.0	15.7	19.5
358. Malacky	4.8	51.4	13.6
359. Sobrance	1.8	21.9	12.8
360. Michalovce	3.5	17.3	17.4
361. Trebisov	3.7	11.0	13.0
362. Kralovsky Chlumec	4.1	17.4	15.6
363. Velke Kapusany	2.1	2.3	14.8
364. Presov	4.7	18.6	8.7
365. Vranov nad Toplou	2.6	28.6	11.3
366. Kosice vonkov	3.1	36.2	10.1

[17] *Recensement tchecoslovaque 1930. Profession de la population*, pp. 122-25, 354, 372.

[18] *Recensement des exploitations agricoles dans la republique tchecoslovaque d'apres l'etat au 27 mai 1930. Volume XCI, Tome I: nature du sol et animaux de ferme* (Prague, 1934), *partie 9 (Slovaquie)*, pp. 2-29, *partie 10 (Slovaquie)*, pp. 2-25.

[19] *Ibid.*

CZECHOSLOVAKIA, CONTINUED

Slovak district by number and name	Industrial workers	500 ha plus	5 ha minus
367. Kosice mesto	12.1	87.5	3.5
368. Moldava nad Bodvou	6.6	30.1	8.0
369. Krupina	1.8	18.6	6.4
371. Modry Kamen	3.0	23.8	9.1
372. Lucenec	10.5	20.9	10.8
373. Feledince	3.6	4.0	8.3
374. Tornala	6.1	15.0	7.3
375. Puchov	6.9	27.6	16.5
376. Povazska Bystrica	2.9	18.0	21.3
377. Velka Bytca	3.8	19.1	19.7
378. Zilina	11.7	45.2	20.0
379. Turcansky Svaty Martin	11.0	40.1	8.0
380. Prievidza	7.2	29.7	18.0
381. Myjava	4.1	30.3	23.7
382. Brezna nad Hronom	11.3	75.2	8.8
383. Banska Bystrica	10.2	54.0	12.8
384. Kremnica	6.0	48.6	15.8
385. Nova Bana	6.9	53.0	16.1
386. Banska Stiavnica	13.0	61.4	7.9
387. Zvolen	3.8	47.4	12.4
388. Roznava	11.9	52.9	7.0
389. Revuca	9.9	55.9	8.4
390. Rimavska Sobota	8.7	34.0	6.6
391. Sabinov	2.3	20.4	11.3
392. Barejov	4.2	22.7	6.3
393. Giraltovce	1.5	13.9	4.3
394. Spisska Stara Ves	2.5	7.6	6.7
395. Stara Lubovna	5.2	37.3	13.2
396. Kezmarok	10.2	43.5	6.9
397. Poprad	12.6	56.6	6.9
398. Levoca	5.3	21.1	6.7
399. Spisska Nova Ves	10.1	50.3	9.3
400. Gelnica	14.1	63.9	10.7
401. Cadca	3.8	21.7	25.4
402. Kysucke Nove Mesto	2.5	13.6	26.3
403. Namestovo	6.1	33.0	9.3
404. Trstena	6.1	36.0	6.9
405. Dolni Kubin	5.9	41.2	8.4
406. Ruzomberok	15.8	70.4	12.8
407. Liptovsky Svaty Mikulas	7.2	60.7	8.5
408. Stropkov	1.2	16.4	5.2
410. Medzilaborce	2.6	38.0	7.7
411. Humenne	6.3	41.4	9.4
412. Snina	1.7	49.6	7.3

CZECHOSLOVAKIA, CONTINUED

Slovak district by number	% of area put to cereals to total arable, 1930[20]	% of Magyars to total population, 1930[21]	% of Communist to total vote, 1929[22]	% of Socialist to total vote, 1929[23]
332.	42.8	0.5	11.8	6.3
333.	49.7	0.7	13.9	8.2
334.	43.7	1.5	8.0	19.2
335.	56.9	62.0	23.5	6.2
336.	60.0	55.5	21.5	3.3
337.	52.7	13.8	15.2	9.6
338.	59.2	31.6	13.9	11.3
339.	61.4	25.7	14.5	4.5
340.	41.1	27.4	9.9	4.6
341.	55.9	79.9	28.5	2.2
342.	23.6	0.2	9.0	2.3
343.	33.9	0.5	11.5	6.3
344.	26.6	9.9	4.6	7.4
345.	18.3	0.4	11.2	7.7
346.	20.6	0.6	7.0	11.4
347.	28.9	0.3	11.2	8.7
348.	32.3	0.1	4.7	12.4
349.	33.7	0.2	7.7	14.6
350.	31.4	2.7	7.7	11.9
351.	25.8	6.8	14.0	26.7
352.	11.2	16.2	10.7	22.5
353.	57.6	76.9	9.6	6.7
354.	50.4	88.2	16.1	1.7
355.	50.5	82.9	29.2	8.4
356.	50.1	70.1	21.0	4.4
357.	59.8	81.5	21.0	4.6
358.	15.8	0.5	4.0	26.2
359.	38.0	1.2	3.8	2.2
360.	34.9	5.9	5.8	3.2
361.	42.5	7.8	7.0	5.3
362.	36.0	78.9	20.6	6.2
363.	35.3	55.7	5.7	1.3
364.	28.5	1.8	6.9	3.6
365.	25.8	0.4	7.9	2.9
366.	26.6	6.4	4.1	5.0
367.	4.6	18.0	14.1	12.0
368.	24.7	56.3	15.7	3.9
369.	23.7	36.4	5.4	4.7
371.	25.5	31.1	5.2	1.3
372.	20.3	25.8	16.5	9.2

[20] *Ibid.*
[21] *Recensement tchecoslovaque 1930: nationalite ethnique*, pp. 35-36.
[22] *Chambre des deputes 1929*, pp. 28-32.
[23] *Ibid.*

CZECHOSLOVAKIA, CONTINUED

Slovak district by number	Area put to cereals	Magyars	Communists	Socialists
373.	31.2	77.4	19.6	1.9
374.	27.8	83.1	15.6	2.5
375.	20.0	0.1	1.7	13.7
376.	18.9	0.0	4.0	3.5
377.	16.6	0.0	1.6	14.5
378.	17.3	0.6	7.4	13.3
379.	15.2	0.4	6.4	20.7
380.	20.1	0.6	13.3	5.5
381.	34.1	0.1	9.6	16.9
382.	3.4	0.4	10.0	25.5
383.	6.9	1.1	15.2	16.3
384.	11.9	0.6	6.9	16.4
385.	10.4	0.4	2.4	23.1
386.	6.8	1.5	3.5	29.6
387.	15.0	0.6	8.8	12.3
388.	8.7	35.1	24.2	10.7
389.	8.6	9.6	13.8	11.4
390.	15.5	13.2	7.7	14.9
391.	23.2	0.6	1.5	3.1
392.	24.2	0.4	2.4	1.7
393.	26.3	0.4	1.0	0.7
394.	22.9	0.3	0.4	1.6
395.	18.9	0.2	0.8	1.3
396.	19.8	0.9	9.8	4.9
397.	14.3	1.6	8.8	9.7
398.	23.2	1.4	5.6	4.0
399.	14.6	2.2	5.3	22.8
400.	5.6	1.4	29.4	13.9
401.	16.0	0.0	2.6	14.3
402.	21.1	0.0	4.8	5.9
403.	19.5	0.0	0.3	1.0
404.	15.3	0.0	0.3	3.3
405.	15.5	0.1	0.7	5.1
406.	6.4	0.2	7.6	7.6
407.	8.8	0.3	7.0	12.2
408.	17.2	0.2	2.4	0.9
410.	11.4	0.1	0.8	3.3
411.	14.8	0.7	4.4	1.8
412.	9.2	0.1	9.8	3.3

EASTERN EUROPE

District	% of Jews to total population[24]
Warsaw	15.4
Lodz	14.4
Ruthenia	14.1
Lublin	12.8
Bialystok	12.0
Lwow	11.0
Bukovina	10.9
Kielce	10.8
Polesie	10.1
Wolyn	10.0
Stanislawow	9.5
Wilno	8.7
Tarnopol	8.4
Nowogrodek	7.8
Krakow	7.6
Bessarabia	7.2
Crisana	7.0
Alfold	6.9
Moldavia	6.7
Macedonia	4.3
Northern Hungary	4.3
Slovakia	4.1
Sofia	3.3
Transylvania	2.5
Muntenia	2.3
Pannonia	2.3
Banat	1.5
Voivodina	1.4
Moravia	1.2
Plovdiv	1.2
Bohemia	1.1
Ruse	1.0
Western Thrace	1.0

[24] *Recensement Bulgarie religion*, pp. 190-209; *Annuaire statistique de la republique tchecoslovaque publie par l'office de statistique de la republique tchecoslovaque* (Prague, 1935), p. 6; *Resultats statistiques du recensement de la population de la grece du 15-16 mai 1928. IV. Lieu de naissance, religion et langue, sujetion* (Athens, 1935), pp. xl; *Annuaire statistique hongrois. Nouveau cours xxxix. 1931. Redige et publie par l'office central royal hongrois de statistique* (Budapest, 1933), p. 11; *Petite annuaire statistique de la Pologne 1937* (Warsaw, 1937), pp. 22-23; *Anuarul statistic al Romaniei 1937 si 1938* (Bucharest, 1939), pp. 74-77; *Resultats definitifs du recensement de la population du 31 janvier 1921* (hereafter cited as *Resultats definitifs Sarajevo*) (Sarajevo, 1932), pp. 1-2. The Jewish population is given in the east European statistics in three different ways, by ethnic origin, by Yiddish language, and by confession. The confessional figures are consistently the largest, and have been used in the present work.

GREECE

District	% of industrial workers to total population, 1928[25]	% of refugees to total population, 1928[26]	% of arable planted to wheat, 1935[27]	% of Communist to total vote		
				1926[28]	1933[29]	1936[30]
Aetolie—A.	6.1	2.6	32.0	1.9	1.6	2.2
Attique—B.	16.1	27.5	41.5	3.2	7.1	6.0
Eubee	7.7	9.1	35.8	2.0	1.9	2.4
Phtiotide—P.	5.5	2.4	45.0	1.3	1.5	2.7
Larissa	9.6	11.4	57.0	14.9	13.6	17.7
Trikkala	4.4	1.3	46.0	5.2	3.2	6.7
Zante	6.3	1.1	18.7	.0	.0	.7
Corfou	7.8	2.0	6.7	2.7	1.1	1.9
Cephalonie	6.2	1.1	3.8	2.5	1.8	4.1
Cyclades	10.2	3.7	5.8	.0	3.4	.3
Argolide—C.	6.2	4.3	34.1	.4	.2	.8
Arcadie	4.9	.6	35.4	.0	.0	.5
Achaie—E.	7.7	4.2	30.6	.9	.4	1.3
Laconie	5.3	1.0	35.8	.0	1.9	1.4
Messinie	5.6	2.0	21.0	.4	3.4	2.7
Drama	9.4	70.3	30.2	7.3	7.0	14.1
Cavalla	17.3	62.7	46.5	14.9	27.5	23.8
Salonique	11.0	48.1	48.0	9.9	7.3	9.6
Chalcidique	5.6	27.5	47.0	2.5	1.0	2.4
Cozane	4.5	31.9	41.5	.0	1.3	6.6
Pella	4.2	53.9	40.0	7.5	6.3	4.0
Serres	6.8	44.7	42.0	3.6	4.3	11.8
Florina	5.6	15.2	33.2	8.1	3.3	7.9
Preveza—A.	4.8	2.4	25.7	.0	2.1	1.4
Jannina	6.6	2.8	21.2	2.9	2.2	5.5
Lesbos	8.4	22.0	29.4	5.4	15.3	14.2
Samos	9.1	10.2	19.1	.0	2.2	5.3
Chio	7.8	18.4	27.0	.0	.0	1.6
Heraclion	5.3	14.1	10.0	2.7	.6	2.7
Lassithi	4.4	2.5	15.7	.0	.0	.0
Rethymno	4.4	6.4	12.0	.0	.0	.8
La Canee	6.5	7.4	14.6	3.0	2.1	1.6
Hevros	4.8	39.0	39.4	16.0	2.5	7.2
Rhodope	9.4	33.1	48.2	13.5	16.8	7.6

[25] *Annuaire Grece 1930*, pp. 27, 76-77.

[26] *Annuaire Grece 1931*, p. 30.

[27] *Statistique annuelle agricole et d'elevage des bestiaux de la Grece 1936* (Athens, 1936), pp. 33, 36.

[28] *Elections des deputes 1926*, pp. xxii-xxiii.

[29] *Annuaire Grece 1933*, pp. 318-21.

[30] *Statistique des elections des deputes du 26 janvier 1936* (Athens, 1938), pp. 316-19.

GREECE, CONTINUED

Province	% of Communist to total vote, 1926
Western Thrace	14.6
Thessaly	10.8
Macedonia	7.6
Asiatic islands	2.9
Rumelie	2.7
Ionian islands	2.1
Crete	1.7
Epirus	1.4
Peloponnesos	.2
Cyclades	.0

HUNGARY

District	% of Communist to total vote, 1945[31]
Abauj	8.8
Bacs-Bodrog-Baja	19.2
Baranya-Pecs	16.5
Bekes	21.2
Bihar	20.8
Borsod-Gomar-Miskolcs	23.0
Csanad	29.1
Csongrad-Hodin-Szeged	18.2
Fejer-Szekesfehervar	12.3
Gyor-Moson	14.8
Hajdu-Debrecen	15.4
Heves	17.6
Jasz-Nagyken-Szolnok	23.0
Komarom-Esztergom	29.9
Nograd-Hont	27.3
Pest-Pilis-Solt-Kisk-Budapest-Kecsk	18.6
Somogy-Kaposvar	5.9
Sopron	11.4
Szabolcs	9.9
Szatmar-Bereg	7.3
Tolna	10.6
Vas-Szombathely	9.2
Veszprem	12.7
Zala	7.2
Zemplen	12.9

[31] Gyula Mike (ed.), *Magyar statisztikai zsebkonyv. XIV Evfolyam 1947*, pp. 213-15.

POLAND

District	% of Jews to total population, 1921[32]	% of Belorussians to total population, 1931[33]	% of Polish Communist to total vote, 1922[34]
Lodz	14.5		1.8
Kielce	11.9		
Thorn	.3		
Posnan	.5		.2
Warsaw city	33.0		6.7
Warsaw province	9.6		.8
Lublin	13.8	.1	.4
Bialystok	14.8	12.5	2.1
Katowice	5.1		
Krakow	7.7		1.0
Lwow	11.5		.2
Stanislawow	10.8		
Tarnopol	9.0		
Luck	11.5	.1	
Brest	12.6	6.6	3.7
Nowogrodek	9.0	39.1	1.5
Wilno	5.9	22.7	.3

The Warsaw city (6.7) and Warsaw province (.8) values are bracketed together as 2.7.

[32] *Annuaire statistique de la republique polonaise. II annee, 1923* (Warsaw, 1924), pp. 12-15.

[33] *Concise Statistical Year-Book of Poland, 1937* (Warsaw, 1937), pp. 20-21.

[34] *Elections a la diete 1922*, pp. 15-101; *Almanac polonais* (Paris, 1926), pp. 53-54.

POLAND, CONTINUED

District	% of Polish Socialist to total vote, 1928[35]	% of Polish Communist to total vote, 1928	% of Ukrainian Communist to total vote, 1928	% of Belorussian Communist to total vote, 1928	Total Communist as % of total vote, 1928
Lodz	25.5	1.0			1.0
Kielce	19.6	6.7			6.7
Thorn	13.4	.0			.0
Posnan	7.6	.0			.0
Warsaw city	9.4 ⎤	14.0 ⎤			14.0 ⎤
Warsaw province	23.1 ⎦ 18.6	2.7 ⎦ 6.6			2.7 ⎦ 6.6
Lublin	16.7	0.7	3.4		4.1
Bialystok	6.3	3.0		(6.5)	9.5
Katowice	13.8	.0			.0
Krakow	21.0	.0			.0
Lwow	7.2	0.3	7.3		7.6
Stanislawow	3.8	.0	7.4		7.4
Tarnopol	0.8	.0	7.8		7.8
Luck	.0	.0	17.5		17.5
Brest	5.9	4.1	28.8	(4.7)	37.6
Nowogrodek	6.2	.0		(28.0)	28.0
Wilno	12.7	.0		(6.1)	6.1

[35] *Elections a la diete 1928,* pp. xxviii-xxix, xxxiv-xxxvii.

POLAND, CONTINUED

District	% of Communist to registered voters, unfree election, 1947[36]	District	% of Communist to registered voters, unfree election, 1947
Opole	97.0	Kalisz	73.4
Kozle	97.0	Kielce	71.0
Gliwice	94.4	Torun	67.9
Lobez	93.2	Czestochowa	67.2
Bedzin	91.3	Lezno	67.1
Katowice	91.2	Bialystok	66.1
Przemysl	90.7	Gniezno	64.9
Bielsko	90.7	Zgierz	63.9
Swiebodzin	88.7	Minsk Maz	63.7
Biskupiec	88.5	Zanosc	62.9
Boleslawiec	88.2	Rzeszow	62.8
Szczecin	87.6	Piotrkow	62.7
Szczecinak	87.4	Lublin	61.8
Lignica	87.1	Radom	61.8
Olsztyn	86.9	Myslenice	61.7
Wroclaw I & II	85.4	Ostrowiec	59.7
Plonsk	84.2	Pruszkow	58.9
Przosnysz	82.2	Bydgoszcz	58.6
Chrzanow	81.0	Pabiana	55.9
Lodz miasto &		Warszawa m.	55.4
Lodz	79.7	Chetin	53.5
Gdynia	78.0	Posnan	50.6
Wloclawek	75.5	Siedlce	41.6
Elk	75.2	Krakow	40.2
Gdansk	74.8	Tarnow	38.1

ROMANIA

Province	% of Communist to total vote, 1922[37]	% of Socialist to total vote, 1922
Moldavia		2.1
Muntenia	1.3	2.0
Oltenia	.5	.9
Dobrudja		.5
Bessarabia		2.8
Bukovina		9.8
Transylvania-Banat		2.7

[36] *Glos ludu* (Warsaw), 22 January 1947.
[37] Ionescu, *loc.cit.*

YUGOSLAVIA

Province	% of Communist to total vote, 1920[38]	% of Socialist to total vote, 1920
Montenegro	36.0	
Macedonia	33.0	
Dalmatia	16.2	
Voivodina	15.0	7.4
Serbia	14.0	
Slovenia	10.3	5.8
Croatia	7.0	5.6
Bosnia	5.4	

District	% of prechani to total population, 1921[39]	% of Communist to total vote, 1920
Banja Luka	57.3	4.6
Bihac	57.0	1.3
Lika Krbava	52.4	1.9
Srjem	46.7	9.9
Veliki Kikinda	44.0	21.2
Tuzla	43.4	4.8
Pancevo	41.4	12.8
Novi Sad	41.3	10.3
Travnik	38.2	7.2
Mostar	37.8	5.6
Sarajevo	34.0	9.0
Modrus Rijeka	32.8	15.8
Pozega	25.9	8.9
Zagreb	23.1	3.1
Virovitica	18.1	18.4
Dalmatia	17.1	16.2
Sombor	14.5	42.5
Bjelova Kuzevic	13.4	1.5
Zagreb city	8.6	26.9
Subotica	7.9	23.4

[38] *Statistichki pregled 1920*, section 56.
[39] *Resultats definitifs Sarajevo*, pp. 1-364.

APPENDIX C: QUESTIONNAIRE USED IN THE
GREEK PRISONS

In the course of interrogation the questionnaire underwent some change for empirical reasons, but the following questions are close to the final form.

1. Man or woman?
2. Year of birth?
3. Place of birth?
4. Nationality?
5. Besides Greek, what languages do you speak?
6. How many years of school did you complete?
7. a) Your principal profession?
   b) What other professions have you practiced?
8. Your father's profession?
9. What was the economic situation of your father's household in the past?
   a) His own house (how many rooms)?
   b) His own land (how many *stremmas*)?
   c) His own shop (kind, number of employees)?
10. What was your economic situation at the time you first became involved with Communism?
    a) At that time were you still dependent on your father's household? (Details.)
    b) Your individual economic situation at that time if you had established your own household? (Details.)
11. Have you ever had, or do you now have, any serious illness? What kind?
12. Do you have any physical defects (blindness in one eye, lameness, stammering, etc.)?
13. Have you ever been a member of the organizations: Workers' aid, OKNE, EAM, ELAS, National solidarity, EPON, Democratic union, Democratic army, KKE? In what year did you first join such an organization?

14. What was the highest rank (position) you held in any of the above organizations?

N varies according to the question asked. The details of property owned, for example, were never given until the interrogators learned to identify the repentant leaders and promised to assist them in some such matter as transfer to a prison nearer home. The leaders would then take the questionnaire to each prisoner in turn, and persuade him to surrender the details desired.

N for date of birth	586	N for extent of education	525
for party membership	568	for ownership of property	470
for profession	565	for date of party membership	440
for chronic disease	532	for amount of property owned	298

Women who were married at the time of their "involvement" were asked to itemize the holdings of their husbands.

APPENDIX D: GLOSSARY

Activist. In the narrow sense, a man fully committed to the party and under party discipline but for one reason or another not drawing a salary from the party treasury. Frequently, however, the term is used more loosely as equivalent to both "cadre" and "*apparatchik*." The *aktiv* of any party is the higher ranking cadres or *apparatchiks* taken collectively.

Aegean Macedonia. That part of traditional Macedonia which today belongs to Greece.

Apparat. Communist neologism denoting the party's hierarchy of command. It is made up of *apparatchiks*, who are full-time salaried revolutionaries. The Greeks use the term *stelechos*, which literally means an officer, whether commissioned or non-commissioned.

Apparatchik. See "apparat."

Armenians. A Christian Indoeuropean-speaking population of perhaps 3.3 millions approximately one-half of whom live in the Transcaucasus as citizens of the Armenian Socialist Soviet republic. Most of the remaining Armenian population live in various countries of the Middle East. Approximately one million Armenians were massacred by the Turks at the close of the nineteenth and the beginning of the twentieth century.

Ashkenazim. The German-speaking Jewish population of eastern Europe, before 1939 concentrated north of the Danube, particularly in Poland.

(β) beta coefficient. In multiple correlation, a measure of the extent to which variations in the Communist (or Socialist) vote are the product of variations in another phenomenon (e.g., cash cropping) when the other factors in the equation have been brought into account. More technically, β is a measure of the relative importance of the independent variables in the regression equation.

Belorussians. A Slavic-speaking population approximately 8 million strong, in general inhabiting the area of the Pripet marshes and having its own Socialist Soviet republic. Between 1920 and 1939 more than a million Belorussians were citizens of the Polish republic.

Bosniaks. The Serbo-Croatian-speaking Moslem population of Bosnia-Herzegovina.

Cadre. The counterpart of *apparatchik* for personnel purposes. One speaks of the cadre bureau or cadre policy. The connotation of *apparatchik* is command.[1]

Cash cropper. Term coined for the present work denoting any peasant, from dwarfholder to *kulak*, whose livelihood is primarily dependent upon the sale of a single crop (tobacco, wheat, wine, raisins), the price of which is determined in the world market.

Caucasians. In this study, Greeks who emigrated from the Russian Caucasus to the Kingdom of Greece after the Greek invasion of Asia Minor in 1920-1922.

Chams. The Greek-speaking Moslem population which inhabited southern Epirus, the part of Epirus under Greek sovereignty; at the close of World War II this population for the most part migrated, or was driven, into Albania.

Chetniks. The Serbian guerrilla forces of Draza Mihailovic.

Cominform. Kommunisticheskoe informatsionnoe biuro, a coordinating organ for some of the European Communist parties, founded in 1947 and dissolved in 1956.

Comintern. Kommunisticheskii internatsional, an agency for coordinating the Communist parties of the world, founded in 1919 and disbanded in 1943.

Communist party. (1) The *apparat,* including the activists. Elite party and cadre party are equivalent terms. In anti-Communist language, the hard core. (2) The party membership. In certain tactical situations large numbers of sympathizers or opportunists may be enrolled in the formal

[1] Cf. R. N. Carew Hunt, *A Guide to Communist Jargon* (New York, 1957), pp. 19-21.

party, but their membership tends to be nominal. Among Communists this party is sometimes referred to as a mass party. (3) The whole movement, *apparatchiks*, voters, fellow travellers, etc.

Correlation analysis. A statistical method which, as applied in the present study, permits us to compare the geographic distribution of the Communist (or Socialist) vote with the geographic distribution of a given social class. More technically, a mathematical procedure for establishing the degree of covariance between two variables and the extent to which this covariance is not the result of accident. See "statistical tests of significance."

Dwarfholder. A peasant whose holding is too small to support his family. Such peasants must seek supplementary employment. In eastern Europe any holding under five hectares (approximately 12.4 acres) is usually considered a dwarfholding, though this figure will vary considerably with the type of cultivation and the fertility of the soil.

EAM. *Ethnikon Apeleftherotikon Metopon*, the Communist-controlled Greek resistance organization of the period of the German occupation.

ELAS. *Ethnikos Laikos Apeleftherotikos Stratos*, the Communist-controlled Greek guerrilla army of 1942-1945.

Ethnic group. Any population sharing a common social inheritance. The extent of this inheritance will vary from population to population, but common language, law, religion, custom, tradition, or some combination of these, are characteristic.

Fellow traveller. A sympathizer who brings kudos to the party by reason of his special standing in society, the world of science, etc. He may or may not belong to the formal party, depending on the circumstances, but in any case he is not ordinarily subject to party discipline.

Gegs. The Albanian population living north of the Shkumbini river, whether in Albania proper, or in Yugoslavia (the Kossovo-Metohija district).

Georgians. A Christian non-Indoeuropean non-Turkic population of some 2.5 million persons which inhabits the Transcaucasus and politically is organized as a Socialist Soviet republic.

Hectare. 2.471 acres.

Hromada. Beloruskaia Sotsialistychkaia Hramada, the principal front organization of the Communist party of Western Belorussia, in its turn a section of the interwar Communist party of Poland.

Ideology. A secular religion; a set of doctrines providing masses of mankind with a basic orientation on the problems of social existence and salvation.

IMRO. Vnatresna makedono-revolucionerna organizacija, also given as *Unutrasnja makedonska revolucionarna organizacija.* A Slavo-Macedonian terrorist organization operating in the interwar period out of Pirin Macedonia.

Kingdom of Saint Stephen. The traditional Hungarian kingdom, founded about A.D. 1000 by King Stephen and comprehending in due course such non-Hungarian populations as Croats, Slovaks, Saxons, Banat Serbs, Transylvanian Romanians, and Ruthenian Ukrainians. The Hungarians tended to regard the whole of Stephen's kingdom, regardless of the ethnic character of the local population, as inalienably Hungarian.

KKE. Kommounistikon Komma tis Ellados, the Communist party of Greece.

Kossovo-Metohija (Kosmet). An area of Yugoslavia inhabited preponderantly by Albanians (Gegs) and under Communist rule granted a measure of autonomy.

Kulak. In Communist terminology, a well-to-do peasant; one who hires others to help him work his land.

Kurds. A Moslem Indoeuropean-speaking population related to the Iranians who inhabit the mountainous area in which the Tigris and Euphrates rivers have their source. Approximately three million Kurds live in Syria, Turkey, the USSR, Irak, and Iran.

Leading cadre. An *apparatchik* or activist assigned at, or directly below, the level of the central committee. Collectively, the party high command.

Lumpenproletariat. In Marxist jargon, the proletariat of thieves, panderers, and ne'er-do-wells.

MADOSZ. Magyar Dolgozok Orszagos Szoevetsege. The front organization of the Hungarian (Szekler) Communists of Transylvania.

Magyars. The Hungarian name for Hungarians.

Moldavians. Official Soviet term for 1.5 million Romanians who live in Bessarabia, a province annexed by the USSR in 1940, the larger part becoming the Moldavian Socialist Soviet republic.

Multiple correlation analysis. An advanced form of correlation analysis which, as applied in the present study, permits us to compare the geographic distribution of the Communist (or Socialist) vote simultaneously with the geographic distribution of several economic and social phenomena. Multiple correlation permits us to measure the relative influence of each of the causal factors in producing the Communist (or Socialist) vote. More technically, multiple correlation is a mathematical procedure for establishing the degree of covariance among several variables and the relative influence of each variable, together with the extent to which this covariance may be ascribed to chance. See "statistical tests of significance."

N. Statistical symbol for the number of cases; in the present work, N usually refers to the number of electoral districts.

Nation. Any population which has developed a common political consciousness and desires to be master of its own destiny. A nation may include more than one ethnic group or only a part of such a group.

Opportunist. A non- or anti-Communist who joins the party, usually after the seizure of power, in order to continue or facilitate his professional career. Opportunists are not as a rule given assignments in the *apparat*.

Partisan. Member of the Yugoslav guerrilla forces organized and controlled by the Communist party and commanded by Josip Broz Tito.

Pirin Macedonia. The part of traditional Macedonia now incorporated in Bulgaria.

Politburo. The political bureau of the central committee of a Communist party. Frequently the locus of supreme power. Now often referred to as the presidium.

Pomaks. The Bulgarian-speaking Moslem population which inhabits the mountain frontier adjacent to Greece.

Prechani. The Serb minority populations living outside the frontiers of the traditional Serbian kingdom, specifically in Bosnia-Herzegovina, Croatia-Dalmatia, and the Voivodina. *Prechanin* is the singular case.

Proletariat. The industrial working class associated with modern industry; in Communist doctrine the principal agent in the historical process which must inevitably eventuate in a classless society. In actual Communist usage, the proletariat is the hortatory equivalent of either the party itself or the movement as a whole.[2]

r (coefficient of correlation). A number between -1.00 and 1.00 which expresses the extent to which the geographic distribution of the Communist (or Socialist) vote is comparable to the geographic distribution of one or another social class. More technically, r expresses the degree of covariance obtaining between two variables.

R (coefficient of multiple correlation). A number between -1.00 and 1.00 which expresses the extent to which the geographic distribution of the Communist (or Socialist) vote is comparable with the geographic distribution of several social and economic phenomena. More technically, R expresses the degree of covariance obtaining among any number of variables greater than two.

R^2 (coefficient of determination). A measure (obtained by squaring R) indicating the extent to which changes in the

[2] *Ibid.*, pp. 121-24.

Communist (or Socialist) vote are the result of changes in a variety of social and economic factors, taken in any given combination. More technically, a measure of the percentage of total variance explained by any combination of the variables entering in a multiple correlation analysis.

Reichsdeutschen. The citizens of the Germany unified by Bismarck and expanded by Hitler. Contrasted with *Volksdeutschen*, which see.

ρ (*rho*). Coefficient of correlation obtained through the use of Spearman's rank-order method, an alternative to the method of linear regression, whose coefficient of correlation is expressed by *r*.

Ruthenes. The Ukrainian population inhabiting Subcarpathian Ruthenia, the easternmost province of interwar Czechoslovakia.

Sejm. The lower house of the Polish parliament.

Sel Rob. *Ukrainske Seliansko-Robitnyche Sotsialistychne Obiednannia*, the principal front organization of the Communist party of the Western Ukraine, in its turn a section of the interwar Communist party of Poland.

SEP. Surrendered enemy personnel. Members of the Malayan Communist guerrilla force who had surrendered to British authority.

Sephardim. The Spanish-speaking Jewish population of eastern Europe, in the interwar period concentrated south of the Danube.

Shumskyism. An ideological deviation affecting the Communist parties of the Ukraine and the Western Ukraine during the interwar period. According to this doctrine, a politically Communist Ukraine should draw its intellectual and literary inspiration from the West rather than from Soviet Russia.

(Σ) *Sigma.* Statistical symbol indicating "the sum of."

Slav. Any speaker of any of a group of closely related Indo-European languages including Russian, Belorussian, Ukrainian, Polish, Sorb, Slovak, Czech, Slovene, Serbo-Croatian, Slavo-Macedonian, and Bulgarian, among others.

Slavo-Macedonians. A Slavic-speaking population sandwiched in between the Serbs on the north, the Bulgars on the east, the Greeks on the south, and the Albanians on the west.

Slavophones. The Slavo-Macedonian minority living in the extreme northwestern corner of Aegean or Greek Macedonia.

SNOF. Slavomakedonski narodnoosloboditelniot front. The Slavophone equivalent of the Greek EAM; the Slavophone anti-Axis resistance organization, controlled by the Communists. Towards the close of the second Greek civil war (1946-1949) the name was changed to NOF.

Sorbs. A Slavic population living in the southeastern corner of the German democratic republic (East Germany).

Srbijanci. The Serbs of that part of Yugoslavia which before 1919 had been the Kingdom of Serbia. *Srbijanac* is the singular case.

$\sigma\beta$ *(Standard error of beta).* In the context of the present work, a measure of the extent to which the geographic distribution of the Communist (or Socialist) vote might conform to the geographic distribution of a *number* of social and economic factors purely as a matter of accident. More technically, a measure of the sampling or chance variability in β used to make statistical tests of significance of the estimated beta coefficient. See "statistical tests of significance."

σr *(standard error of r).* In the context of the present work, the extent to which the geographic distribution of the Communist (or Socialist) vote might conform to the geographic distribution of a *given* social class purely as a matter of accident. More technically, a measure of the sampling or chance variability in r used to make statistical tests of significance of an estimated correlation coefficient. See "statistical tests of significance."

Statistical tests of significance. Statistical devices used in correlation analysis for determining the extent of correlation or covariance between any two or more variables which could be the result of accident or chance. More technically, a scientific method based on the laws of probability for making a decision at a predetermined level of risk about the statistical significance of an empirical finding.

Steni aftoamina. Narrow self-defense, the execution squad of the secret police of KKE.

Sudeten Germans. Those *Volksdeutschen* who lived in Bohemia and Moravia, the Czech provinces of Czechoslovakia.

Szeklers. The Hungarian population of southeastern Transylvania, separated from the main mass of Hungarians by Romanian populations.

Tobacco worker. In the Balkans a term usually denoting the laborer who sorts and cures tobacco in the warehouse.

Tosks. The Albanian population living south of the Shkumbini river.

Ustasha (plural *Ustashe*). In interwar Yugoslavia a Croatian terrorist organization; in Axis-occupied Yugoslavia the Croatian Fascist equivalent of the Nazi SS. The dominant figure in both organizations was Ante Pavelic.

Vardar Macedonia. That part of traditional Macedonia now incorporated into Yugoslavia. Its capital is Skopie (in Serbo-Croatian Skoplje, in Greek Skopia, in Turkish Uskub). Vardar Macedonia is referred to by Serb nationalists as South Serbia.

Volksdeutschen. The German minority populations of eastern Europe, in Bohemia-Moravia referred to as Sudetens, in Hungary as Swabs, in Romania as Saxons. The ancestors of these people had migrated to eastern Europe long before the unification of Germany by Bismarck. The term is contrasted with *Reichsdeutschen* (which see).

INDEX

activist, described, 8-9, 12; and heretical mass movements, 14; religious character, 15; social composition, 26-27, 35-37; defined, 229. *See also* aktiv, apparat, cadre, hard core, repentants.

Aegean Macedonia, *see* Macedonia

aktiv, 229

Albania, Communist party of, social composition, 21, 52; size, 51; Western education of leading cadres, 63-64; relations with Yugoslav party, 147-48

Albanians, 144-45, 147-48

Alexander, king of Yugoslavia, 116

Almond, Gabriel, 183ff

anti-faction faction, 115

Anti-Fascist council of national liberation (AVNOJ), 124

anti-Semitism, *see* anti-Zionism

anti-Zionism, 167-69

apparat, compared with Christian hierarchy, 9; as elite party, 11; mass following, 38; defined, 229

apparatchik, *see* activist, apparat, cadre

Armenians, 174, 176-77, 189-90, 229

Ashkenazim, 150, 229

authoritarianism, in Malaya, 178-79; in eastern Europe, 198-99

Axis, 96-97, 118-19

Balkan Communist federation, 114

Balkan federation, and IMRO, 94-95; and Bulgarian Communist party, 94, 95, 114; Yugoslav-Bulgarian negotiations for, 99; and Macedonian unification, 101; Cominform version, 103; as a supra-national state, 193-94

Belorussians, 80, 85, 223, 230

Benaroya, Abraham, 161

Berman, J., 166, 169

beta coefficient, 73, 229

Bethlen, Count Istvan, 156-57, 157n

Bled agreement, 99

Bolshevik party, *see* Soviet Union, Communist party of

Bosnia-Hersegovina, 127, 128, 144

Bosniaks, location, 123; and Partisan army, 124, 125-26; and Yugoslav nationalism, 142, 144; and Communism, 189; identified, 230

bourgeoisie, 3, 199-200. *See also* middle class

Broz, Josip, *see* Tito

Bulgaria, Communist party of, social composition, 35, 52; electorate, 40, 44, 57, 78; size, 51; and union membership, 65; and Balkan federation, 94, 95, 114

Bulgaria, election returns, 211; basic statistics, 212

Bulgarian Macedonia, *see* Macedonia

Bulkes camp, 32, 101n

cadre, 230. *See also* activist

cash cropper, 56n, 56-57, 74-75, 212, 218-219, 221, 230

Caucasians, 60, 230

Chams, 142, 143-44, 230

Chetniks, 119ff, 230

Chinese, and Malayan Communism, 180-82, 194, 196

Christianity, compared with Communism, 4-7, 15-16

Ciliga, Ante, 79n, 107n, 111n; position on national question, 112, 118n

Cizinsky, M., 115 and n

Clementis, V., 157

coefficient, of correlation, 39, 208, 234, 235; of determination, 74-75, 234-35; of multiple correlation, 74, 209-10, 234

Colakovic, R., 109-10, 115n

Cominform, 102, 103, 194, 230

Comintern, 94-95, 108; and Jugoslav national question, 111, 112 and n, 113-14, 117; and Bulgarian territorial claims, 114; and

239

ethnic group, 85-86, 231
ethnic purification, 131, 148-49

Farkas, M., 165, 169
Federacion, 161-62
Federation balkanique, la, 95
fellow traveller, 9-10, 231
front member, 10, 11

Gegs, 145, 146, 147, 231
Geminder, B., 165, 168
Georgians, 172, 173, 174, 232
Germans, distribution, 131-33;
Volksdeutschen and Reichsdeutschen, 132-33, 134-35, 235, 237;
and the Communist vote, 133-34;
expulsion, 134-35; and Communism, 189. See also Sudeten Germans
Gero, E., 162, 165, 169
Gomulka, W., 49-50, 166, 169
and n
Gotsi, 98 and n, 102
Gottwald, K., 36, 165
Greece, basic statistics, 221; election returns, 221-22
Greece, Communist party of, and repentant prisoners, 25; social composition, 35; leading cadres, 58-59; and union membership, 65; and the Greek civil war, 100-02; role of Jews in, 161-62
Greek civil war, 101, 102, 104
Greek Macedonia, see Macedonia
Greek prisoners, 22 and n, 23, 24
Greek Thrace, 100 and n
Green Apple, 176, 189
guerrillas, defined, 10-11; forcible recruitment of, 13-14; social composition, 45-49, 46n; Slavo-Macedonian, 97, 125-26; Bulgarian, 98-99; Greek, 102, 103-04; Yugoslav, 119, 120, 121-26. See also Democratic army, Green Apple

ha, see hectare
hard core, 8-9, 11, 36-37, 187. See also activist, apparat, cadre, leading cadre
hectare, 232

Horthy, Admiral Miklos, 154
Hoxha, Enver, 63-64
Hromada, 82, 83, 84-85, 210, 232
Hungarians, see Magyars
Hungary, Communist party of, size, 51; social composition, 52; and union membership, 65; role of the Jews, 162-63; and empire building, 192-93; electorate, 222. See also kingdom of St. Stephen, MADOSZ, Magyars
Hungary, election returns, 222

ideology, 232
IMRO, 93, 94-96, 105, 110, 116-17, 232
Independent peasant party (Poland), 82, 83, 85
Indians, 181, 182
industrial workers, and the Communist vote, 39-41; and the Socialist vote, 39-41; and the political right, 41-42; and guerrilla armies, 46-47; voting behavior, 52; and union membership, 65; in Bulgaria, 212; in Czechoslovakia, 214; in Slovakia, 216-17; in Greece, 221. See also proletariat
intelligentsia, 63-64, 191

Jajce resolution, 120-21
Jews, Ashkenazim and Sephardim, 150, 229, 235; and the Communist electorate, 158, 160; and the Polish party, 160-61, 164n, 166, 169 and n; and the Greek party, 161-62; and the Hungarian party, 162-63; divisions among, 163-65; and gentiles, 163n; and the Romanian regime, 165; and the Czechoslovak party, 165-66; concentration in police, 166; and the Bolshevik party, 173; and Communism, 189-90; distribution in eastern Europe, 220 and n, 223

Kardelj, E., 45-46, 126
Karolyi, Count Michael, 151
Khrushchev, N. S., 3-4
kingdom of St. Stephen, 152, 158, 192-93, 232